This book is to be returned on
or before the date stamped below

MONOCHROME
MEMORIES

MONOCHROME MEMORIES

Nostalgia and Style in Retro America

Paul Grainge

Westport, Connecticut
London

Library of Congress Cataloging-in-Publication Data

Grainge, Paul, 1972–
   Monochrome memories : nostalgia and style in retro America / Paul Grainge.
     p. cm.
   Includes bibliographical references and index.
   ISBN 0–275–97618–1 (alk. paper)
   1. Popular history—United States—History—20th century. 2. Nostalgia—United States—History—20th century. 3. Memory—Social aspects—United States—History—20th century. 4. Visual communication—Social aspects—United States—History—20th century. 5. Black-and-white photography—Social aspects—United States—History—20th century. 6. United States—Civilization—1970– 7. Mass media—Social aspects—United States—History—20th century. 8. Nineteen nineties. I. Title.
   E169.12.G68   2002
   973.9′07′2—dc21   2002025323

British Library Cataloguing in Publication Data is available.

Library of Congress Catalog Card Number: 2002025323
ISBN: 0–275–97618–1

First published in 2002

Praeger Publishers, 88 Post Road West, Westport, CT 06881
An imprint of Greenwood Publishing Group, Inc.
www.praeger.com

Printed in the United States of America

The paper used in this book complies with the Permanent Paper Standard issued by the National Information Standards Organization (Z39.48–1984).

10 9 8 7 6 5 4 3 2 1

To my family

Copyright Acknowledgments

Portions of chapters 1 and 2 appeared in a different guise as "Nostalgia and Style in Retro America: Moods, Modes and Media Recycling," in *The Journal of American and Comparative Culture*, 23, no. 1 (2000): 27–34, reprinted by permission of Bowling Green State University Popular Press. A short version of chapter 3 appeared as "*Time*'s Past in the Present: Nostalgia and the Black and White Image," in *The Journal of American Studies*, 33, no. 3 (1999): 383–392, reprinted by permission of Cambridge University Press. An earlier version of chapter 4 appeared as "Advertising the Archive: Nostalgia and the (Post)national Imaginary," in *American Studies*, 41, nos. 2/3 (2000): 137–157, reprinted by permission of the Mid-America American Studies Association. A version of chapter 6 appeared as "Reclaiming Heritage: Colourization, Culture Wars and the Politics of Nostalgia," in *Cultural Studies*, 13, no. 4 (1999): 621–638, reprinted by permission of Taylor & Francis (http://tandf.co.uk/journals).

Reproductions of *Time* magazine covers appear courtesy of Time/Rex Features.

Contents

Illustrations

Preface

I began this book as a project on contemporary American nostalgia, broadly conceived. Working against criticism that, it seemed to me, collapsed nostalgia too quickly into some diagnostic condition or end-of-century malaise, my attentions were drawn to the proliferating styles of nostalgia that had come to abound in the commercial and visual markets of Europe and America. Fairly quickly, one particular style or mode of nostalgia came to interest me above others: the black-and-white image. Not only was monochrome infused with an atmospheric quality of the past, it also seemed remarkably popular within regimes of contemporary visual taste. When I began to conceive the project in 1997, it appeared that no self-respecting café bar could do without a black-and-white print on the wall; monochrome was the signature of designer chic for the likes of Armani and Calvin Klein; even sepia was staging a comeback within commercial photography and portraiture. Initially, the popularity of the black-and-white image seemed ripe for a single chapter. However, monochrome soon took on a larger significance; it became clear that, as a cross-media phenomenon, black and white provided a perfect means of exploring a particularized discourse of visual nostalgia.

In seeking to examine the use and status of the black-and-white image, anchored to questions of American memory, I have drawn upon a range of theories and methodologies. This book is indebted to critics across a broad disciplinary spectrum, but it has also, on certain terms, had to invent its own field of study. Just as there is little sustained work on nostalgia as a cultural style, so consideration of the black-and-white image generally proceeds from specific disciplinary positions concerned with the use of monochrome in photographic, documentary, and/or cinematic practice. In the modest terms of this project, I hope to have offered, or at least to have explored, a new means of locating the reproduction and circulation of nostalgia within contemporary cultural artifacts, paying due attention (through the study of black-and-white imagery) to the resolute interdisciplinarity and intertextuality that such a project demands.

Writing this book has generated its own brand of appreciative memory. It began as a doctoral thesis undertaken in the School of American and Canadian Studies at the University of Nottingham, and I would like to thank the University of Nottingham and the Arts and Humanities Research Board for their generous financial support. In helping the book to completion, my debt of gratitude extends in various directions. I owe much to the scrupulous supervision of Paul Giles and Douglas Tallack, whose critical generosity and guidance have been crucial, and to Mark Jancovich, who has been consistently, and characteristically, supportive of the project. My thanks also extend to Richard King, George McKay, and Max Page for reading and discussing several chapters of the book, to Rob McMinn for providing useful source material, and to several anonymous readers who provided valuable suggestions for improvement, both in terms of individual chapters and for the manuscript as a whole. In shepherding the book to published form, Elisabetta Linton and the team at Greenwood Press and Klara and Eric King have all been remarkably efficient.

Of the numerous friends who made life so entertaining and critically enriching during the writing process (and beyond), my thanks go especially to Martyn Bone and James Lyons and to the endless hospitality of June and Mike Morris. Generously reminding me that weekends are sacred, I have any number of reasons to thank Claire Tyler. Suffering all of my nocturnal scribblings and dinnertime witterings, she has become my center of gravity in life and love, and has no doubt heard a lot more about postmodernism than she would otherwise have cared for. With endless humor, she has significantly enlarged my capacity for nostalgia in recent years. Finally, I owe the greatest debt, and most sincere thanks, to my family, whose love and unconditional support have always meant everything to me. I therefore dedicate this book to my parents, David and Jane, to my sister, Catherine, and to the memory of my grandfather, Ernest Julian Edwards [1910–1998].

MONOCHROME
MEMORIES

Introduction:
Putting It in Black and White

Chapter One. He adored New York City. He idolized it all out
of proportion. Uh, no, make that: He, he, romanticized it all
out of proportion. Now . . . to him . . . no matter what the
season was, this was still a town that existed in black and
white and pulsated to the great tunes of George Gershwin.

Woody Allen, *Manhattan*

Gershwin's "Rhapsody in Blue" begins with a soaring clarinet glissando
that seems to befit the rising New York skyline in the memorable opening sequence of *Manhattan*. The music of Gershwin, himself Brooklyn-
born, is used in the film's prelude to accompany a vivid series of New
York city images, all in black and white. Interspersed with an iconic
geography of parks, bridges, monuments, and buildings, a host of street
scenes and urban vistas form a montage of mercurial city delights.
"Rhapsody in Blue" initiates a mood, an atmosphere, a sense of time and
the past. It is Woody Allen's use of monochrome, however, that provides
Manhattan with a sustained feeling of nostalgia. Black and white creates
a quality of pastness in a film that is set in the present. New York is given
a suspended temporality: a case, one might say, of nostalgia for now, of
putting the classic in the contemporary.

Woody Allen has used black-and-white photography in several of his
films, including *Manhattan* (1979), *Stardust Memories* (1980), *Zelig* (1983),
and *Celebrity* (1998). It is perhaps unsurprising, considering this directorial disposition, that he should have become one of the principal

opponents of movie colorization at the end of the 1980s. This was a short-lived debate that set a host of liberal directors and film bodies against the commercial machinations of Ted Turner. Having procured the back catalogue of MGM, Turner sought to recoup his investment by digitally "colorizing" a series of old black-and-white films, maximizing their profit potential by securing copyrights for them as new commodities. Defending artistic and creative rights, Woody Allen made a strident case for the integrity of black and white. His argument had two parts. First, he said that black and white had particular aesthetic and expressive properties. Writing in *The New York Review of Books*, he commented: "If I had portrayed New York City in color rather than black and white in my movie *Manhattan*, all the nostalgic connotations would have vanished. All the evocations of the city from old photographs and films would have been impossible to achieve in Technicolor."[1] Second, he gave black and white a value of authenticity. This was linked to the authority vested in the originality of the art work, and was measured against the colorized simulacra of the "new classic." In Woody Allen's public pronouncements against color conversion, monochrome became an aesthetic that, for the sake of American film heritage and in the name of good taste, should be saved from the dubious benefits of technological "enhancement."

As it turned out, Woody Allen's fears about colorization were premature. Despite early commercial success, and largely irrespective of liberal opposition, colorization never took off. With the public's waning interest in the novelty of colorized classics, and with cable channels like American Movie Classics showing a host of black-and-white "oldies," Ted Turner closed down his operations in 1994. Monochrome memory was itself becoming marketable in a range of cultural media, principally in advertising and magazine journalism, but also within film, on cable television, and in the image industries that sell posters and prints through main street chains and home improvement wholesalers. It is here that my own interests begin. Central to *Monochrome Memories* is an examination of why, and to what effect, the black-and-white image was taken up and used stylistically in American visual culture during the 1990s. While seemingly specific as a field of interest, I would argue that black and white opens up a series of pregnant debates about cultural nostalgia, visual taste, and the politics of memory in what might be dubbed, with postmodern sympathies, "retro America."

The late 1980s saw an explosion of color in the visual media, enabled by new digital technologies and printing processes. From movie colorization to the large-scale transition to color within magazine publishing and the newspaper industry, color was sold as an aesthetic value. Moving to a full-color format in 1989, *Time* magazine trumpeted its new color capacity, providing what it called a more "exciting" and "livelier" medium for both readers and corporate promotion. In the same year, Ted Turner brushed off claims of cultural vandalism by saying that colorizing film was about "making an improved version."[2] Color was associated with excitement and improvement, an aesthetic mode penetrating the arcane vestiges of black and white wherever they may be. However, by the early 1990s, the saturation of color within a crowded visual marketplace had given black and white a new life. Monochrome was able to punctuate the visual norm; it became a mark of depth in a culture of surface, an aesthetic of slowness in a climate of speed. Black and white was part of, but also seemingly beyond, the world of corporate and media image production. The visuality of monochrome seemed to efface its own relation to the sphere of capitalist simulations, sustaining the illusion that it was somehow removed from the market culture in which it was necessarily produced. Harnessing the temporal and authenticity "effects" of monochrome, an increasing number of picture editors, filmmakers, ad designers, and other cultural producers utilized black and white to appeal fundamentally to the *aura of the archive*.

If the black-and-white image has become an idiom of visual pastness, an aesthetic of memory, and the archive, its popularity might be examined in light of debates over the selling, staging, and significance of the past within contemporary culture. Critics in various disciplinary fields have drawn attention to the restless, even obsessional, interest in history, memory, and tradition that has developed within Europe and America since the mid to late 1980s. Some have read this negatively, suggesting that memorial culture is a regressive malady, the commodified result of a rapacious heritage industry, and/or symptomatic of (post)modern culture's frantic hyperrealization of the past in a moment of temporal estrangement.[3] More positively, a number of critics have read the form and presence of memory in terms of a broadly enlivened and reevaluative dialogue with the past.[4] The debates that center upon contemporary memory have revealed a spectrum of theoretical assumptions and political investments. Writing from the perspective of cultural studies and focusing upon the production of visual memory within the dominant media, Marita Sturken writes that "cultural memory is a central aspect of how U.S. culture functions and how the nation is defined."[5] I proceed with this idea in mind. By locating the production of visual pastness in the news magazine, global advertising, Hollywood film, and syndicated television, I consider how, *as an aesthetic mode of nostalgia*, black and white has been used to establish and legitimate particular kinds of memory in American cultural life.

Three basic questions underpin my focus on the black-and-white image. What is the effect of monochrome as a representational mode? Why has monochrome become a popular style in a visual culture governed by the color image? And to what degree, and with what significance, has monochrome been used to consolidate a sense of history and heritage, memory and time? These are related to a broader set of issues surrounding the aestheticization of nostalgia in contemporary culture: specifically, the relation of memory modes to particular regimes of style and to the production of cultural discourses about national memory. Unlike theories that dismiss contemporary memory practices, especially those shaped by media industries, as specious and amnesiac, I want to explore how the black-and-white image has been used to perform specific cultural and memory work. By examining the use and signification of monochrome within 1990s media, I look at the way that a particular "nostalgia mode" has been used stylistically within visual culture and has been taken up within discursive figurations of cultural memory and identity.

NOSTALGIA MODES AND MEMORY CRISIS

One idea that found expression in a variety of cultural prognoses in the 1980s and 1990s, from the postmodern theory of Fredric Jameson to the public jeremiads emanating from Lynne Cheney as head of the National Endowment for the Humanities (NEH), was that of "memory crisis." While the explanations and political agendas that claimed this condition may have differed, amnesia was diagnosed as a pervasive ailment in American life and was set within a discourse of cultural crisis. There is nothing especially new about the perception of crisis in American life, or indeed, memory crisis. A sense of cultural decline, matched with a fear of widespread societal forgetting, has arisen at various historical moments when the pace and project of modernity has put adverse pressure on established traditions and cultural ideologies. For example, Michael Kammen suggests that a new self-consciousness about American tradition grew in a period beginning in the 1870s; memory became a force of reconciliation after the Civil War, a strategy of assimilation responding to the flood of immigration, and a means of adjusting to the impact of industrialization.[6] Similarly, Lawrence Levine has examined the sense of decline and the attendant force of nostalgia that grew in relation to various determinants of crisis in the 1920s. This focused significantly on the dilution of American purity by "alien" elements and ideologies, set within a period of "profound ambivalence" felt toward sweeping socioeconomic change.[7] The status of memory, both its social use and its potential loss, has at different historical junctures become joined to questions of continuity and rupture, development and dislocation, cohesion and crisis.

The contemporary memory crisis has been framed, and can be understood, in two different ways. For neoconservative critics, like Cheney and William Bennett, at the end of the 1980s, it became a matter of *what* (*or not*) is remembered. This was notably outlined in two documents published during their respective tenures at the NEH, titled *American Memory* (Cheney, 1987) and *To Reclaim a Legacy* (Bennett, 1984), which outlined the failings of the American educational system. The "crisis of memory" was taken up in debates about historical illiteracy, failing educational standards, and the threat posed to consensual notions of American tradition by the curricular claims of the culturally marginalized. Memory crisis was linked to cultural debates about pedagogy and the preservation of national patrimony in a climate of pressing multiculturalism. For left-wing critics like Fredric Jameson, the contemporary memory crisis has come to mean something else altogether; it speaks more profoundly to the matter of *how* (*or not*) we remember in the culture of late capitalism. If, as Andreas Huyssen suggests, "the very structure of memory (and not just its contents) is strongly contingent upon the social formation that produces it,"[8] memory crisis has been theorized in terms of a formation where new technologies and multinational organizations of capital have engendered a culture of hyperreality and capitalist hyperdevelopment, where changing relations of space and time have produced a culture "haunted by the explosion of temporality in the expanding synchronicity of our media world."[9] While memory has been in a state of "crisis" ever since Plato warned against the impact of the written word on active remembrance, a specific discourse of amnesia developed in the late 1980s. This grew in relation, and as a response, to a postmodern formation shaping the way that memory has come to be lived, taught, experienced, and understood.

In broad historical terms, postmodernism replicates previous concepts of memory crisis by generating cultural fears about the "loss of a sense of time's continuous flow."[10] Richard Terdiman relates this experience to the late nineteenth century, outlining determinants in the reconfiguration of the experience of memory brought about "by the inadequacy of available memory mechanisms to the needs of a transformed society."[11] Postmodernism reiterates themes of flux and forgetting that, since the shaping of modernity in the "long nineteenth century," has seen cultural stress come to bear upon traditional forms of memory. However, postmodernism is anchored to transformations in the experience of temporality and the real that have made issues of memory crisis seem even more intractable. The desire for memory as stable, reassuring, and constant has always been plagued by the fear of its instability and unreliability, as well as its disposition toward fantasy. The trope of "memory crisis" in postmodern culture is by no means new in this regard. However, it has been configured in specific ways. For Jameson, this bears centrally upon transitions in the form and structure of capitalist postmodernity that, he suggests, have engendered a profound waning or blockage of historicity.

In a culture distinguished by the spatial logic of the simulacrum, Jameson argues that historicity has been replaced by a new aesthetic "nostalgia mode." This describes an art language where the past is realized through stylistic connotation and consumed as pastiche. Symptomatic of a crisis in the postmodern historical imagination, the nostalgia mode satisfies a desperate craving for history while reinforcing the past as "a vast collection of images, a multitudinous photographic simulacrum."[12] The representational economy of the nostalgia mode enfeebles a "genuine" sense of history. And yet, the production of pastness in postmodern culture is also "a tangible symptom of an omnipotent, omnivorous, and well-nigh libidinal historicism."[13] In Jameson's influential theory, the historical past is replaced by fashionable and glossy *pastness*. As a concept, the nostalgia mode is divorced from any necessary, or properly existential, sense of longing, loss, or even memory. It is instead a cultural style. Jameson defines nostalgia less in terms of an experiential mood than as an aestheticized mode. In mnemonic terms, the effective content of nostalgic longing has been rivaled and replaced by the contentless of nostalgic affect.

I want to use an idea of the "nostalgia mode" but in a way that departs from Jameson. *Monochrome Memories* maintains a sense of nostalgia's relationship with postmodernism, existing as a retro style, but it rejects the assumption of amnesia and historicist crisis common to much postmodern critique. Essentially, I want to consider the memory politics of stylized pastness, in particular the visual pastness of the black-and-white image. In his critical nostalgia for a modern affirmation of history—a position that leads to questionable assumptions about cultural access to an unmediated past—Jameson fails to account for memory and identity being negotiated by the nostalgia mode. Lamenting the indiscriminate pastiche that distinguishes late capitalism, he gives little sense that meaningful narratives of history or cultural memory can be produced *through* the recycling and/or hybridization of past styles. As an aesthetic of pastness, a particular kind of nostalgia mode, monochrome developed a specific capital in the economy of visual taste during the 1990s. As a chromatic punctuation of the visual norm, black and white assumed a marketable cachet, largely based on its figurative "authenticity" and difference from a culture of surface spectacle and color simulacra. However, monochrome was also taken up in a discursive sense. Black and white became a strategic mode, deployed intertextually and from specific institutional/critical positions to visualize a sense of American memory, heritage, patrimony, and past. In a time when American identity was, and continues to be, undermined by transnational political and economic restructuring, when ideas of national commonality were being challenged by an emergent politics of difference, and in a moment when the metanarratives of American history were straining for legitimacy against the multiple pasts of the marginalized, the black-and-white image became linked to the cultural and political aestheticization of national memory.

As a feeling and formation, postmodernity has been distinguished in many different ways: by the specific relationship of space and time, the instability of temporal and referential moorings, the profusion of simultaneity and simulacra, the globalization of image flows. There are numerous sobriquets and schemas that can define the particularity of the postmodern. In sociological terms, Zygmunt Bauman suggests that the most conspicuous features of postmodernity are "institutionalized pluralism, variety, contingency and ambivalence."[14] If one sense of memory crisis relates to a representational regime of simulation and pastiche—what Jameson calls the "perpetual present" of postmodernism—another derives from a deepening sense of plural and discontinuous *histories*: that is to say, the fundamental reconception of the cultural center, of the singularity of American experience, of history with a capital "H." If the late 1980s and early 1990s saw a discourse of cultural crisis taking hold in America, this was partly a response to a series of transitions undermining the perceptual unities of national meaning. While multiculturalism became a lightning rod for jeremiads about national decline in the early 1990s, a sense of dissolving national identity must also be measured against factors such as the end of the cold war and the accelerated process of globalization. As it was framed in public discourse, memory crisis was linked to the destabilization of cultural moorings, in particular the securities of consensual nationhood and common citizenship that have underpinned and authorized postwar liberal ideologies.

The suggestion of memory crisis can be related in significant ways to hegemonic struggles over centered American identity, including the sense of a common national past. One must always, of course, pose the question at the outset: "Whose memory crisis are we dealing with?" By what measure is it possible, and in whose interests does it serve, to call a culture amnesiac? Does the "loss" of memory really mean the loss of a particular kind of memory or way of remembering? As formulated by liberals and neoconservatives in the burgeoning culture war of the late 1980s and early 1990s, "memory crisis" had very acute political stakes. Liberal visions of national fraying and disuniting joined neoconservative diatribes against deculturation and the collapse of tradition. In the bellicose disputes over "political correctness," the American "memory crisis" was discursively intertwined with a series of debates about education and the status and teaching of history. This was nowhere more effectively displayed than in Arthur Schlesinger Jr.'s polemical "reflections" on multiculturalism, *The Disuniting of America*. In it, he attacked the "cult of ethnicity" and what he called the "therapeutic" recourse to history and the past. Schlesinger wrote: "For history is to the

nation what memory is to the individual. As an individual deprived of
memory becomes disoriented and lost, not knowing where he has been
or where he is going, so a nation denied a concept of its past will be
disabled in dealing with its present and its future."[15] *The Disuniting of
America* poured fuel on the fire of neoconservative attacks directed at
multiculturalism and the beleaguered state of educational standards. If
the book sought "to produce and license ignorance about multiculturalism," as Michael Bérubé suggests, it grew out of fears concerning the
breakdown of historical knowledge and the degeneration of American
heritage.[16] In 1987, Lynne Cheney complained of "a system of education
that fails to nurture memory of the past."[17] Berating the impact of "the
victim revolution that is sweeping campuses," George Will spoke in
1991 of the "collective amnesia and deculturation" that results from a
basic failure to transmit the chords of American cultural patrimony.[18]
Memory crisis was, in this context, linked to the protection of a consensual and objective "tradition," conceived as an indisputable set of shared
historical experiences, common symbols, and agreed literary classics.
Tradition became a byword for a particular and exclusive version of
cultural inheritance, the memory of which was (seen to be) challenged
by hostile multiculturalism and the pedagogical tyrannies of "tenured
radicals."

It is not in the scope of this book to trace the political fortunes of
multiculturalism during the 1990s. It is perhaps enough to say that
multiculturalism was mainstreamed and transformed during the
Clinton presidency into the basis of a new kind of national consensus. If
the United States has always been multicultural, Jon Cruz suggests that
"only recently has this been recognized and *named* as such in the context
of the modern state's attempt to work out a politically pragmatic blend
of cultural benevolence and statecraft to configure its own legitimacy."[19]
The 1990s saw a figurative victory for multiculturalism in the culture
war, but this hardly meant that America was suddenly, and successfully,
dealing with difference. In many respects, it meant retooling the terms of
consensus in a struggle to preserve the stakes of commonality and the
fundamental constituents of nationhood. In 1996, Avery Gordon and
Christopher Newfield wrote that "recent years have enhanced the pres-
tige of common culture as the primary defensive barrier to the dangers
posed by the existence of ethnicity and race. Plurality is increasingly
seen as a dangerous thing."[20] If consensual frameworks of national
meaning were challenged in the 1990s by an increasing awareness of
local and global conflicts structured around relations of race, class, ethnicity, sexuality, and gender, this did not temper various attempts in
cultural and political discourse to shore up traditional narratives of
nation. Indeed, attempts were made to reconfigure the idea of common
ground against the claims of multicultural difference, to reframe na-

tional exceptionalism in the context of contemporary globalization, and to recoup American identity as somehow unitary and unconflicted. Memory became an instrumental site of hegemonic contestation in this context.

There are numerous incidents where the negotiation of a national past intersects with the challenge of multiculturalism. Curatorial debates at the Smithsonian over exhibitions such as the "West as America" (1991) and the Enola Gay (1995) both raised anger and protest at revisionist histories daring to present, respectively, the frontier experience as a question of capitalist exploitation, sexism, and genocide, and the Hiroshima bombing as one of several possible actions on the part of the U.S. government. As the self-appointed guardian of American memory, Steven Spielberg turned *Schindler's List* (1993), *Amistad* (1997), and *Saving Private Ryan* (1998) into cultural master memories, humanist dramas infused with themes of redemption and collective (national) remembrance. More in response to globalization than multiculturalism, controversy arose in 1992, when quilt historians accused the Smithsonian of abandoning responsibility for the nation's heritage by allowing commercial reproductions of early American quilts to be made by laborers in the People's Republic of China. In different ways, these indicate the negotiation, representation, and battles of ownership fought over common national memory. In the so-called "struggle to define America" that took place in the 1990s, hegemonic interests were frequently served by, and inscribed within, discursive recourse to an authoritative sense of the national past.[21]

Several critics have examined the larger political and economic contexts informing the struggle over multiculturalism in the 1990s.[22] Many agree that the culture wars were a single, if symbolic and politically pregnant, manifestation of a much broader sense of national identity crisis. While the end of the cold war denied America its defining ideological "Other," the more sustained effects of globalization were serving to reshape national boundaries and, with it, imagined communities. Frederick Buell suggests that "the culture wars were, of course, one of the most visible responses to the global slippage felt by many in the United States."[23] This slippage does not simply describe the economic challenge by Japan and other tiger economies to U.S. fiscal authority at the beginning of the 1990s. It speaks more profoundly of the ideological crisis of the nation state brought about by the global cultural economy. The "fetishizing of tradition" was a form of hegemonic positioning in the culture wars. However, the discourse of common memory must also be understood in relation to particular disorientations produced by the global restructuring of capital.

If the comforts of national heritage and the coherence of place-bound identity have been challenged by the intensity of global cultural confrontations, theorists of globalization have discussed the protective national strategies utilized to conserve local identities.[24] David Morley and Kevin Robins suggest that "the driving imperative is to salvage central, bounded and coherent identities." Discussing the struggle for meaningful communities and secure social identities in a global world of difference and Diaspora, they point to cultural constructions that are "about the maintenance of a protective illusion, about the struggle for wholeness and coherence through continuity." They continue: "At heart of this romantic aspiration is . . . the search for purity and purified identity."[25] Although their focus is Europe, this speaks well of the vested attempts in America to construct, in a variety of cultural discourses, a distinguishable sense of nationhood for the 1990s. Fought in a preservationist mode in the culture war debates at the beginning of the decade, American identity came to be figured in terms of new postnational imperatives by the end of the 1990s. In part, this reflected the increasing role and engagement of the United States in the emerging order of contemporary globalization, powerfully embracing a neoliberal global formation based on cross-border flexibility and cultural/capital flow. Despite transitions in the discursive context in which American identity came to be fought and forged, however, the desire to articulate the coherence of U.S. nationhood remained. Jon Cruz writes of a particular conjuncture in the 1990s where "on the one hand, a *centrifugal capitalism* began to push outwards, disengaging from domestic commitments in pursuit of transnational strategies. On the other hand, a *centripetal culture* shaped in part by political developments and aided by new tiers of internal mass-media development augmented the process of identity formations."[26] In the midst of a sea change in global relationships, a paradox emerged whereby the fractured ideological basis of the nation state met with a vigorous articulation of national identity.

Cruz suggests that "if economic capital seeks flight, cultural capital seeks stable moorings." Broadly speaking, I am concerned with the unsettled moorings of American national identity—largely produced by the challenge and effects of multiculturalism and globalization—and the attempt to resecure these moorings through an appeal to an aestheticized memory and past. In this context, I examine how a discourse of "black and whiteness" functioned in and through the dominant media. Stuart Hall asserts that "there is always something decentered about the medium of culture, about language, textuality and signification, which always escapes and evades the attempt to link it directly, and immediately, with other structures."[27] I am not suggesting that the black-and-white image was always used consciously, or with calculation, to shore up particular narratives of nationhood. Instead, I am concerned with locating in its use what Hall calls "the shadow, the imprint, the trace, of those other formations, of the intertextuality of texts in their institutional positions, as texts as sources of power, of textuality as a site representation and resistance." I want to consider the memory politics of monochrome, examining the way that black and white helped legitimate in the 1990s an archival identity for a strained national culture undergoing both diversification and demystification.

NOSTALGIA AND CULTURAL STYLE

While practically concerned with the culture of the 1990s, the critical interests of *Monochrome Memories* are not restricted to this period alone. Examining black-and-white as an aesthetic mode of nostalgia can suggest a framework for the discussion of nostalgia that moves beyond psychological discussions of fin-de-siècle memory and the more dismissive criticism of nostalgia's tendency to sentimentalize and/or dehistoricize the past. Modern theories of nostalgia arguably veer toward one of two conceptual poles, which can be simply defined as the mood and mode. If the nostalgia mood is a feeling determined by a concept of longing and loss, the nostalgia mode is a consumable style that has been commonly characterized as amnesiac. The mood/mode distinction is not a binary opposition but, instead, represents the conceptual tendencies of a theoretical continuum. Examining nostalgia as a cultural style involves a particular negotiation of theories that read nostalgia in terms of cultural longing and/or postmodern forgetting. Mediating between the positions of mood and mode, I take issue with, and seek to refine, various generalized assumptions emanating from nostalgia theories that not only proceed from, but are fairly governed by, notions of loss and amnesia.

There are perhaps two major theoretical sleights, developing from different ends of the mood/mode axis, that need to be addressed. First is the assumption that nostalgic forms and styles in cultural production somehow reflect or embody nostalgic moods in cultural life. In this view, the popularity of, say, retro fashion, products of the heritage industry, or the resurgence of television reruns would be explained in terms of dissatisfaction with the present. Such a position would fail to account, however, for the specific histories and representational economies that explain the emergence, and define the character, of particular nostalgic styles. The rerun, for example, is not simply a reflex symptom of nostalgic loss, but the complex result of television syndication going back to the 1950s and the industrial deregulation and technological advances in the 1980s that led to the explosion of cable. While the rerun may well tap the nostalgic propensities of certain demographic markets, it must also be understood in a culture where the past is one of many styles taken up within particular regimes of taste. The commodification and aestheticization of nostalgia is not, by necessity, the cultural flush produced by a broadly experienced nostalgic fever. Neither does this mean to say, however, that it has no relation whatsoever to the production of cultural memory narratives.

The second assumption that demands interrogation, evident in the work of Jameson, is the view that nostalgia modes in cultural production are amnesiac and perform no memory function at all. Jameson believes in a fundamental crisis of collective memory and relates the nostalgia mode to a beleaguered historical imagination. However, this does not account for the way that nostalgia modes perform memory work through the stylistic and affective play of "pastness." There has been a considerable amount of work recently on the *construction* of memory. Just as biologists have reconceived the brain's memory function—from a case of dormant biochemical proteins waiting simply to be recovered to a dynamic process constituted by ever-shifting arrangements of neurons within the cerebral cortex—so the process of collective memory has also been scrutinized within the humanities and social sciences. Memory has become less a question of the accuracy or authenticity of mnemonic retrieval than a matter of its development in relation to particular collective contexts, social dynamics, and political stakes. Critics have examined the invention of tradition, the construction of heritage, and the performance of nostalgia, principally as they relate to identity formation and the maintenance of political hegemony.[28] In this context, aestheticized modes of nostalgia need not be judged in terms of postmodern depthlessness, but they can be examined politically in the context of particular negotiations of cultural identity and historical meaning.

If the black-and-white image can be thought of as an aestheticized mode of nostalgia, it cannot be reduced to schemes that would see it either in terms of generalized longing for the past (relating to an experience of loss) or as a desperate hyperrealizing of it (responding to a condition of amnesia). The popularity of monochrome has emerged in relation to particular taste regimes and definitions of style; it has developed as a result of the saturation of color in contemporary visual media and as one of many available codes in a profligate image culture. It is not, in this sense, a visual proclivity that has become popular through a sudden incidence of cultural nostalgia. At the same time, however, a discourse of "black and whiteness" developed in the 1990s where the temporal and authenticity effects of monochrome became a visual means of articulating issues and identities figured around the construction, representation, and preservation of national memory. In a context where the politics of difference and the emerging climate of postnationalism were beginning to question the coherence of American identity, monochrome memory became a style and site for the articulation of a figuratively coherent and stable past. It functioned in response to a certain kind of "loss," mainly to the hegemonic legitimacy of a dominant liberal consensus that has authorized its power in the postwar period through appeal to cultural commonality and the principle of the nation state.

To explore fully the place and stakes of aestheticized nostalgia in American cultural life, *Monochrome Memories* is composed of two parts, one dealing generally with the theoretical status and cultural significance of nostalgia as a style, and the other looking specifically at the memory work performed by the black-and-white image *as* a nostalgia style. Part I provides a conceptual and contextual survey of the nostalgia mode. Chapter 1 examines nostalgia as it has been theorized in psychological, sociological, cultural, and postmodern discourses, distinguishing between "mood" and "mode" as conceptual tendencies. Chapter 2 provides a broad treatment of commodified/aestheticized nostalgia in cultural life during the 1980s and 1990s, focusing upon Reagan, recycling, and retro. This explores nostalgia affectively, as a political and commercial investment in "pastness" rather than a content-specific experience of loss. Taken together, these chapters establish the theoretical parameters and a cultural basis for the consideration of black and white as a contemporary nostalgia mode. Part I establishes both my critical position—mediating between the conceptual tendencies of loss and amnesia—and demonstrates the disconnection of nostalgia from loss in a range of cultural examples.

Having established the sense and scope of nostalgia, defined as a mode, part II turns more specifically to the memory politics of monochrome; it examines a particular mode of visual nostalgia in the 1990s and the cultural work it performed in the context of debates about the status and articulation of American national memory. Examining different kinds of mass media, and challenging ideas of postmodern amnesia, part II explores monochrome memory in two related ways: as it has been used to arrest meaning in a world of color imagery, and as it has been taken up discursively in the negotiation of nation. Chapters 3, 4, and 5 consider the way that monochrome was deployed in the 1990s, exploring its use and function within the news magazine, corporate brand advertising, and Hollywood film. Not only did black and white punctuate the color norm in each medium, it helped to produce a sense of national and/or postnational memory. *Time* magazine deployed black and white within a particular signifying regime, using it to transform news facts into "shared" history, the brand campaigns of Apple and Gap produced an archival sense of cultural heritage, reconstituting memory in (post)national terms, and *Schindler's List* and *Forrest Gump* used the documentary techniques of black and white to authorize master memories of the episodic past. Chapter 6 anchors the discussion of "monochrome memory" within the context of the American culture wars. Returning to issues of "memory crisis" at the beginning of the 1990s, the final chapter considers an overtly politicized discussion about the stakes and status of monochrome memory; it examines the way that black and white was taken up and defended in debates about aesthetic and cultural integrity. Treating the liberal defense of the black-and-white movie "classic," the chapter relates the black-and-white image to a particular struggle fought over the preservation of national heritage; it examines the "colorization debate" as an example of the desire to stabilize through black-and-white aesthetics the configuration and transmission of American cultural identity.

Much of the work on memory that is informed by cultural studies has examined the political nature of subjugated histories—the Foucauldian "countermemories" that disrupt and deconstruct the narrative coherences of official history. *Time Passages* by George Lipsitz examines the interplay between commercialized leisure and collective memory in postwar America, considering "how the infinitely renewable present of electronic mass media creates a crisis for collective memory, and how collective memory decisively frames the production and reception of commercial culture."[29] More recently, *Tangled Memories* by Marita Sturken investigates cultural memory as a "field of negotiation," focusing upon the contested narratives surrounding the traumas of Vietnam and the AIDS epidemic. Both treat, in different ways, the role of cultural memory "in producing concepts of the 'nation' and of the 'American people.'"[30] I want to complement this body of work but concentrate more on the endeavor to fix, rather than on the dialogic fluidity of, cultural memory. Of course, this does not mean to say that memory *is* or *could ever be* fixed. Instead, it suggests that hegemonic attempts have been made to stabilize and define its permanence, albeit within changing contexts of national identity formation.

In treating monochrome memory, one must not critically overdetermine the popular meaning and reception of black and white as a visual image. George Lipsitz is correct when he says that "images and icons compete for dominance within a multiplicity of discourses."[31] While not ignoring issues of reception, my emphasis is on the significance, genesis, and essential *production* of visual memory within the mass media. I focus upon the representational—or what should more accurately be called the nonrepresentational—properties and politics of "black and whiteness." Todd Gitlin writes: "Where we stand in history, or even whether there is a comprehensible history in which to stand, we grapple for ready-made coordinates. And so, as time passes, oversimplifications become steadily less resistible. All the big pictures tend to turn monochromatic."[32] I examine this sentiment in a literal manner. Concentrating upon products of the multinational media, I ask how the black-and-white image has been taken to signify a "comprehensible" national history; how, in related ways, the temporal and authenticity effects of monochrome have been used to transcend the culture of simulacrum. I ask, quite simply: What does it mean to put things in black and white?

NOTES

1. Woody Allen, "True Colors," *New York Review of Books*, 13 August 1987: 13.

2. See *Time*, 5 June 1989: 1; Greg Dawson, "Ted Turner" (interview), *American Film*, 14, no. 4 (1989): 39.

3. See, respectively, Robert Hewison, *The Heritage Industry: Britain in a Climate of Decline* (London: Methuen, 1987); Michael Kammen, *Mystic Chords of Memory: The Transformation of Tradition in American Culture* (New York: Vintage, 1993); Fredric Jameson, *Postmodernism, or, The Cultural Logic of Late Capitalism* (London: Verso, 1991); and Pierre Nora, "Between Memory and History: Les Lieux de Mémoire," trans., Marc Roudebush, *Representations*, 26 (Spring 1989): 7–25.

4. See, in particular, Linda Hutcheon, *The Politics of Postmodernism* (London: Routledge, 1989); Roy Rosenzweig and David Thelan, *The Presence of the Past: Popular Uses of History in American Life* (New York: Columbia University Press, 1998).

5. Marita Sturken, *Tangled Memories: The Vietnam War, the AIDS Epidemic, and the Politics of Remembering* (Berkeley, CA: University of California Press, 1997): 2.

6. Kammen, *Mystic Chords of Memory*: 93–296.

7. Lawrence Levine, *The Unpredictable Past: Explorations in American Cultural History* (New York: Oxford University Press, 1993): 189–205.

8. Andreas Huyssen, *Twilight Memories: Marking Time in a Culture of Amnesia* (New York: Routledge, 1995): 252.

9. Huyssen, *Twilight Memories*: 100.

10. Richard Terdiman, *Present Past: Modernity and the Memory Crisis* (Ithaca, NY: Cornell University Press, 1993): 5. See also Susannah Radstone, ed., *Memory and Methodology* (Oxford: Berg, 2000): 1–22.

11. Terdiman, *Present Past*: 20.

12. Jameson, *Postmodernism*: 18.

13. Jameson, *Postmodernism*: 18.

14. Zygmunt Bauman, *Intimations of Postmodernity* (London: Routledge, 1992): 187.

15. Arthur Schlesinger Jr., *The Disuniting of America: Reflections on a Multicultural Society* (New York: W. W. Norton, 1991): 45.

16. Michael Bérubé, *Public Access: Literary Theory and American Cultural Politics* (London: Verso, 1994): 225–241.

17. Quoted in George Lipsitz, *Time Passages: Collective Memory and American Popular Culture* (Minneapolis, MN: University of Minnesota Press, 1990): 23.

18. George Will, "Literary Politics," *Newsweek*, 22 April 1991: 72.

19. Jon Cruz, "From Farce to Tragedy: Reflections on the Reification of Race at Century's End," in Avery F. Gordon and Christopher Newfield, eds., *Mapping Multiculturalism* (Minneapolis, MN: University of Minnesota Press, 1996): 28.

20. Avery F. Gordon and Christopher Newfield, eds., *Mapping Multiculturalism* (Minneapolis, MN: University of Minnesota Press, 1996): 8.

21. See James Davison Hunter, *Culture Wars: The Struggle to Define America* (New York: Basic Books, 1991).

22. See Todd Gitlin, *The Twilight of Common Dream: Why America is Wracked by Culture Wars* (New York: Henry Holt, 1995); Nikhal Pal Singh, "Culture/Wars: Em-

pire in an Age of Democracy," *American Quarterly*, 50, no. 3 (1998): 471–522; Frederick Buell, "Nationalist Postnationalism: Globalist Discourse in Contemporary American Culture," *American Quarterly*, 50, no. 3 (1998): 548–591; Cruz, "From Farce to Tragedy": 19–39.

23. Buell, "Nationalist Postnationalism": 554.

24. See, in particular, David Morley and Kevin Robins, *Spaces of Identity: Global Media, Electronic Landscapes and Cultural Boundaries* (London: Routledge, 1995); Frederick Buell, *National Culture and the New Global System* (Baltimore, MD: Johns Hopkins University Press, 1994); and Rob Wilson and Wimal Dissanayake, eds., *Global/Local: Cultural Production and the Transnational Imaginary* (Durham, NC: Duke University Press, 1996).

25. Morley and Robins, *Spaces of Identity*: 122.

26. Cruz, "From Farce to Tragedy": 28.

27. Stuart Hall, "Cultural Studies and Its Theoretical Legacies," in David Morley and Kuan-Hsing Chen, eds., *Stuart Hall: Critical Dialogues in Cultural Studies* (London: Routledge, 1996): 271.

28. For a journalistic summary of recent biological research on memory, see James Geary, "A Trip Down Memory's Lanes," *Time*, 5 May 1997: 43–49. The literature on the invention and construction of memory is developing into a vast field, treated from a range of disciplinary perspectives. Chosen selectively, see Eric Hobsbawm and Terence Ranger, eds., *The Invention of Tradition* (Cambridge: Cambridge University Press, 1983); David Brett, *The Construction of Heritage* (Cork: Cork University Press, 1997); Susan Bennett, *Performing Nostalgia: Shifting Shakespeare and the Contemporary Past* (London: Routledge, 1996); Barry Schwartz, "The Social Context of Commemoration: A Study in Collective Memory," *Social Forces*, 61, no. 2 (1982): 374–402; and M. Christine Boyer, *The City of Collective Memory: Its Historical Imagery and Architectural Entertainments* (Cambridge, MA: MIT Press, 1994).

29. Lipsitz, *Time Passages*: vii.

30. Sturken, *Tangled Memories*: 1.

31. Lipsitz, *Time Passages*: 13.

32. Todd Gitlin, *The Sixties: Years of Hope, Days of Rage* (New York: Bantam Books, 1993): xiii.

I

MOODS AND MODES

1

Theorizing Nostalgia
Isn't What It Used to Be

If anyone has the right to remark that nostalgia is not what it used to be, it is surely the seventeenth-century Swiss physician Johannas Hofer. Examining the particular kind of melancholy experienced by Swiss mercenaries when removed from their homeland, Hofer conceived the term "nostalgia" in 1688. Drawn from the Greek *nostos* (meaning return home) and *algos* (meaning pain), nostalgia described the homesickness, or "*Heimweh*," that soldiers could suffer and even die from when fighting away from their native land. Symptoms involved despondency, weeping, and sometimes suicide; nostalgia was a disease caused by "the quite continuous vibration of animal spirits through those fibers of the middle brain in which impressed traces of ideas of the fatherland still cling."[1] As a medical complaint, numerous theories were advanced to explain the likely causes of nostalgia. These ranged from the relentless clanging of cow bells to adjustments in atmospheric pressure when descending from alpine regions. Nostalgia was originally conceived as a specifically Swiss condition. Gradually sanctified by the medical profession, nostalgia attained broad clinical recognition in 1835, when Hofer's neologism entered the *Dictionnaire de l'Académie*. Moving progressively into the realm of psychiatry, nostalgia retained a medical resonance as late as 1946, appearing on a list issued by the U.S. Surgeon General of maladies experienced during the Second World War.

The speed with which nostalgia became semantically unmoored from its early medical basis makes a ripe tale for linguistic and cultural history. While nostalgia began to lose its pathological associations at the turn of the century, Fred Davis estimates that until the 1950s the word was confined within America to psychiatrists, academic psychologists, and a minority of lay speakers.[2] Few could have foreseen the prolific dissemination of "nostalgia" as a cultural term in the late twentieth century. While at the beginning of the century the modernist triangulation of Freud, Proust, and Faulkner may have problematized and poeticized the experience of memory, melancholy, and nostalgia, the conception of mnemonic yearning was invariably that of a personal kind. The sociologist Maurice Halbwachs theorized "collective memory" during the 1920s and 1930s, arguing that memory is a socially constructed notion depending on collective frameworks of interpretation.[3] However, the sociocultural dimensions of nostalgia were not given serious attention until the late 1970s. Critical treatments of nostalgia were, until this time, principally literary or philosophical in their concerns, reflections on artistic longing, or existential meditations on the nature of authentic being.[4]

It was from the early 1970s that nostalgia became a routine keyword in America for the capaciously sentimental, and variously commodified, past. The reasons for this are varied, but critics have generally explained a burgeoning "culture of nostalgia" through factors that include the dislocations caused by the 1960s and the ensuing search for stability, a growing media culture feeding upon its own creations, and the broad commodification of memory within film, fashion, architectural design and the heritage industry. Nostalgia was a sentiment but also a growing style. While complex, related, and often symbiotic, the distinction between sentiment and style, mood and mode, has come to underpin many contemporary theories of nostalgia. Since the late 1980s, when memory became a topic of concerted critical interest, nostalgia has been taken up in critiques of reactionary conservatism, in accounts of retro phenomena, in relation to the growing memorial tendencies in Europe and America, and as central to particular theories of postmodernism. David Lowenthal wrote in 1989, echoing an essay in *Harper's* by Christopher Lasch: "Perhaps our epoch is awash not in nostalgia but in a widespread *preoccupation* with nostalgia among intellectuals and the mass media." Discussing the expansive use of the term in contemporary culture, he went on to say: "Nostalgia is apt to be confused with *any* perspective on the past and every historical enterprise mistaken as nostalgic."[5] The media currency and commercial profitability of nostalgia grew exponentially in the postwar period, alongside a heightened critical concern with its status, significance, and, since the 1970s, its inveterate place in America's cultural lexicon.

The purpose of this chapter is to examine the conceptual presuppositions behind modern cultural theories of nostalgia, helping to establish a framework for the discussion of contemporary styles of nostalgia in

American life. There are perhaps two dominant tendencies at work, captured in the distinction between *mood* and *mode*. The nostalgia mood articulates a concept of experience—what Raymond Williams might call "a structure of feeling." Theoretically, nostalgia is understood as a socio-cultural response to forms of discontinuity, claiming a vision of stability and authenticity in some conceptual "golden age." This approximates the conventional sense of nostalgia as a yearning. Critics who examine nostalgia in this way are invariably concerned with the question of what is chosen from the past and why—with how, and in whose interest, the past is made to relate to the present. With a different emphasis, the nostalgia mode articulates a concept of style, a representational effect with implications for our cultural experience of the past. To the likes of Fredric Jameson, the central issue is not how the past is made to relate to the present. Rather, the nostalgia mode questions the ability to apprehend the past at all in a postmodern culture distinguished by the profound waning of history. As a term, the "nostalgia mode" is a specific concept put forward by Jameson but also indicative of theories that treat memory as contingent upon culture and that examine the specificity of (post)modern memory practices.

The difference between mood and mode is largely a matter of critical orientation. In each case, a conceptual emphasis, or what might be called a main gravitational presumption, can be seen to operate. The nostalgia mood is principally defined in relation to a concept of *loss*. Notions of authenticity and time—endemic to the experience and rhetoric of nostalgia—are structured around a principle of absence and longing, or what Susan Stewart calls a "generalized desire for origin, for nature, and for unmediated experience."[6] By contrast, the nostalgia mode has no necessary relation to loss or longing. As a commodified style, the nostalgia mode has developed, principally within postmodern theory, a theoretical association with *amnesia*. When authenticity and time have themselves become victims of postmodern speed, space, and simulacra, forms of stylized nostalgia have been framed in relation to an incumbent memory crisis. As Jameson writes: "This mesmerizing new aesthetic mode itself emerged as an elaborated symptom of the waning of our historicity, of our lived possibility of experiencing history in some active way."[7]

It is important not to exaggerate or schematize the difference between mood and mode; nostalgic sentiments in social life can, of course, be related to nostalgic styles in cultural production. Particular periods or eras that have been characterized as nostalgic have frequently witnessed a proliferation of cultural forms and genres that, at some level, reflect and embed a prevalent economic and/or politically determined mood. The end of the nineteenth century is a case in point, where huge transitions in the urban and industrial reorganization of American life gave rise to various kinds of nostalgic and mythic invocation, especially figured in artistic and narrative renditions of the vanishing West. There is some argument that modernity itself has come to be characterized by a "paradigm of nostalgia." Bryan S. Turner, for example, describes nostalgia as an "ontological condition" arising from estrangement and alienation; he considers the powerful articulation of loss by artists and intellectuals living within, and responding to, the vicissitudes of our modern world. Tracing the endurance of the "nostalgic metaphor" in cultural life, especially within the classic sociology of Tonnies, Weber, and Durkheim at the turn of the twentieth century, Turner suggests that the "nostalgia paradigm is a persistent and prevalent feature of western culture, in literature, art, medical history and social theory."[8]

While nostalgic moods and nostalgia modes are related, this connection should not simply be assumed. Reducing sentiment and style to a fixed and causal relation can underestimate the way that, as a cultural style, nostalgia has become divorced in contemporary culture from a necessary concept of loss. Writing in 1994, Donna Bassin argued: "The current nostalgia among baby boomers for their fifties childhood is evidenced by the increased seeking and collecting of retro artifacts and the surging increase of flea markets and vintage stores."[9] Not only does this assertion ignore the significant popularity of retro and vintage styles among the *children* of the baby boomers to whom Bassin refers, it overdetermines the relationship between middle-age longing and acts of consumption. Bassin does not account for the taste regimes that make retro artifacts popular, the broad development of nostalgia as a commodified genre, or the means by which "the fifties" might exist simultaneously with other kinds of period nostalgia. If there *is* something new about the contemporary moment of nostalgia, it may lie in the ambivalence of the mood/mode relation—that is to say, styles of nostalgia cannot be contained or conflated within schemas of loss, or be read simply in terms of baby-boom longing, fin-de-siècle syndromes, or other kinds of personal and cultural anxiety.

This chapter examines loss and amnesia as grounding critical orientations in modern theories of nostalgia. As a mood, critics have focused upon the social function and cultural politics of nostalgia. It has largely been discussed in terms of its use and appropriation by the political right, but more recent criticism has tried to recoup the significance of nostalgia for the left. This can be traced from the early sociological work of Fred Davis through to more contemporary work informed by feminism and cultural studies. Alternatively, the nostalgia mode has been theorized by critics who perceive a cultural shift reshaping our experience of memory and time. This can be seen in the modernist position taken by Pierre Nora and the differing postmodern perspectives offered by Fredric Jameson and Andreas Huyssen. Conceptually, I want to find a position *between* the prevailing tendencies of loss and amnesia—a critical vantage point that can mediate between dominant narratives of cultural longing and postmodern forgetting. My own position will in this sense depend on a discussion of the two main orientations within nostalgia theory in order that my focus on the memory politics of monochrome can be critically realized in the space left between them.

MOOD

To understand nostalgia as a mood, distinguished by a sense of loss, we must return to the medical conception developed by Johannas Hofer. His conjunction of the classical *nostos* and *algos* at the end of the seventeenth century was an exercise in medical invention, the creation of a mental disease. As Jean Starobinski writes: "The word *nostalgia* was coined for the express purpose of translating a particular feeling (*Heimweh, regret, desiderium patriae*) into medical terminology."[10] By giving "homesickness" a clinical authority and semantic designation, its effects were exposed to rational inquiry. Nostalgia was understood as a form of melancholic loss arising from physical and geographical displacement from the homeland. As an emotional disturbance related to the workings of memory, doctors of the Romantic era conceived nostalgia as a psychosomatic condition. In a time when the demographic displacements of urbanization were shaping the structures of modernity, it is perhaps not incidental that a clinical theory should develop based on the fundamental longing *to return home*.

As nostalgia moved into the realm of psychiatry at the end of the nineteenth century, focus changed from the patient's desire for the literal geography of home to the feelings evoked by past experience. In a medical sense, nostalgia was conceived less as a clinical disease than a matter of reaction and adaptation. These themes would be taken up most famously by Sigmund Freud. In his influential work on mourning and melancholia, Freud theorized the regression of the neurotic to a lost object and / or history. He wrote: "Mourning is regularly the reaction to the loss of a loved person, or to the loss of some abstraction which has taken the place of one, such as one's country, liberty, an ideal, and so on. In some people the same influences produce melancholia instead of mourning and we consequently suspect them of some pathological disposition."[11] Within psychiatric literature, nostalgia became a pathological longing for a lost object particularized in the past. If modern nostalgia critique has often become hostile and disparaging, associating the experience with distortion and regression, it inherits a tradition where nostalgic melancholy has long been seen as something to be cured. Indeed, metaphors of illness and pathology are inscribed in many contemporary theories of nostalgia. Allison Graham argues that a *"plague* visited upon American culture in the mid-1970s, a kind of *illness* whose chief manifestation has been the commercialization of nostalgia." While Susan Stewart talks of the "social *disease* of nostalgia," Robert Hewison comments that "we have no real use for a spurious past any more than nostalgia has any use as a *creative emotion"* (italics added).[12] The nostalgia mood has frequently been given a character of weakness, a feeling defined by crippling reservoirs of pathological longing.

Having lost its clinical currency by the middle of the century, nostalgia developed a critical edge. Tracing its discursive development in the postwar period, Jackson Lears pinpoints the 1970s as the time when "nostalgia's stock began to rise both within the academy and outside it."[13] With the ideology of progress under pressure, intensified by the maelstrom of the 1960s, and with a new generation of social and cultural historians reclaiming and redeeming the preindustrial past, nostalgia developed a new intellectual legitimacy. Lears points to left-wing intellectuals such as E. P. Thompson, Herbert Gutman, and Raymond Williams, all of whom sought to give new seriousness to preindustrial cultures. Together with the so called "nostalgia wave" developing in the sphere of popular culture and with media outpourings helping to model and define it as a cultural phenomenon (*TIME* magazine asked the question in 1971: "How much nostalgia can America take?"), nostalgia was ripening as a theoretical subject in its own right.[14]

The first sustained study of collective nostalgia came in 1979 with Fred Davis's *Yearning for Yesterday: A Sociology of Nostalgia.* Attempting to account for nostalgia and its function in social identity formation, Davis argued that "the current nostalgia boom must be understood in terms of its close relationship to the era of social upheaval that preceded it."[15] Davis is theoretically concerned with nostalgia as it relates to the experience of discontinuity. Underpinning his analysis is an attempt to account for the dislocations of the 1960s and the resulting currency of nostalgia produced in the 1970s. He suggests that nostalgia does not derive from some inherent quality found in the past, but occurs "in the context of present fears, discontents, anxieties and uncertainties." Davis writes: "Nostalgia thrives on transition, on the subjective discontinuities that engender our yearning for continuity."[16] While nostalgia can service politically conservative ambitions, it can also function more broadly as a lens that "we employ in the never-ending work of constructing, maintaining and reconstructing our identities." Focusing upon American life and society, Davis allows for the constructive, as well as for the reactionary, license of collective nostalgia.

Throughout *Yearning for Yesterday,* nostalgia is defined as a mood; it is a feeling characterized by the perception of loss and the prescription of longing. While providing a qualitative description of the nostalgic experience, Davis also considers the manifestation of nostalgia within art and commerce. He writes:

So frequently and uniformly does nostalgic sentiment seem to infuse our aesthetic experience that we can rightly begin to suspect that nostalgia is not only a feeling or mood that is somehow magically evoked by the art object but also a distinctive aesthetic modality in its own right, a kind of code or patterning of symbolic elements, which by some obscure mimetic isomorphism comes, much as in language itself, to serve as a substitute for the feelings or mood it aims to arouse.[17]

Here, nostalgia is framed as a cultural style, an *aesthetic modality*. However, its symbolic elements emerge from, and are governed by, the fundamental experience of nostalgic longing. The nostalgia mode is not a genre but a "substitute for the feelings" of the nostalgia mood. It represents what Davis calls "the artistic symbolization of an emotion." The idea of nostalgia art developed by Davis is very different in this regard from that conceived by Fredric Jameson. By way of focusing their respective theories of nostalgia art, Davis and Jameson both discuss *American Graffiti* (1973). For Davis, this is an example of a failed nostalgia film in that it refuses to maintain a contemplative distance from the past. He writes: "Rather than evoke a nostalgic sense of the past, [it] made events appear as but a slightly oblique version of the present."[18] It is the very presentness of *American Graffiti*, however, that for Jameson makes it the inaugural postmodern nostalgia film. It illustrates a troubled historical imagination "where the desperate attempt to appropriate a missing past is now refracted through the iron law of fashion change and the emergent ideology of a generation."[19] The difference between Davis and Jameson is conceptual. They stand at different ends of a theoretical continuum that distinguishes the feelings of the nostalgia mood (based upon longing) from the style of the nostalgia mode (born from a condition of amnesia).

Davis is significant in providing one of the first systematic explorations of social and cultural nostalgia. He establishes various conditions and specifications that define the nostalgia mood and that distinguish it from remembrance and recollection. It must relate to lived experience, it depends upon a notion of discontinuity, it imbues the past with special qualities, and it is necessarily selective. There is a lapsarian dynamic to the experience and rhetoric of nostalgia, and it is the political potency vested in this sense of loss that has been especially explored by cultural critics. If nostalgia approaches the past as a stable source of value and meaning, Stuart Tannock is keen to acknowledge "the diversity of personal needs and political desires to which nostalgia is a response."[20] This

reflects a tendency in recent cultural analyses for redeeming the function
and utility of nostalgia, focusing upon the way it has been taken up in
the articulation of social and cultural identity.[21] Nostalgia need not be
seen as a troubled emotion but can, instead, respond strategically to the
ambivalence surrounding sociocultural transformation and/or ideologies of progress. Tannock writes that the nostalgic vision can offer "at
one and the same time, both a deferral of, and an alternative to, the first,
everyday world of the present."[22] In different ways, there has been a
renewed tendency in recent social, historical, and cultural theory to
write against the idea that nostalgia is a bankrupt, and politically regressive, disease.

Nostalgia has no prescribed political orientation. It can be engaged by
dominant and subordinate groups alike and used for ends that are
enabling as much as disabling, progressive as well as reactionary. It
would be wrong to conflate nostalgia with conservatism. This does not
mean to say, however, that critics have not scrutinized the conservative
appropriation of nostalgia, especially in hegemonic strategies of the New
Right during the 1980s. By the end of the 1980s, nostalgia had become a
subject of pointed critical interest.[23] This was the result of a number of
factors, but significant among them was the success—and rhetoric—of
neoconservatism as it developed under Reagan and Thatcher. Cultural
criticism has, in this context, focused upon the selectivity and political
mystifications of nostalgic memory as it has been taken up within social
and political discourse. To cite three examples: Stephanie Coontz examines the "crisis" of the American family and the "nostalgia trap," which
has served to idealize a series of family myths that occlude any real grasp
of contemporary family dilemmas; James Combs considers the "nostalgic myth" in U.S. politics that greased Reagan's assault on the welfare
state and buttressed the growth of hawkish militarism; and Janice Doane
and Devon Hodges provide an ideological critique of the "rhetoric of
nostalgia" that has informed the resistance to contemporary feminism in
American life and literature.[24]

The last of these is of particular interest in the way it considers the
politically infused trope of cultural degeneracy. In *Nostalgia and Sexual
Difference* (1987), Doane and Hodges consider the reactionary politics of
nostalgia and the resistance to feminism within male literature, from
novels to cultural critique. They use poststructuralist theory to analyze
strategies of representation, examining "a frightening antifeminist impulse" they call nostalgic. Nostalgia is here defined as "a retreat into the
past in the face of what a number of writers—most of them male—
perceive to be the degeneracy of American culture brought about by the
rise of feminist authority."[25] Nostalgia responds to the "discontinuity"
that feminism represents to patriarchal hegemony. Considering writers

as diverse as Harold Bloom, Christopher Lasch, John Irving, and Ishmael Reed, the authors show how a belief in "natural" sexual difference is held up and sanctified as a norm that contemporary feminists are then seen to threaten. Doane and Hodges conceive nostalgia as a "rhetorical practice" that has idealized a past deeply complicit with patriarchal authority; they demonstrate how narratives of decline and degeneracy have been used to shore up the status and legitimacy of existent power relations. Their analysis is critically prescient, for it anticipates a number of key rhetorical issues that would emerge in the academic "culture war" of the late 1980s and early 1990s. Linked to the rise of (feminist/multi-cultural) identity politics, narratives of cultural degeneracy were mobilized from various critical positions in response to, and as a reaction against, the so-called "politicization" of educational practices and institutional structures.[26]

There are several key presuppositions in theories that conceive nostalgia as a mood. Whether examined as rhetoric or a structure of feeling, the nostalgic experience emerges from, and is made to relate to, a grounding concept of loss. Responding to a felt or figurative discontinuity, the nostalgic mood locates meaning and stability in a glorified past. Critics of the nostalgia mood are concerned with specific representations of the past and how these may respond to present social and political needs. Focus will sharpen on *what* is chosen from the past, *why* exactly, and *whose interest* it serves. As a form of idealized remembrance, the nostalgia mood can be taken up in ways that are reactionary and progressive. Whichever it may be, the mood is based on the principle and experience of longing. In the next section, I consider theories of nostalgia that are organized around, or specifically conceive, nostalgia as a mode. Describing the aestheticization and commodification of nostalgia within the contemporary cultural terrain, critics are less concerned with the content of nostalgic longing than with its stylistic form and significance in a world of media image, temporal breakdown, and cultural amnesia. At issue here is not the substance of nostalgic loss but the specificity of postmodern memory itself.

MODE

In commercial and aesthetic terms, nostalgia has long been a "mode" in American cultural life, whether viewed in terms of the bygone West pictured at the end of the nineteenth century by Frederic Remington, the "colonial" revival in building and furniture design that emerged in the 1880s, the resurgence of folk arts and handicraft traditions during the 1930s, or the protoheritage sites of Greenfield Village (1933) and Colonial Williamsburg (1934). It is in the postwar period, however, that

nostalgia was broadly commodified in the burgeoning heritage industry. Michael Kammen has assiduously traced this development, describing the period from 1945 to 1990 as one distinguished by "nostalgia,
heritage and the anomalies of historical amnesia."[27] Kammen maps the
democratization of tradition since the Second World War and, with it,
the prodigious growth of nostalgia bound in ideas of heritage. He links
nostalgia to the cultural consequences of swift social change, the need
for stable anchors and consensus in the wake of upheavals like Vietnam
and Watergate, an entrepreneurial spirit intent on selling the past, the
growing interest in historical preservation and Americana, a broadening
enthusiasm for "vernacular culture," and the impact of the media in
disseminating popular, "instant" history. Kammen weaves the sentiment of the nostalgia mood and the selling of the nostalgia mode in a
complex history examining the invention, celebration, marketing, and
mythologizing of America's national past.

Kammen is useful in bridging theoretically the concept of nostalgia as
a social and collective mood with definitions that conceive it as a
commodified and amnesiac mode. Historically, Kammen suggests that
nostalgia emerged as a pan-Atlantic phenomenon in the postwar period,
compensating for "our genuine distance from the past in time as well as
knowledge and understanding."[28] Like Fred Davis, he gives nostalgia a
social function, helping people and cultures adapt to rapid and momentous change. Kammen grows more scathing about the "wistful nostalgia
of the seventies and eighties," however. He suggests that nostalgia's
growing commercialization has turned the past into a playground of
what he calls "history without guilt."[29] Kammen concentrates less on the
social function of nostalgia than on its "tendentiously capricious memories" within mass culture. He writes:

The pervasiveness of nostalgic yearnings, the peculiarity of disremembering
amidst pride in the past, an expanded role for the media in presenting
"memories" and the commercialization of tradition supply some of the central themes that have characterized our own time with its strangely superficial sense of history and heritage—a commodity to be packaged in hundreds
of ways ranging from docudramas to "collectibles" at flea markets.[30]

As nostalgia proliferates in cultural and commercial life, it intensifies a
"superficial" sense of history. Kammen is bothered by the fatuous capacity of idealized history, and his sense of amnesia develops from this
concern; it is a consequence of the selectivity of nostalgic memory rather
than a conditional response to the deep restructuring of mnemonic experience. To place Kammen along the proposed theoretical continuum, one
might say that, within his framework of cultural history, nostalgia is *a
mood that has been increasingly realized as a mode*. Nostalgic loss has been

transformed into a marketable style, a kind of entertainment. This has engendered a saccharine and ultimately forgetful history. Kammen suggests that an "entrepreneurial mode of selective memory has achieved amazing commercial success, though the price of selective memory has been indiscriminate amnesia."[31] In his account of the growing heritage "imperative" or "syndrome" within American cultural life, Kammen understands nostalgia as a mood verging on, or veering into, a commercialized mode. Amnesia describes the unhappy consequence of sanitized memory rather than being, as for many postmodern critics, a symptom of an emergent cultural condition.

It is in postmodern discourse that the nostalgia mode reaches its theoretical apogee. In this context, amnesia is not a side-effect of commercialized nostalgia, as it is for Kammen, but is central to a crisis in the contemporary historical imagination. Jean Baudrillard suggests: "when the real is no longer what it used to be, nostalgia assumes its full meaning."[32] Here, "nostalgia" refers not to any longing for a specified golden age, but to a "panic-stricken production of the real and referential" in a new era of simulation and hyperreality. Of particular significance, and influencing later theories of postmodernism like that of Fredric Jameson, is Baudrillard's claim that history itself has become a "lost referential." He suggests that in response "nostalgia endlessly accumulates: war, fascism, the pageantry of the belle époque, or the revolutionary struggles, everything is equivalent and is mixed indiscriminately in the same morose and funereal exaltation, in the same retro fascination."[33] For Baudrillard, as for Jameson, nostalgia is never a mood or a feeling in any simple sense, but is tied to the mourning for memory itself. While these arguments are not without their own critical nostalgia—largely for an idea of deep historicism and the capability, supposedly lost, of looking at the "real" past—my concern in this section is less with the nostalgic subtext of particular works than with the explicit and conceptual "nostalgia mode" developed within postmodern theory.[34] Ultimately, this bears upon the work of Fredric Jameson and a series of influential essays that formed the basis of *Postmodernism, or, The Cultural Logic of Late Capitalism*.

In Jameson's theory, nostalgia is not a mood of longing but a "mode" within art, symptomatic of the postmodern "crisis of historicity." This crisis describes a situation whereby the present can no longer be conceived as history or lived in active ways. Unable to organize the past and future into a temporal scheme, Jameson argues, "we seem increasingly incapable of fashioning representations of our own current experience."[35] If postmodern society cannot deal with time and history, it has consequences for cultural production; the nostalgia mode does not represent, approximate, or idealize the past, but it helps reconstruct it for the present as a vast collection of images. The nostalgia mode does not find utopian meaning in the past, but indiscriminately plunders it for style, refracting the past through fashion and glossy images of "pastness."

The significance of Jameson is the neo-Marxian framework he brings to his postmodern theory. Postmodernism is never merely a style in his argument. Neither does it signify a major cultural break, nor a total paradigm shift. Instead, postmodernism is a new cultural dominant that corresponds to the third stage of late, multinational capitalism. He uses the term as a periodizing concept but one that is based on the reconstellation of historical elements in new and intensified forms, not on a fixed division between radically different epochs. Jameson identifies not a break but a profound shift occurring in the social, cultural, and economic order. He locates this in the 1960s, where new forms and modes of experience began to grow in relation to multinational consumer capitalism. A distinguishing feature of this economic system, along with its media technologies, business organization, and global character, is the commodification of previously uncommodified areas. This speaks of its cultural logic, meaning the penetration of (late) capitalist energies into the cultural sphere and, ultimately, representation. As culture and aesthetic production become commodities in their own right, they expand throughout the social realm and provide both for the aestheticization of daily life and for the effacement of distinctions between high and mass culture. Critically, this means that Jameson can examine postmodern cultural forms—media images, political spectacle, music, film, architecture—and find them not simply reinforcing but constituting the economic order. Although Jameson has provoked wide discussion about the legitimacy of his argument and methodological dependence on cultural forms, his theory is significant in drawing a basic relationship between postmodernism and capitalist materiality.

If in different historical moments our lived experience of space and time can change according to particular modes of production, Jameson believes that late capitalism has brought with it the "spatialization of time." This concept underpins much of his theory. Many features of postmodernism that Jameson identifies, like pastiche and schizophrenia, derive from a contention that space has overcome time in the way we live, think about, and experience the world. A strong sense of (temporal) continuity is difficult to achieve in a postmodern state of information flow, media imagery, flexible accumulation, market volatility, global production, and accelerated consumption, in a postmodern culture of surface, simulation, fragmentation, and instantaneity. Themes of time and temporality belong to high modernism, along with models of depth. Postmodern life, on the other hand, is marked by flux and discontinuity. This has led to the breakdown of the temporal order and a profound waning of our sense of history. Jameson writes that "our entire contemporary social system has little by little begun to lose its capacity to retain its own past, has begun to live in a perpetual present and in a perpetual change that obliterates traditions of the kind that all earlier social formations have had in one way or another to preserve.[36] There has been, in effect, a compression whereby the past and the future have been sucked into a state of temporal presentism. It is this state that ultimately leads to postmodern schizophrenia (the loss of self in undifferentiated time) and pastiche (the flat and random collage of dead styles). Both are constitutive of a new depthless culture that has given rise to a new relationship between postmodernism and the past.

To understand Jameson's "nostalgia mode" fully, it is important to grasp this relationship. The loss of temporality in our perpetual present has, so the argument goes, caused new attachments to instant impact over continuity. There is a fixation on images and appearance as temporal depth is replaced by spatial surface. Jameson writes: "The new spatial logic of the simulacrum can now be expected to have a momentous effect on what used to be historical time."[37] The past, he goes on to say, is modified by this. Genuine historical consciousness that would enable distinctions to be drawn between past and present, thereby organizing time historically, is replaced by simulation and pastiche. This may satisfy our need for *images* of the past but will do nothing in the way of relating the past to a temporal scheme. Mnemonic capacities are replaced by random intensities; our conception of the past becomes spatial, instant, depthless. Jameson provocatively suggests that "we are condemned to seek History by way of our own pop images and simulacra of that history, which itself remains forever out of reach."[38]

The breakdown of memory and historical time will have implications for nostalgia understood as a form or idealized remembrance. If the nostalgia mood is based on a dialogue between the present and the past, this dialogue is problematized in a world of perpetual presents. Part of the postmodern "waning of effect," in Jameson's argument, involves the loss of historicist pathos and deep nostalgia. Indeed, his use of "nostalgia" is separate from any concept of golden ages, visions of stability, or connotations of past utopia. Nostalgia is no longer conceived as a yearning but as a consumable mode. It does not relate the present to the past but transforms the past into image and stylistic connotation. This mode is discussed specifically in terms of art and the "nostalgia film." Here, content is less significant than feel; it is exemplified not only by *American Graffiti,* with its recreation of the atmospheric and stylistic peculiarities of the 1950s (or "fifties-ness"), but also by *Star Wars* (1977) and its evocation of old genres and the reinvention of serials like *Buck Rogers.* Now that the modernist period of individual expression and originality has arguably passed, marking the death of the (creating) subject, superficial ensembles of past style have become a primary mode of cultural production. The nostalgia film exemplifies this. Using pastiche, nostalgia films imitate the spirit, style, dash, and design of previous times, crafting a product that, when it treats the past, offers little more than simulation and "fashion-plate image."

It is necessary to focus at some length on *Postmodernism*, for Jameson posits an influential concept of nostalgia that can be distinguished from more conventional ideas of loss, absence, and an idealized past. Jameson's ambitious attempt to cognitively map the life and logic of postmodernism is not without its criticisms. Ien Ang, for one, chastises any totalizing theory that sees postmodernism as a structural *fait accompli*, "a homogenized, one dimensional and increasingly global reality."[39] In the terms set out by Ang, Jameson fails to consider the profound uncertainty of capitalist postmodernity. Specifically, he does not consider how audiences negotiate meaning in a media-saturated world, or, indeed, how meaning and memory may be refigured in a changing cultural and semiotic terrain. Nevertheless—and without wishing to paint Jameson as some über-theorist of postmodern nostalgia—he is significant for two reasons. First, Jameson develops a concept that usefully conceives something new about nostalgia and its aesthetic place in cultural life, examining it generically as "art," "film," and "mode." Second, his theory is based on presuppositions that operate in other critical works concerned with (post)modernity and time. This, put simply, is the premise that our current climate is one marked by historical amnesia. Two critics who develop this concept are Andreas Huyssen and Pierre Nora. Although their work is markedly different in historical scope and political orientation, they each theorize a basic change in the way that people relate to the past; they notice a shift in our experience of history and memory. Nostalgia is not examined directly, yet both critics help to emphasize, like Jameson, the question of *how* we apprehend the past as much as what is drawn from it.

In his novel *Slowness*, Milan Kundera writes of a "secret bond between slowness and memory, between speed and forgetting."[40] One could argue that postmodernity is beset by the promise and perils of speed in its various forms, whether information highways or media blizzards. Speed has come from the reconfiguration of space. One of the clearest examples of this is the speed of communication that has developed from satellites, media technology, and electronic networks. Despite its wonders, many argue that speed does very little to nourish memory or a sense of continuity. This belief is present in Jameson's work and is taken on by Huyssen too. Amnesia is seen to be the consequential illness of a postmodern climate of rapid change, instant communication, and constant consumption. The equation between speed and forgetting defines our contemporaneity. If Michael Kammen looks for the historical indices of amnesia, examining everything from the need to forget after Vietnam to the commercially sanitized history purveyed by the likes of Disney, Andreas Huyssen provides a more fundamental cultural diagnosis. Rather than focusing on definitive historical conditions that explain amnesia for any one country, he examines the "twilight" status of memory itself in Western culture.

Like Jameson, Huyssen believes that our experience of time has changed dramatically. Central to this transformation is the speed and style of high-tech media. The point for Huyssen is not the breakdown of historical time and cultural memory, but the way they have each been shaped by a social formation where the past has become subject to new forms of representation. Huyssen does not give up memory as some older modernist privilege but explores how a new postmodern variety has developed in relation to media representation and the "quickening pace of material life." It has been argued that new media technologies have induced cultural amnesia by diluting the process of active remembrance. Huyssen is unconvinced by this, accepting that contemporary culture suffers from an amnesiac virus but, at the same time, is witnessing the struggle of memory against it. He looks at a contemporary paradox, or dialectic, whereby a waning sense of historical consciousness has been matched simultaneously by a virtual obsession with the past. Trying to think memory and amnesia together, Huyssen believes that we are experiencing mnemonic fever as a reflex *against* forgetting. He considers there to be a basic need to "mark time" in a culture losing its temporal anchor. He states that memory "represents the attempt to slow down information processing, to resist the dissolution of time in the synchronicity of the archive, to recover a mode of contemplation outside the universe of simulation and fast-speed information and cable networks, to claim some anchoring space in a world of puzzling and often threatening heterogeneity, nonsynchronicity, and information overload."[41] Memory represents a battle. This is not judged on the grounds of cultural politics, be they struggles fought over the "natural woman" in contemporary literature or the kind of history the Enola Gay should tell as an exhibit in the National Air and Space Museum.[42] The battle for memory, in Huyssen's view, is a question not simply of negotiated political meaning, but of the need, *the imperative*, to live with a sense of temporality.

Huyssen proceeds, like Jameson, from an idea of cultural shift. They both identify something new in the way we live time and experience the past, each agreeing that amnesia defines the postmodern moment. Huyssen does not give up the concept and significance of memory, however. One can see that important questions are being asked and different conclusions drawn about the nature of memory and its relation to the cultural configuration of postmodernism. Nostalgia, as a form of memory, is deeply involved in these debates. How do changing structures of temporality affect the meaning and experience of nostalgia? What effect do the media have on the status of nostalgia as a style or mode? Is nostalgia a product of, or a defense against, the so-called virus of amnesia? Huyssen does not theorize nostalgia as a mode in the same way as Jameson does, but he does consider the various ways in which memory, recollection, history, nostalgia, all the means of marking time, relate to a postmodern social formation obliged, even compelled, to arrest the past in the face and fear of memory's dissolution.

Although working with historical parameters that extend far beyond specific discussions of postmodernism (namely, the difference between peasant and modern cultures), and keeping his discussion focused on France, Pierre Nora also considers memory in contemporary culture. He focuses on French culture, but his theoretical distinction between "environments of memory" and new "sites of memory" has been applied to other cultural, in particular American, paradigms.[43] Nora's basic contention is that the "acceleration of history"—meaning the historical perception with which "our hopelessly forgetful modern societies, propelled by chance, organize the past"—has replaced older forms of spontaneous memory. Instead of environments of memory, *milieux de mémoire*, we now have sites of memory, *lieux de mémoire*. These include museums, archives, cemeteries, festivals, monuments—anything that represents a conscious endeavor to maintain a sense, or trace, of memory. For Nora, these are "moments of history torn away from the movement of history."[44] They are, in a particular sense, material, symbolic, and functional modes of memory entirely divorced from experiential moods of memory.

Nora believes that "we speak so much of memory because there is so little of it left." Memory is now a matter of conscious construction and preservation, rather than instinctive and impromptu feeling; it is artificially (hyper)realized in response to our basic estrangement from the past. According to Nora's argument, a transformation has occurred in the relationship between memory and history—memory being suppressed and destroyed by history's compulsion to crystallize and exteriorize its "magic" in artificial representations—and our sense of the past has been deeply altered because of it. While his theory has become an influential touch-point in thinking through memory's cultural and historical specificity, Nora demonstrates a troubling nostalgia for "real" or unbidden memory. Yearning for a moment when society's experience of the past was fluid and not manifest in stillborn sites, Nora's memorial lament shares something in kind with Jameson's neo-Marxian nostalgia for "genuine historicity." While argued on different critical grounds, both suggest a deleterious transformation in our experience and understanding of the past, linked to modern and / or postmodern conditions of change.

Jameson, Huyssen, and Nora all have different critical objectives. Jameson wants to historicize postmodernism, cognitively mapping its new territory with examples drawn principally from America; Huyssen examines the status of memory in contemporary culture, addressing the media as a representational form but with a specific cultural interest in Germany; Nora considers the transformation of modern memory from a spontaneous experience to a constructed "site," his theoretical application being France. What connects them all, however, is the belief in a critical change that (post)modern culture has experienced in its relationship with the past. It is held that forms of memory have been influenced, inscribed, even destroyed, by the pace of change in the contemporary milieu. There is nothing timeless about the way we apprehend the past. Indeed, there is nothing timeless about historical time. Accepting the cultural contingency of memory, each critic develops a theory or principle of amnesia; they understand contemporary memory practices in terms of depthlessness (Jameson), struggle (Huyssen), and inauthenticity (Nora). Nostalgia is embroiled in these different schemes of beleaguered mnemonic experience. Whether a stylistic mode resulting from a crisis of historicity, a way of "marking time" in a culture of amnesia, or a memory "site" in a climate where moments have replaced the movement of history, nostalgia is theoretically positioned in relation to an era where memory is fading in the form and structure of everyday life. Nostalgia is set in relation to a new cultural configuration where the experience of memory and moods of temporal longing may be felt and signified in particular ways, or where they no longer exist or function at all.

NOSTALGIA MODES
AND NONREPRESENTATIONAL CODES

The mood / mode distinction should not be taken to suggest mutually exclusive categories. Critics frequently address nostalgia as a feeling *and* a style, as a cultural orientation *and* a representational effect. The relationship between the two will often be understood, however, through conceptual presuppositions that I have characterized in the distinction between loss and amnesia. To illustrate, one might compare Fred Davis and Fredric Jameson. Davis is concerned with nostalgia as a collective mood, a way of adapting to social change and responding to the experience of discontinuity. When Davis considers nostalgia as a cultural style, it is an aesthetic figuration of this mood, "the symbolization of an emotion." In his theory, the mode grows from and helps enact the mood; nostalgia is a collectively felt and culturally realized experience of longing. By contrast, Fredric Jameson is concerned with nostalgia as a mode, a form of pastiche symptomatic of the postmodern crisis of historicity. When Jameson considers nostalgia as a mood, it is only as a casualty of the depthless and spatial logic of late capitalism. The mood has become a bankrupt emotion and has been replaced by the simulations of a new cultural mode; nostalgia is a stylistic regime defined by the historical waning of effect. While Davis has little sense that nostalgia may have become a consumable style reflecting economies of taste and textuality rather than compulsory feelings of loss, Jameson disconnects stylized nostalgia from any concept of memory at all.

To examine nostalgia as a contemporary cultural style, a theoretical scheme is required that can mediate between the poles of loss and amnesia. Concentrating upon the context and use of particular media practices in contemporary life, a culturalist position should avoid, or at least be wary of, schemes that reduce aestheticized nostalgia to necessary manifestations of longing or forgetting. In moving toward a consideration of the black-and-white image in 1990s America, I want to account for the manner in which styles of nostalgia have become divorced from any *necessary* concept of loss, but also for how particular nostalgia modes have been used affectively in the mass media to perform specific cultural and memory work. Basically, I wish to tread a path that will neither ignore the broad development of nostalgia as a style— bound in specific regimes of taste, inscribed in modes of textuality, and enabled by new forms of technology—nor underestimate the function of aestheticized nostalgia as it has been taken up within discourses of cultural and national identity.

As it applies to an examination of the black-and-white image, the said process of mediation involves critically intersecting two cultural/theoretical projects. The first is represented in a varied body of work concerned with the construction of memory, a diverse critical enterprise that deals with the means by which the past has been staged or invented to authorize and articulate particular cultural and historical identities and political/critical positionalities.[45] The second project derives from the field of cultural studies and is specifically concerned with the way that nonrepresentational cultural effects such as color and music may (or may not) make connections with the ideological, the economic, and the political. While Lawrence Grossberg explores music and the "affective economy" of rock, film theorists such as Steve Neale and Richard Dyer have focused on the technological use and cinematic conventions of color and light in classical and postclassical Hollywood.[46] In each case, there is a fundamental concern with nonrepresentational effects (and affects) in cultural production and everyday life. At issue are abstract sign systems such as color and sound that have no referent—that is, they do not constitute representations of reality in and of themselves—but are nevertheless infused with codes, and are articulated within discursive formations, that help to create particular kinds of feel and meaning.

By focusing upon the use of monochrome in contemporary visual media, I am concerned with the nonrepresentational effects of "black and whiteness." I am less concerned with the content of any particular image than with the temporal and authenticity effects produced by monochrome as a mode of nostalgia. In critical terms, this involves locating the reproduction and circulation of nostalgia within specific cultural examples rather than speculating on whether nostalgia is endemic to the disposition and temper of American (postmodern) life. Defining nostalgic practices and predispositions may have validity in establishing broad historical structures of feeling. Critically, however, Christopher Lasch is perhaps right to comment that "what is needed is not an explanation of our nostalgic national condition but an explanation of the widespread *preoccupation* with nostalgia in the intellectual community and the mass media, and the infiltration of political and cultural commentary by this particular catchword."[47] Effectively, I want to anchor a set of critical questions that can be asked of the signifying and political functionality of nostalgia in the visual narratives of the dominant media.

Before turning to the memory politics of monochrome, it is necessary to expand on the commodification and aestheticization of nostalgia in contemporary American culture. Chapter 2 considers the cultural dimensions—and provides some more precise examples—of nostalgia as a style or mode. It will focus upon the disjunction between nostalgia modes and forms of longing in American culture, suggesting that the selling and circulation of nostalgia has become less dependent on the content of any specific (and idealized) past than upon the *affective economy of pastness*. In such a context, the prevalence of black and white in 1990s visual culture cannot be explained simply as the "symbolization of an emotion"; it does not reflect or reveal a general incidence of nostalgic longing. Neither does it reveal the frantic thrashings of a drowning memorial consciousness, a culture whose image world responds desperately to the threat and presence of postmodern forgetting. Instead, it can be understood within a climate where memory, nostalgia, and the past had become, certainly by the 1990s, an amplified site of affective investment—that is to say, a moment where the production of pastness had been enabled by new technologies, enlivened by regimes of taste and textuality, and increasingly mobilized for commercial, cultural, and political ends. This chapter has examined tendencies within nostalgia critique; chapter 2 historicizes the cultural production of nostalgia in American life during the 1980s and 1990s. Having established the conceptual terrain, I want now to provide some contextual bearings.

NOTES

1. Johannas Hofer, " Medical Dissertation on Nostalgia," first published in 1688 and translated by Carolyn K. Anspach, *Bulletin of the History of Medicine,* 2 (1934): 384. A concise treatment of nostalgia as a term is given by Jean Starobinski, "The Idea of Nostalgia," trans. William S. Kemp. *Diogenes,* 54 (1966): 81–103.

2. Fred Davis, *Yearning for Yesterday: A Sociology of Nostalgia* (New York: Free Press, 1979): 4.

3. Maurice Halbwachs, *On Collective Memory,* trans. and ed. Lewis Coser (Chicago, IL: University of Chicago Press, 1992).

4. See Ralph Harper, *Nostalgia: An Existential Exploration of Longing and Fulfillment in the Modern Age* (Cleveland, OH: Press of the Western Reserve University, 1966).

5. David Lowenthal, "Nostalgia Tells It Like It Wasn't," in Malcolm Chase and Christopher Shaw, eds., *The Imagined Past: History and Nostalgia* (Manchester: Manchester University Press, 1989): 29; see also, Christopher Lasch, "The Politics of Nostalgia," *Harper's* (November 1984): 65–70.

6. Susan Stewart, *On Longing: Narratives of the Miniature, the Gigantic, the Souvenir, the Collection* (Baltimore, MD: Johns Hopkins University Press, 1984): 23.

7. Fredric Jameson, *Postmodernism, or, The Cultural Logic of Late Capitalism* (London: Verso, 1991): 21.

8. Bryan S. Turner, "A Note on Nostalgia," *Theory, Culture & Society,* 4, no. 1 (1987): 147–156. The "nostalgia paradigm" in social and cultural discourse is, in Turner's argument, distinguished by four dimensions of loss. These include a sense of lost grace, the loss of personal wholeness and moral certainty, the loss of individual freedom and genuine social relationships, and the loss of simplicity and personal authenticity.

9. Donna Bassin, "Maternal Subjectivity in the Culture of Nostalgia: Mourning and Melancholy," in Donna Bassin, ed., *Representations of Motherhood* (New Haven, CT: Yale University Press, 1994): 164.

10. Starobinski, "The Idea of Nostalgia": 84.

11. Sigmund Freud, "Mourning and Melancholia," *On Metapsychology: The Theory of Psychoanalysis,* trans. and ed., James Strachey (London: Penguin, 1991): 252. For a broad treatment of Freud and memory, see Richard King, "Memory and Phantasy," *Modern Language Notes,* 98 (1983): 1197–1213.

12. Allison Graham, "History, Nostalgia and the Criminality of Popular Culture," *Georgia Review,* 38, no. 2 (1984): 348; Susan Stewart, *On Longing:* 23; Robert Hewison, *The Heritage Industry: Britain in a Climate of Decline* (London: Methuen, 1987): 138.

13. Jackson Lears, "Looking Backward: In Defense of Nostalgia," *Lingua Franca* (December/January 1998): 60.

14. Gerald Clarke, "The Meaning of Nostalgia," *Time,* 3 May 1971: 77.

15. Davis, *Yearning for Yesterday:* 90.

16. Davis, *Yearning for Yesterday:* 49.

17. Davis, *Yearning for Yesterday:* 73.

18. Davis, *Yearning for Yesterday:* 90.

19. Jameson, *Postmodernism*: 19.

20. Stuart Tannock, "Nostalgia Critique," *Cultural Studies*, 9, no. 3 (1995): 453.

21. See, for example, Lawrence Levine, *The Unpredictable Past: Explorations in American Cultural History* (New York: Oxford University Press, 1993); and Lears, "Looking Backwards."

22. Tannock, "Nostalgia Critique": 459.

23. David Lowenthal comments upon his own rather casual treatment of nostalgic sentimentality in 1985 compared with his entrance into the growing debates over the politics and cultural consequences of nostalgia four years later. See the difference in analysis between Lowenthal, "Nostalgia Tells it Like it Wasn't": 18–32, and his previous work, *The Past is a Foreign Country* (Cambridge: Cambridge University Press, 1985).

24. Stephanie Coontz, *The Way We Never Were: American Families and the Nostalgia Trap* (New York: Basic Books, 1992). In a similar account, Arlene Skolnick has examined the rhetoric of nostalgia that pervades many discussions about family life and the changes that have occurred since the 1950s. See Arlene Skolnick, *Embattled Paradise: The American Family in an Age of Uncertainty* (New York: HarperCollins, 1991). The discussion of Reagan and feminism can be found, respectively, in Combs, *The Reagan Range*; and Janice Doane and Devon Hodges, *Nostalgia and Sexual Difference: The Resistance to Contemporary Feminism* (New York: Methuen, 1987).

25. Doane and Hodges, *Nostalgia and Sexual Difference*: xiii. See also Jean Pickering and Suzanne Kehde, ed., *Narratives of Nostalgia, Gender and Nationalism* (Basingstoke, U.K.: Macmillan, 1997).

26. In the academic culture war, the concept of degeneracy can be seen in both conservative and liberal critique, from the work of Allan Bloom to that of Russell Jacoby. Barry Sarchett writes: "even though Jacoby and Bloom do not share similar political positions, they do share a common discursive formation that demands a narrative of decline as a rallying call for a lost authority." In each case, this is figured around the perception of failing educational standards and compromised intellectual integrity, brought on by the (theoretical) professionalization and (cultural) politicization of the American academy. See Barry S. Sarchett, "Russell Jacoby, Antiprofessionalism, and the Cultural Politics of Nostalgia," in Jeffrey Williams, ed., *PC Wars: Politics and Theory in the Academy* (New York: Routledge, 1995): 253–278.

27. Michael Kammen, *Mystic Chords of Memory: The Transformation of Tradition in American Culture* (New York: Vintage Books, 1993): 7.

28. Kammen, *Mystic Chords*: 534.

29. Michael Kammen, *In The Past Lane: Historical Perspectives on American Culture* (New York: Oxford University Press, 1997): 157.

30. Kammen, *Mystic Chords*: 536.

31. Kammen, *Mystic Chords*: 536.

32. Jean Baudrillard, *Simulacra and Simulation*, trans. Sheila Faria Glaser (Ann Arbor, MI: University of Michigan Press, 1994): 6.

33. Baudrillard, *Simulacra and Simulation*: 44.

34. With his critical interest in popular culture and postmodern aesthetics, Jim Collins suggests that "Underlying all of Baudrillard's claims is a basically Adorno-like combination of nostalgia and paranoia." Similarly, Neville Wakefield argues that Jameson indulges "in a nostalgia for a paradise lost of stable meanings and fixed coordinates of value." Suggestive here is the potential for certain kinds of critical nostalgia to embed themselves within theories that themselves proclaim the end of

memory, longing, and nostalgia. See Jim Collins, *Uncommon Cultures: Popular Culture and Post-Modernism* (New York: Routledge, 1989): 117; and Neville Wakefield, *Postmodernism: The Twilight of the Real* (London: Pluto Press, 1990): 62.

35. Jameson, *Postmodernism*: 21.

36. Fredric Jameson, "Postmodernism and Consumer Society," in E. Ann Kaplan, ed., *Postmodernism and its Discontents* (London: Verso, 1990): 28.

37. Jameson, *Postmodernism*: 18.

38. Jameson, *Postmodernism*: 25.

39. Ien Ang, *Living Room Wars: Rethinking Media Audiences for a Postmodern World* (London: Routledge, 1996): 2.

40. Milan Kundera, *Slowness* (London: Faber & Faber, 1996): 34.

41. Andreas Huyssen, *Twilight Memories: Marking Time in a Culture of Amnesia* (New York: Routledge, 1995): 7.

42. The Enola Gay exhibition went on display in the Smithsonian's National Air and Space Museum in June 1995, having been chastised by a number of columnists and ex-servicemen as an "antinuke morality play." A good account of this is given by Mike Wallace, "The Battle of the Enola Gay," *Mickey Mouse History and Other Essays on American Collective Memory* (Philadelphia, PA: Temple University Press, 1996): 270–318.

43. See in particular Genevieve Fabre and Robert O'Meally, eds., *History and Memory in African-American Culture* (New York: Oxford University Press, 1994).

44. Pierre Nora, "Between Memory and History: Les Lieux de Mémoire," trans. Marc Roudebush, *Representations*, 26 (Spring 1989): 12.

45. See Barbara Kirschenblatt-Gimblett, *Destination Culture: Tourism, Museums, and Heritage* (Berkeley, CA: University of California Press, 1998); Eric Hobsbawm and Terence Ranger, eds., *The Invention of Tradition* (Cambridge: Cambridge University Press, 1983); Susan Bennett, *Performing Nostalgia: Shifting Shakespeare and the Contemporary Past* (London: Routledge, 1996); and David Brett, *The Construction of Heritage* (Cork: Cork University Press, 1996).

46. See Lawrence Grossberg, *Dancing in Spite of Myself: Essays on Popular Culture* (Durham, NC: Duke University Press, 1997): 145–165; Steve Neale, *Cinema and Technology: Image, Sound, Colour* (London: Macmillan, 1985); Richard Dyer, *White* (London: Routledge, 1997). Written more from a psychoanalytic perspective, see also Caryl Flinn, *Strains of Utopia: Gender, Nostalgia and Hollywood Film Music* (Princeton, NJ: Princeton University Press, 1992).

47. Lasch, "The Politics of Nostalgia": 66.

2

Pastness
and the Production of Nostalgia

In describing the recent and growing popularity of old photographs, Raphael Samuel suggests that within popular taste the content of an image is often secondary to questions of color and tone. As such, the difference between a print of a 1906 football team and that of women demonstrating for suffrage will be of little consequence, so long as both are in sepia. He writes: "Pictures seem to recommend themselves for reproduction because they are, in some ineffable sense, 'atmospheric,' blurring the hard lines of detail in some more generalized aura of pastness."[1] Samuel is specifically concerned with the commercial circulation of visual images and their contribution to British "theatres of memory." His comment is suggestive, however, of larger conceptual distinctions that can be made between the content, or "detail," of nostalgic longing and the more random, and affective, economy of stylized pastness. If the nostalgia mood represents a particular conception of the past, thought to be more stable and complete, the nostalgia mode describes an aesthetic register with a far more indiscriminate relationship with the past. This chapter is concerned with the status and production of "pastness" in American culture during the 1980s and 1990s; it provides a wide-ranging survey of how nostalgia has developed as a mode, market, and style.

In the last three decades of the twentieth century, nostalgia was commodified and aestheticized in American culture as perhaps never before. One may posit a variety of contributory factors, including diversifying markets for memory, the growth of the heritage industry, the political aesthetic of Reaganism, the demographic size of a baby-boom generation entering middle-age and the attendant selling of the "boomer" past, the proliferation of technologies of time-shifting and digital reproduction, and a representational economy of recycling and pastiche. In no singular way, these all helped develop nostalgia as a cultural style—a consumable mode, as much as it can be said to be an experienced mood. Mocking the prevalence of American pop-cultural kitsch appreciation in the late-1990s, the irreverent online magazine *The Onion* ran a headline story that cautioned about an imminent national retro crisis, stating: "U.S. Dept. of Retro Warns: 'We May Be Running Out of Past.'" In many ways, this was satirically engaged with the kind of crisis scenario envisaged by critics who often read the proliferation of nostalgia as a sign of (1) creative bankruptcy, (2) millennial longing, (3) temporal breakdown, (4) postmodern amnesia, (5) other kinds of prescriptive malaise. The reservoir of American popular nostalgia has been generously tapped in recent times, and this has encouraged a trend in rather foreboding cultural diagnoses. There is a critical tendency across various disciplines to explain the new preponderance for the past in terms of what Jim Collins has called, and criticized as, a *"Zeitgeist* model"—that is to say, a mode of analysis that accounts for (and generally laments) the rising stock of heritage, tradition, memory, and nostalgia by relating them to a governing narrative or cultural temper.[2]

The zeitgeist model is especially prevalent in accounts of the initial "nostalgia boom" of the 1970s, a phenomenon that can be seen to include films like *The Sting* and *American Graffiti*, sitcoms such as *Happy Days*, the flourishing of "retrochic" in the fashion industry, the turn toward historic preservation in city architecture, and the burgeoning interest in heritage evidenced in, and inspired by, dramas like *Roots*. Explaining the growing currency of nostalgia emergent in the 1970s, critics often refer to a sense of national crisis or—to use a phrase made popular at the time—"malaise." Fred Davis relates the cultural incidence of nostalgia to a sense of dislocation, mainly caused by sociopolitical factors such as crippling inflation, the humiliations caused by the Arab oil embargo and the withdrawal from Vietnam, the tarnishing of the presidency caused by the Watergate scandal, and the confusions of sexual morality and family values that, collectively, led Jimmy Carter to speak in 1979 of an American "crisis of confidence." In aesthetic terms, Allison Graham relates the production of nostalgia within popular culture to a moment of creative exhaustion, a time where "popular art no longer springs from creative associations with a contemporary social reality."[3] She suggests that America is drawn to its recent history and the recreation of cultural artifacts because of a certain alienation and detachment from vital issues experienced in the present. In different ways, these arguments link nostalgia to a prevailing cultural experience and condition, the consequence of sociopolitical disorientation and creative enervation.

While the production of nostalgia in the 1970s may have grown in tandem with a sense of cultural crisis, even a feeling of loss and malaise, it cannot be reduced to this explanatory model; the commodification and aestheticization of nostalgia in the 1970s and beyond cannot be contained within hermetic theories of crisis and decline. For one thing, these do not adequately grasp the "modish" existence of nostalgia in cultural life or the way that images of the past *and* the future circulate together in reconfigured forms within the textual and taste cultures of postmodern life. While the selling of the past may have developed in accordance with social ruptures, notably in the 1970s, theories that reduce commodified nostalgia to a climate of enveloping decline and dislocation do not always account for the more particular technological, economic, and design histories behind specific nostalgia modes or for the economy of *pastness* that has developed within the textual and affective regimes of contemporary culture.

This chapter considers nostalgia as a cultural style, addressing the subject from three different perspectives within the context of the 1980s and 1990s. Beginning with the Reagan aesthetic and the political expediencies of pastness, it then considers the question of cultural recycling and the impact of cable, video, and digital markets/technologies on the reproduction of the past. In a final section on "retro," the focus turns toward nostalgia in fashion and display, considering issues of taste and textuality as they relate both to representational strategies of pastiche and to the commercial staging of "heritage." This chapter does not aim or claim to provide an exhaustive account of nostalgia as a contemporary cultural style. It is purposefully diverse in its approach, moving between politics, technology, textuality, and taste in ways that do not seek to harmonize them within any single account of, or explanation for, the place and significance of stylized nostalgia. Ultimately, it provides a contextual survey, historicizing the popularity of "pastness" in a culture that is not so much reeling from discontinuity and the experience of loss, as able to transmit, store, retrieve, reconfigure, and invoke the past in specific ways.

THE REAGAN AESTHETIC

Any attempt to measure the feeling or degree of nostalgia within American cultural life runs the risk of becoming a fitful exercise in cultural pulse-taking. It is perhaps more reasonable, and useful, to account for the *discourse of nostalgia* within any period. This concentrates less on how America "feels" than on what it feels it needs—what terms and categories have become gradually, or even suddenly, meaningful. Michael Kammen makes some attempt at mapping such a discourse in the contemporary period by suggesting that "nostalgia" became a media buzzword between the mid-1970s and the mid-1980s. His evidence for this comes mainly from critical comments in periodicals, broadsheets, and news magazines, addressing and ultimately railing against the promiscuous degree of nostalgia observed within American life. He pins 1985 as the year when "warnings started to flash" in journalistic features, beginning to question nostalgia as a detrimental "disease" and "fallacy."[4] The media have played a central role in diagnosing and detailing America's "nostalgic condition." Christopher Lasch goes as far as to suggest that the "nostalgia boom" of the 1970s first took shape as a media promotion, "a non-event that proclaimed the demise of the sixties."[5] While the media will frequently create news stories and inflate them into the realm of cultural phenomena, the media discourse of nostalgia in the 1980s did not emerge in a complete vacuum. This decade saw the development of nostalgia as a markedly self-conscious mode, both in commercial *and* in political spheres. Reaganism, in particular, was a political credo with a pact with the past. A certain Rockwellian nostalgia lay at the rhetorical heart of the Reagan presidency, harmoniously combined with investments in progress and technological promise.

Identifying Ronald Reagan as the man, and the moment, when nostalgia crystallized as a style in American political life is simplistic. It was Reagan, however, who refined nostalgia into a political aesthetic and who unmoored the experience of nostalgia from a concept of loss by turning it into a performative style. From the outset, Reagan's previous careers in radio, film, television, and then radio again gave him a certain iconic capital, being perceivably of the (popular culture) past. Gary Wills writes that "Reagan gives our history the continuity of a Möbius strip. We ride its curves backwards and forwards at the same time, and he is always there."[6] Unlike Jimmy Carter, who saw in the past a better America, a time before the contemporary worship of "self-indulgence and consumption," Reagan invoked the past as a well of American spiritual essence of which he himself was a part. The shift from past to pastness in political rhetoric was partly the result of Reagan's own symbolism. He was "the great American synecdoche, not only a part of our past but a large part of our multiple pasts."[7] Reagan had the aura of pastness about his very being; he was identified with American history by the proxy of popular culture and his enduring place within it for much of his life. According to Wills, "Reagan not only represents the past but resurrects it as a promise of the future. He has Edison's last breath in his lungs."[8]

Reagan played upon his own symbolic cachet, developing a mythic conception of the American past where ideas of small-town normalcy and its composite institutions—family, church, community, and business—were supposedly manifest.[9] Reagan's politics of nostalgia invoked a vision of America unaffected by the social ruptures of the 1960s and the political and economic humiliations of the 1970s; it was central to a strategy of aggressive nationalism that Todd Gitlin situates in terms of Reagan's desire to "preside over the in-gathering of a majority and the invocation of a unity."[10] In important ways, Reagan played upon a reinvigorated sense of national mission in a climate of acute sociopolitical discordance. In the context of sustained economic travails, a politically ignominious hostage debacle, and the more general fallout from a decade of so-called "narcissism," James Combs suggests: "Reagan had to re-enchant the world, to imbue the profane present with the aura of the sacral past in order to forestall or reverse the rapid decomposition of value orientations."[11] If, as some would say, the Presidency was Reagan's last great acting role, then the executive script involved a large degree of mythic invocation, riding slipshod over historical particularity and factuality to construct a useable past that would support a variety of right-wing political adventures.[12]

No treatment of nostalgia as a cultural style in contemporary America could fail to mention the significance of Reagan. He developed a particular form of neo-kitsch, feeding on the past and the present in ways that transmogrified popular culture into a compendium of national motifs. Sidney Blumenthal suggests that familiarity was the quintessence of the Reagan aesthetic, familiar personalities, songs, jokes, lines, stories, and images. If postmodernity is defined by the cannibalization of past styles, Reagan became the cannibal-in-chief. Blumenthal writes that "his rhetoric was filled with shards of kitsch ripped from popular culture. The stream of kitsch allusions emanating from Reagan was endless."[13] It is indicative that both Wills and Blumenthal, writing in 1988, the year Reagan left office, should be drawn in their preliminary observations to Reagan's political style. The significance of Reagan was in part his ability to embody a vision of America that was both emotive and comforting. Style, in this sense, was substance. Wills contends that Reagan "renews our past by resuming it. His approach is not discursive, setting up sequences of time or thought, but associative; not a tracking shot, but montage. We make the connections. It is our movie."[14]

Reagan did not invent the nostalgic style in American political culture, but he may have given it a particular twist in politicizing the conjunction of nationalism and nostalgia through a neo-kitsch aesthetic. Lawrence Grossberg maps a new relationship that developed between "the people and the nation" in the 1980s with the rise of a new conservative hegemony. Rather than redefine the contents of "common sense" as in Thatcherite Britain, Grossberg argues that the American New Right set about "restructuring the terrain of the national popular."[15] Explaining the neoconservative premise that the crisis of America in the 1980s was affective—a lack of passion for values and beliefs—Grossberg suggests that attempts were made to reconstruct investments in the nation through people's affective relationship with popular taste and culture. One site of this was the proliferation of, and investments in, images of the family; another was the rearticulation of the 1960s and the generation of images of precountercultural youth cultures. The crux of Grossberg's argument is that hegemonic conservatism constructed America as a "purely affective investment," the focus of passionate commitment but without standing for anything. He calls this "nationalism with no content," an "empty fullness" possible in postmodern culture where the strength of feeling is difficult to achieve for *any* meaning or value. Nostalgia here functions less in the creation of an imaginary past than in providing an iconic terrain for affective commitments to the nation.

In the Reagan aesthetic, nostalgia was a question more of atmosphere than of detail. Harvey J. Kaye comments: "Since he did not tie his past-to-be-recovered to any particular period in American history, Reagan was not temporally limited in his staking of claims on the past."[16] Reagan deployed the aura of pastness, he even symbolized it, but in ways that did not so much speak of the past than secure through kitsch and camp Reagan's own credentials as a political and cultural icon—one of commitment to national commitment. One of Grossberg's key ideas in theorizing a postmodern climate is that of a dominant sensibility characterized by ironic cynicism. He writes: "The cynicism dictates that nothing matters; and yet, even within the cynicism, something has to matter if only to avoid allowing your cynicism to matter too much."[17] Reagan's political aesthetic advanced nostalgia as a cultural style that focused "maps of mattering," if not, in Grossberg's vocabulary, "maps of meaning." It was a form of nostalgia without a concomitant sense of longing or loss. Rather than construct national identity through an imaginary past thought to be retrievable, the New Right used the past as a stimulus of passionate believing. In the 1984 presidential campaign, Assistant White House Chief of Staff Richard Darman wrote a memo that advised speechwriters to create a particular kind of rhetoric. It said: "Paint Ronald Reagan as the personification of all that is right with or heroized by America. Leave Mondale in a position where an attack on Reagan is tantamount to an attack on America's idealized image of itself—where a vote against Reagan is in some subliminal sense a vote against mythic "AMERICA."[18] For Reagan, nostalgia was not an exercise in ritualist yearning; it was an aesthetic mode that became fundamental to his projection and embodiment of a mythical national essence.

The concept of affect is useful for theorizing the disconnection of nostalgia from loss in the political terrain of the 1980s. According to Grossberg, "affective politics" were central to the hegemonic strategies of neoconservatism. Affect is a structure of belonging; it describes the energy and passion with which people invest in particular sites of meaning. Neoconservatism, however, made passion a value in itself. The political meaning of "the family," "drugs," "the economy," and "America" became less significant than the degree of belief and commitment each one inspired (or was made to inspire) as a site of affective investment. According to Grossberg, this represents a process of depoliticization whereby the production of passion replaces the capacity for real political debate. Nostalgia was a particular form of passion within this affective economy, a feeling divorced from any culturally realized sense of longing, loss, or necessary meaning. Nostalgia, in other words, was no longer a yearning that derived from the articulation of values and virtues thought to exist in the past; it was, instead, ritualized within a certain political performance. Grossberg suggests that in a world where politics has become freed from the constraints of meaning, where passion has become a replacement for politically informed choice and engagement, "nostalgia is suspect in a scandalized public domain, for it can be measured and judged."[19] What is left is "nostalgia for nostalgia, nostalgia for a mood." Reagan's success was partly achieved through his sustained invocation of mood: upbeat, reassured, and greased with a constant stream of hometown rhetoric. Nostalgia was central to a political aesthetic that invoked the past randomly but relentlessly in strategic attempts to "redistribute affective investments in the nation."

RECYCLING

It is perhaps not incidental that in 1985, during the high point of Reagan's new politics of old values, a new 24-hour cable station called "The Nostalgia Network" should be launched, offering a "unique blend of non-violent, feel-good programming with traditional values." Products of popular culture cannot be divorced from the political climate in which they emerge. If the new conservatism was put in place through people's relation with popular culture, one might be especially inclined to relate the nostalgia embedded within the Reagan aesthetic to certain manifestations in film, television, and music. A different kind of analysis might look more closely at the satiric pastoralism of Garrison Keillor, for example, whose national radio show, *The Prairie Home Companion*, became a hit in the mid-1980s and inspired Keillor's cult book, *Lake Wobegon Days* (1985); it might investigate the nostalgic recreation of family values in the enormously popular sitcoms, *The Cosby Show* and *The Wonder Years*; it might examine the very currency of "traditional values" proffered by a cable station such as the Nostalgia Network. All of these can be set in the context of a political culture where the (nostalgic) past was being heavily trafficked in what one critic has called Reagan's "orgy of re-illusionment."[20] While there is considerable scope for ideological critique of this sort, the production of nostalgia in the 1980s cannot be explained, or examined, through the interests and agenda of the New Right alone. In this section, I want to consider the development of stylized nostalgia from a different perspective: not as it relates to any particular political project, but as it has been enabled by technological advancements and produced by specific consumer industries.

It is useful to examine the Nostalgia Network in greater detail in this case. While not the largest or most conspicuous U.S. nostalgia channel—compared with the likes of Nick at Nite or American Movie Classics, for example—it nevertheless represents patterns of market segmentation that have come to characterize American media culture in the last few decades. Indeed, the genesis of the network must be measured, first and foremost, not in relation to Reagan, but in the context of the massive expansion in cable television during the 1980s. In 1976, 90 percent of television viewers watched programs broadcast by the three major networks—ABC, CBS, or NBC. By the mid-1980s, this figure had dropped to 75 percent. Making use of new satellite technologies that could reach large geographical areas and encouraged by the deregulation of the cable industry's pricing structure in the free-market frenzy of the 1980s, there was a proliferation of cable networks, including the likes of MTV and CNN.[21] The Nostalgia Network was one of a large number of cable creations that emerged in the 1980s, helping to segment television viewing by targeting specific demographic groups. Exploiting a vast television market and targeting post-49-year-olds, The Nostalgia Network combined niche information and lifestyle programs with acquired shows like *The Love Boat*, *The Rockford Files*, and *The Streets of San Francisco*. In the early 1990s, the network reached a subscription peak of 9,000,000, tapping into one of the fastest growing segments of the population in that of middle-aged "baby-boomers."

Market demographers generally split the baby-boom generation into two categories: those born between the end of the Second World War and the mid-1950s, and those born between the mid-1950s, and the mid-1960s.[22] Together, they comprise well over a quarter of the population. With high disposable incomes and increased leisure time, the aging baby-boom generation has become a major target group within the marketing community. If cable networks acquire revenue through subscription fees and paid advertising, the Nostalgia Network provides a programming service, as well as an advertising platform, aimed at the post-49 market. Competing with such as The History Channel, TV Land,

Home and Garden Television, and American Movie Classics, The Nostalgia Network is a lifestyle channel that targets the interests, concerns, and entertainment predilections of the "graying sector." Ron Neeson, who hosts an information program on the network called "Issues and Answers," suggests that while those in the post-49 market are diverse, they may nevertheless share certain attitudes toward money, leisure time, entertainers, food, and music. Of his own program (the title of which, "Issues and Answers," was bought by The Nostalgia Network, having been a long-running show on ABC), Neeson comments: "We try to deal with serious issues, particularly issues to people over 50, not a lot of shouting and yelling." He continues: "We try to provide information because that's the other thing people over 50 are looking for, information: what to do with their own money, what's the government going to do to them or for them, what candidates best represent them and so forth."[23] Just as MTV, with its fast-cut format and high degree of yelling, serves a youth market, so the Nostalgia Network provides a programming option at the other end of the demographic scale.

The Nostalgia Network is not about the past per se, but about niche marketing and the taste and value differentials of particular demographic segments. Significant here is perhaps the connotative drift experienced by the very word and concept of "nostalgia." In commercial terms, it need not depend on a specific idea of the past; it can designate anything that has been culturally recycled and/or appeals to a market where pastness is a value. It is not, in other words, symptomatic of cultural or consumer longing, but is an index of commodities, media products, and programming orientations that draw upon notions of tradition, or use an idea of the past to position themselves within particular niche markets. After a drop in viewing figures in the mid-1990s, The Nostalgia Network underwent a process of rebranding. This entailed the adoption of a new name to portray the contemporary aspects of its revamped schedule. "Nostalgia Good-tv" was deemed by management a better description of its value-oriented rather than past-oriented programming. As President and CEO of The Nostalgia Network, Squire Rushnell, identified the station:

Audiences have been set adrift in a cluttered, fast-paced television environment characterized by sex, violence and social cynicism. Nostalgia Good-tv provides an entertainment oasis that is especially attractive to viewers, because we offer more than old programming; we present innovative, original programs built around friendly personalities who uplift, relax and entertain without assaulting one's sensibilities.[24]

Rushnell plays upon a certain nostalgia for an idea of television as warm and wholesome; there is a picture of decline based around the apparently cluttered, violent, sex-ridden television culture of the 1990s. He is also quick to emphasize, however, that Nostalgia Good-tv is not about returning to a golden age or reliving a better past. It is about innovation and originality. In a business climate where cable stations must fight desperately for broadcast audiences, Nostalgia Good-tv caters to an older media generation, a specific demographic market whose values are sponsored and then serviced in the development of contemporary niche programming.

"Nostalgia" has become something of a genre in a media culture of "narrowcasting"—a term denoting the pursuit of narrow but profitable segments of the viewing audience. As a commodity, "nostalgia" designates a particular kind of programming in the radio as well as the television industries. Capitalizing on the growing market for radio syndication in the 1990s, the Nostalgia Broadcasting Corporation (a company that operates NBG Radio and that went public in 1996) offered four networks of radio programming, including the Financial Network, Nostalgia Network, Sports Network, and Entertainment Network. According to its own corporate profile, "the company's approach to radio syndication is to produce and/or acquire specialty audio shows and enroll radio station affiliates to broadcast these programs. NBG's new product development is market driven; niche radio programming important to specific national advertisers is the first target."[25] Nostalgia is therefore one of four niche options in this context. NBG sells two radio shows—*The Golden Age of Radio* and *Big Band Classics*—to stations filling what radio insiders have come to call an "Oldies" format.

With the marked increase in the number of radio stations and television channels in the 1980s and 1990s—all trying to fill schedules and in competition for listeners and viewers—syndication became an extremely lucrative business. The rerun became an especially cheap and reliable source of material in this context, providing a base component of contemporary broadcast nostalgia. Of course, the rerun has a long syndication history. In television, it dates back to the 1950s, where the production costs of live television became too expensive and stations came to rely on filmed, and hence repeatable, programming.[26] The expansion of the cable industry and the growth of commercial radio in the 1980s, however, gave the rerun an invigorated life. Old serials and sitcoms were not only targeted at the post-49 market, but also framed in programming formats that helped foster a cult youth following. Nick at Nite is perhaps the best example of this, launched in 1985 as part of the evening schedule of the children's cable station, Nickelodeon. Hosted by Dr. Will Miller and then by Dick Van Dyke, Nick at Nite specializes in old sitcoms and television reruns. The concept of the rerun is expedient for Viacom, the company that owns Nickelodeon, because it has at its disposal a large stock of old network programming. Accounting for the success of Nick at Nite, Lynn Spigel writes: "The popularity of Nick at Nite's reruns probably has less to do with the universal appeal of television art—its ability to last through generations—than with the network's strategies of representation. Nickelodeon created a new reception context for old reruns by repackaging them through a new camp sensibility."[27] This "repackaging" involves a certain playfulness in the way sitcoms are introduced, employing stars like David Cassidy to host special program marathons. It also derives from original programming such as Nickelodeon's own 1991 sitcom *Hi, Honey, I'm Home*. This show was based on a black-and-white rerun family displaced into the 1990s, a conceit that would be replicated and reversed by Hollywood in *Pleasantville* (1998), a film in which two teenagers from the 1990s filmed in color are displaced into a black-and-white 1950s sitcom. By replaying and recontextualizing reruns in programming formats aimed at particular demographic segments, cable stations have sold nostalgia both as generational reminiscence and as postmodern camp. A measure of its success, Nick at Night had over 53 million subscribers in 1991, a million more than MTV.[28]

Within the broadcast industries, the commodification of nostalgia has not been a market response to generalized cultural longing but can be explained through commercial imperatives such as market segmentation and media syndication. Cable channels like The Nostalgia Network, radio syndicators like the Nostalgia Broadcasting Corporation, and more specific programs such as Nick at Nite are fairly indiscriminate about the constitution of "nostalgia" in their broadcast formats. As a generic category, nostalgia can encompass anything from ballroom dancing and Big Band interviews to multilingual versions of *The Streets of San Francisco* and rerun marathons of *The Partridge Family*. The content and "meaning" of nostalgia is, in many respects, secondary to strategies of production and the imperatives of niche consumption. If nostalgia is a marketable mode in the broadcast industries, it has become so in the context of the fragmentation of the television and radio audience. While nostalgic loss may well be experienced and played upon in contemporary media culture, the commodification of nostalgia perhaps more accurately demonstrates the contingencies of niche marketing than any particular index of cultural longing.

To explain the proliferation of stylized nostalgia through any simplified theory of cultural longing would be to misread the development of nostalgia as a register and mode, as it has been both taken up affectively within political discourse and deployed strategically within consumer culture. Instead of one explanatory master-narrative (discontinuity, crisis, enervation, fin-de-siècle anxiety), the commodification and aestheticization of nostalgia in American culture must be set in relation to a cumulation of factors. It is important, in this context, to mark the significance of new technological innovations and their ability to rescue, recycle, and reconfigure the past in the cultural and media terrain. The digital and video revolutions, in particular, have transformed our ability to access, circulate, and consume the past. The surfeit of information in contemporary culture, enabled by information technologies like computers, cable television, VCR, and digital recording, has had a dramatic impact, both on our engagement with the past and on our sense of the archive. Whether through the click of a mouse or the push of a TV or CD remote, the past has become, in the words of Jim Collins, "a matter of perpetually reconfigurable random access."[29] If nostalgia is a style based on a particular economy of "pastness," one must recognize the cultural influence of technologies that enable the recoupment of images, styles, and sounds drawn from the past.

In a *Herald Tribune* article entitled "New Nostalgia on Record," Bernard Hollard suggests that "classical music is recycling with the best of them."[30] Owning the tapes of classical recordings made thirty or forty years ago, Hollard notes that companies will prefer to pay the reuse rights rather than hire an orchestra to record a new version. Sony Classical, for example, has gathered many performances from its back catalogue and reissued them on compilation CDs. What lies behind this strategy are the digital technologies that enable old recordings to be produced and sold as high-quality merchandise. Selling the musical past has grown exponentially with CDs. Whether jazz, classical, punk, or folk, there has been an extremely profitable outpouring of musical box sets and single-album reissues since the 1980s. These are produced by record companies who own the master tapes of old recordings and can make profits through reselling their archives as "classics." Nostalgia has become a musical category in its own right within this context. The music magazine *Gramophone* gathers under this title compilation CDs by artists such as Nat King Cole, Billie Holiday, Ella Fitzgerald, Peggy Lee, Sarah Vaughan, Dean Martin, and Frank Sinatra.[31] In the music industry, "nostalgia" denotes a particular kind of "prerock" performer—mainly jazz artists, crooners, and torch singers—who can be sold under ready rubrics such as "timeless" and "legendary."

If the record industry experienced a commercial windfall in the digital remastering of old music, the film and television industries have also capitalized on the possibilities of cultural recycling opened up by video. As a technological and aesthetic form, video has enormous possibilities for repetition and recycling. From a commercial point of view, it provides the film and television industries with a means of repackaging their products, enabling consumers to watch again their favorite movies and shows, including the "classics" that might otherwise have been laid to rest in company vaults. A video revolution occurred in the 1980s. While in 1978 there were just 440,000 VCRs, by 1983 there were 4.1

million. By 1990, 75 percent of American homes owned a video re-corder.[32] One consequence of this technological tide has been a newly figured relationship with the here-and-now of television "presence." Central to the impact of video is the capacity for "time-shifting." Practi-cally, this gives the individual far more control over the way that televi-sion can be watched; viewers are released from network programming schedules with the possibility of replay and are given more choice through the advent of home rental. Douglas Gomery states that by the beginning of the 1990s revenue from tape rentals was exceeding $10 billion a year.[33] The video market vastly increased the interest in movie watching. By the mid-1980s, more than 100 million cassettes were being rented each month.[34] Marketing the filmic as well as the televisual past became integral to this new media environment. Catering to niche mar-kets, companies like Rhine Records and Video Yesteryear have come to specialize in old movies, adding to the range of films drawn from studio archives that are broadcast and sold through cable and video outlets. Marketing the past has, in short, become a lucrative byproduct of the new relationship being forged in the age of video between institutions, texts and viewers.[35]

"Nostalgia" has grown as a commercial niche, developing in the con-text of certain demographic, industrial, and technological transforma-tions that have enabled, and given life to, a newly recyclable past. The ability to resuscitate the past does not, in itself, explain or guarantee the currency of nostalgia in commercial and cultural life, however. One must also account for the manner in which nostalgia has insinuated itself into particular textual and taste economies. To judge nostalgia as a quite explicit *style*, I want in the final section to look at the phenomenon of "retro" and the commercial selling of "heritage." The former brings together issues of taste and textuality as they relate to a postmodern culture where the past is not simply *more* recyclable, but structured into a particular representational regime. The latter concentrates on the pro-liferating means by which the past is staged as a tourist attraction and consumer atmosphere. Together, they can round off this chapter's brief survey of the contemporary "nostalgia mode" by accounting for some of the ways in which temporality has become a determined style value.

RETRO

In the late-1990s, *The Onion* cautioned satirically: "if current levels of U.S. retro consumption are allowed to continue unchecked, we may run entirely out of past by as soon as 2005."[36] What is perhaps interesting in this "news" feature is that comic inventions such as a national retro clock—standing at 1990, an "alarming 74 percent closer to the present than 10 years ago when it stood at 1969"—are in some sense quite accurate. For example, Rudi Franchi, who owns a shop in Boston called The Nostalgia Factory, explains that, since he turned his personal collection of memorabilia into a specialist collectors' shop in 1970, the greatest change he has noticed while selling "overpriced junk and trendy trash" is the speed with which items become collectible. From Pez dispensers to cereal boxes, Franchi says: "No sooner is an item introduced to the market than it shows up at a shop like mine."[37] The lapse of time between an item entering the cultural terrain and returning as "retro" has become a matter of years rather than of decades.

"Retro" has become a term used to describe the past as it is figured within style narratives of the chic and trendy. Dictionary definitions of retro give it is as a prefix, meaning backward (as in retrospect) or, in medical terms, contrary to the usual or natural course (as in retrograde). In his treatment of "retrochic," Raphael Samuel explores its more contemporary application, used to describe any style, advertisement, or product that is based on some essential quality of pastness.[38] As a term, "retrochic" was coined in France in the late 1960s by the Paris avant-garde. It was applied to the growing taste in revival or period styles emerging from certain countercultural examples of alternative consumerism. It began as an impromptu antifashion but was soon taken up as a profitable style, fashion critics calling the trend in mainstream commercial design "the nostalgia industry." Retro also had a particular meaning in French film, the *"mode retro,"* coined as a term in *Cahiers du Cinema,* describing a new genre of film concerned with European fascism. (This became widely discussed after the 1974 release of Louis Malle's *Lacombe Lucien.*) In this case, "retro" referred not to stylistic kitsch, but to the cinematic reexamination of the Occupation.[39] While the *mode retro* has a particular meaning in French film history, the idea of stylistic "retro" has developed a broad international currency based on borrowing, quoting, and pastiche. Retro is the word that perhaps best describes versions of postmodern nostalgia: playful, ironic, and where the past is a storehouse of fashion.

Critics from Raphael Samuel to Umberto Eco have argued that there is nothing fundamentally new about repetition and recycling within modes of cultural and aesthetic production.[40] What is perhaps new about retro, however, is its cavalier and eclectic regard for the past. Retro is less concerned with historical particularity than with scripting kitsch pastness into particular style regimes. Retro does have a loose period orientation. Within the fashion and music industries—where the term has been most fully developed—it describes kitsch drawn from the 1960s, 1970s, and 1980s. Cinematically, this has been expressed in retro films such as *Boogie Nights* (1997) and *The Wedding Singer* (1998). Whatever the periodic focus of retro, the past is almost always judged through layers of fashion iconicity; previous styles inspire revelry more than reverence, nostalgia without loss. In his discussion of "retro-modernism," Jim Collins suggests that the significance of the retro phenomenon, broadly defined, is in the reconfiguration of "taste cartographies" brought about by the semiotic excess of postmodern culture.[41] This refers to a process of hybridization that circulates ideas of old and new, classic and cutting-edge, within compound notions such as the "modern classic." His use and understanding of "retro" in this context goes beyond the designation of fashion raids on popular post-1960s kitsch. It suggests a representational economy that can mix and reconfigure past and present, historicity and contemporaneity, in textual syntheses that disturb older distinctions between tradition and innovation. This, he suggests, has a profound impact on evaluative criteria and the forms of cultural authority that legitimize such criteria; it introduces a new "variability of value" where distinctions between past and present, like those of high and popular culture, are less clearly demarcated.

Retro nostalgia has become a subject of pointed critical debate in arguments about the substance of postmodern historicism. Critics such as Fredric Jameson and Allison Graham lament the fact that postmodern culture has become self-consuming. Graham suggests that "Feeding only on itself, the culture can refer only *to* itself; its crimes are those of absolute solipsism."[42] This arguably fails to see the particular negotiations of meaning (and evaluative criteria) undertaken by the retro mode, however. To its defenders, "retro" is not a mark of cultural solipsism or creative bankruptcy, but a way of acknowledging that the past exists through textual traces in cultural and ideological mediation with the present. There is, in other words, a more acute sensitivity in the retro mode to the fact that access to the past is never direct or natural but realized through a complex history of representations. For Linda Hutcheon, the parodic rereading of the past, evidenced in postmodern culture, is not ahistorical, dehistoricizing, or even nostalgic, but it demonstrates an increasing semiotic awareness of the textuality of the past. She writes: "Postmodern historicism is wilfully unencumbered by nostalgia in its critical, dialogical reviewing of the forms, contexts and values of the past."[43] Put another way, the modish nostalgia that defines postmodern historicism is unencumbered by any attendant sense of nostalgic *loss*. Kaja Silverman reads this in the context of fashion, suggesting that the stylized nostalgia of retro problematizes the binary of "old" and "new." She argues that retro fashion inserts the wearer "into a complex network of cultural and historical references. At the same time, it avoids the pitfalls of a naïve referentiality; by putting quotation marks around the garments it revitalizes, it makes clear that the past is available to us only in a textual form, and through the mediation of the present."[44] Retro borrows from the past without sentimentality, quotes from the past without longing, parodies the past without loss. As a term, "retro" developed a broad market currency in the 1990s, describing anything from home furnishing and thrift store fashion to "Britpop" and forms of digital sampling. "Retro" was popularized both as a commercial category and as a cultural practice; it designated a wide range of forms and activities where the past was taken up with a particular, often ironic, self-consciousness.

While it is perhaps the epitome of postmodern nostalgia, retro irony is not the only way that nostalgia has been coded within the taste regimes of contemporary culture. A quite different example can be found in the heritage industry, with its staged authenticity of local and national traditions. As a collective term, "the heritage industry" is an expansive cultural/commercial notion, including tourist attractions, architectural initiatives, and preservation projects that market the past as a spectacle and a site. The reasons for the growth of an international heritage culture are varied and have been treated at length by a number of critics. It has been explained in terms of anything from the democratization and popularization of tradition in the postwar period to the growth of particular tourist economies, from the need to affirm political legitimacy and social identity in a global culture to the symptomatic result of historical and creative national decline.[45] What interests me in this burgeoning field is not the evolution of the American heritage industry (which emerged after the Second World War) or the historical representations of particular heritage spectacles. Rather, it is the way that "heritage" and "bygone" have become cojoined in the marketing of consumer atmosphere.

Drawing upon the architectural showcasing of urban heritage that grew in American cities from the 1970s, M. Christine Boyer considers the current wisdom of city building that connects stagings of the bygone past with an idea of a city's image, livability, and cultural capital. She writes: "Increasingly in the 1970s and 1980s, the centers of American and European cities were seized with nostalgia for past architectural styles, transforming enclaves of their architectural patrimony into city tableaux arranged for visual consumption."[46] From Boston's Quincy Market to New York's South Street Seaport, Boyer reads postmodern fragmentation and amnesia into the economic imperatives of city development. She is highly critical of the process by which historic styles and images are plundered in the creation of historicized commercial stage sets. Not unsimilarly to Pierre Nora, she objects to the creation of "imposed scenes" that do not remain part of "living memory." The return to tradition within contemporary cityscapes has, she argues, turned collective memory into a series of conflicting and privatized fragments that are estranged from any unified totality. Whether or not one agrees with Boyer's concept of authentic, "living" memory, set against a postmodern architectural ethos of fragments and dissonance, she usefully examines how the bygone past has been taken up in "the new public theatres of late capitalism." Boyer suggests that a development like the South Street Seaport, which opened in 1983, uses history to script consumers within narratives based on a mercantile past, engaging modes of consumption through the fictive pleasures of bygone trade. The historical tableau extols a nostalgia that is then used for commercial ambiance; the aura of pastness is figured within an image spectacle that is profitable and visually fashionable, where memory is an adjunct of consumption.

The bygone past has become a marketable experience; it is a look, a feel, an atmosphere to be consumed. It can be witnessed in city building but also in the atmospheric surrounds created by the leisure industry, where hotels promise to "echo the graciousness of a bygone era," or, as one Arkansas establishment put it, "recapture the warmth of a bygone era for non-smoking adults."[47] Staging the bygone has become central to the valuation of consumer quality and experience. It has also become integral to the techniques of display at specific heritage sites. Exploring the question of authenticity at New Salem, a heritage site marking the home of Abraham Lincoln, Edward Bruner suggests that authenticity is measured in terms less of material originality than of "historical verisimilitude."[48] Within museal discourse, this designates a movement away from a concentration on artifacts and toward that of "experience," a strategic necessity for an industry modeling itself upon, and competing within, an expanding tourist economy. Barbara Kirschenblatt-Gimblett suggests that heritage represents "the transvaluation of the obsolete, the mistaken, the outmoded, the dead and the defunct."[49] In other words, heritage adds value to buildings, products, districts, and histories that are no longer, or have never been, commercially viable. The *process* of adding value will often necessitate a particular kind of restaging, however. Rather than classify and exhibit the past, heritage sites will more often than not display it in ways that are performative and interactive, typified in "living" heritage sites like Plimoth Plantation, Colonial Williamsburg, and New Salem. The contemplation of the historical archive has given way to a more personally experienced, nostalgically inflected engagement with theatrical "pastness." As a mode, nostalgia has become a matter of atmosphere within a heritage and tourist economy privileging experience, immediacy, and adventure.[50]

My consideration of retro and heritage is, admittedly, brief. The basic point I want to make is that nostalgia has been taken up within different kinds of taste regime; it has become a style value in representations of the past that are hybrid, ironic, and playful, and that, alternatively, summon and stage a particular idea of the authentic. Both have evolved within, and are in some sense a response to, the cultural exigencies of postmodernism. In the context of film theory, Jim Collins suggests two kinds of response to the expanding volume, access, manipulability, and circulation of signs in postmodern cultural life. One is to play in the array of signs and the other is to retreat from them and appeal to a past purity. Writing quite specifically about film genericity, he labels this as the difference between "eclectic irony" and "new sincerity."[51] There is no reason why this difference cannot be seen to operate on a more general level, however. In some sense, it signifies the difference between retro phenomena and the staging of the bygone past. One involves the hyperconscious reworking *of* the past and the other appeals to an authenticity located *in* the past. As a style value, nostalgia can embrace or be seen to escape postmodern culture, depending on its figuration within particular representational and taste regimes.

AESTHETICIZING "AMERICA"

Nostalgia modes do not emerge from nostalgia moods or reflect them in any simple way. If nostalgia has developed as a cultural style in contemporary American life, it cannot be explained through any single master narrative of decline, crisis, longing, or loss. This does not mean to say that modes of nostalgia have not developed in the context of crisis, or that longing and loss are not powerful and operative narratives within certain kinds of discourse. Instead, it resists a critical reduction where nostalgia modes become the reflex result of anxieties and dissatisfactions with the present. As a cultural style, nostalgia has developed in accordance with a series of political, cultural, and material factors that have made "pastness" an expedient and marketable mode. Pastness became a site of affective investment in the 1980s and 1990s, a mode and register that emerged in an information culture able to access, circulate, and reconfigure the textual traces of the past in new and dynamic ways, that took up nostalgia in particular representational and taste regimes, that turned nostalgia into a performative politics and commercial category, and that generally disjoined nostalgia from any specific meaning located in the past.

One might argue that the production of pastness can be related, if not to schemes of loss and amnesia, then at least to particular temporal inclinations of the postmodern: to cultural and ideological factors that have produced a certain, although by no means one-dimensional or unidirectional, revisiting of history, memory, and the past. In a culture where metanarratives of history and progress have been severely undermined and where information technologies have enabled an endless number of texts to exist simultaneously, our relationship with the past has been intellectually and culturally problematized, but also, and at the same time, *enlivened*. In bringing about the deconstruction of history— meaning the way that the past has become increasingly subject to cultural mediation, textual reconfiguration, and ideological contestation in the present—postmodern culture has arguably given memory a new discursive import.[52] This line of argument still threatens to recoup nostalgia into the kind of metanarrative this chapter has been at pains to avoid, however. Instead of seeking broad sociocultural "explanations" for the presence of the past in contemporary life, I focus in part II on a particular nostalgia style of the 1990s. Helping to sharpen cultural questions in a more sustained and discursively specific manner, an examination of the form and function of monochrome in contemporary culture may provide a critical framework for an applied discussion of visual memory modes.

The popularity of the black-and-white image in American and other visual markets of the 1990s must be set in relation to contemporary taste regimes and to the image strategies of consumer culture. Black and white is neither the result of cultural longing nor a symptom of postmodern forgetting. While its resurgent cachet might be understood broadly within a culture of simulacra—a visual conjuncture that in the 1990s put added value on the temporal and authenticity effects of monochrome—black and white became, at root, a transient style in the aesthetic regimes of middlebrow taste. The revival of the black-and-white image in the 1990s must be understood in specific terms. It relates to the saturation of color in the visual marketplace, to the taste regimes that have made memory and temporality categories of cultural value, and to the broad commodification and aestheticization of nostalgia in architecture, commerce, film, and fashion. Black and white is a disposable style, subject to the contingencies of taste. No specific claims can be made about the resolute meaning or the visual durability of the black-and-white image in contemporary life. It is one of many stylistic codes that appear and disappear in the commercial and cultural sphere, one of a number of images that are figured and refigured within different visual contexts. I would argue that having been a transient code with multiple meanings, black and white nevertheless became a pervasive memory style in the 1990s, a nostalgia mode where the (representational) content of the past was often less significant than black and white's (nonrepresentational) feeling of pastness.

In part II of this book I examine how the "feeling"—or what might be called the "affective economy"—of the black-and-white image functioned *discursively* in the dominant media, exploring the way that monochrome became linked to particular negotiations of American memory. This engages a framework of analysis concerned implicitly with the articulation of American cultural nationalism in the 1990s. Janice Radway has argued that America should no longer be venerated as an organic or homogenous thing.[53] Drawing upon a concept developed by Wahneema Lubiano, she argues that the "myth of America must be de-aestheticized"—that is to say, national identity must be recognized as fluid, contested, and fundamentally heterogeneous; the idea of nation must be "dislodged from its attachment to essentialized notions of culture and geography."[54] This view underwrites a cultural and critical reconception of American identity that took place largely in the 1990s. With the dissemination of multicultural and global perspectives, the concept of America as a bounded, internally coherent entity has been questioned both socially and intellectually.[55] If the 1990s can be ascribed with a particular historical and discursive specificity, it rests with a confluence of factors, emerging in the aftermath of the cold war, which caused a particular problem for dominant (liberal) frameworks of national/cultural legitimation. With the shift toward the transnationalization of capital in the 1990s and the problematizing of national identity in the spatial and imaginative order of the global cultural economy, essential and exceptionalizing notions of American identity were increasingly thrown into question. Traversed by the forces of difference on local and global levels, the United States was compelled both to confront and to reconfigure the grounds on which cultural nationalism had come to be forged and authorized. In cultural and critical discourse, focus moved away from ideas of commonality and coherence and toward the question of heterogeneity and difference.

Despite challenges to traditional frameworks of national meaning (heretofore based on a consensus forged around the elimination of difference and the essentializing of national culture), efforts were nevertheless made in the 1990s to shore up what Radway has called the ghostly presence of a phantasmatic, unitary "American" culture.[56] American identity may well be fluid, contested, and subject to historical change, but there has remained a particular (hegemonic) imperative to *re-aestheticize* American identity as stable, unitary and unconflicted. Monochrome memory represents a particular, and quite literal, process of aestheticization within media culture. In a juncture where the concept of "America" had come under increasing scrutiny and pressure, the black-and-white image became linked discursively in the 1990s to questions about the construction, representation, and preservation of national memory. The temporal and authenticity effects of the black-and-white image were used, in one sense, to transcend the color norms of a profligate image culture. In more political terms, however, monochrome was deployed intertextually, and from particular institutional positions, to aestheticize the archival history and memory of a national identity under strain. Having established the theoretical and contextual basis for nostalgia as a mode or style, in part II of this book I examine the memory work performed by one particular example. In moving from a broadly conceptual to a culturally and visually specific analysis, I turn to the memory politics of monochrome.

NOTES

1. Raphael Samuel, *Theatres of Memory: Past and Present in Contemporary Culture* (London: Verso, 1994): 359. Samuel is concerned with "theatres of memory" in contemporary Britain, but his comments are equally valid for America's own historicist "scopophilia."

2. Jim Collins, *Architectures of Excess: Cultural Life in the Information Age* (New York: Routledge, 1995): 7.

3. See Fred Davis, *Yearning for Yesterday: A Sociology of Nostalgia* (New York: Free Press, 1979); Allison Graham, "History, Nostalgia and the Criminality of Popular Culture," *Georgia Review,* 38, no. 2 (1984): 364.

4. Michael Kammen, *Mystic Chords of Memory: The Transformation of Tradition in American Culture* (New York: Vintage, 1993): 656.

5. Lasch, "The Politics of Nostalgia," *Harper's* (November 1984): 70.

6. Gary Wills, *Reagan's America* (New York: Penguin, 1988): 440.

7. Wills, *Reagan's America*: 1.

8. Wills, *Reagan's America*: 445.

9. See James Combs, *The Reagan Range: The Nostalgic Myth and American Politics* (Bowling Green, KY: State University Popular Press, 1993).

10. See Todd Gitlin, *The Twilight of Common Dreams: Why America is Wracked By Culture Wars* (New York: Henry Holt, 1995): 76.

11. Combs, *The Reagan Range*: 26.

12. See Mike Wallace, *Mickey Mouse History and Other Essays on American Memory* (Philadelphia, PA: Temple University Press, 1996): 250–268. Wallace examines the historical pedigree Reagan claimed for contemporary right-wing policies. This included suggestions that the Contras fought with the moral equivalent of the Founding Fathers, a pseudoanalysis of the rise of federal government in order to justify budget cuts and tax reforms, and persistent mythic constructions of good and evil to legitimate versions of anticommunism.

13. Sidney Blumenthal, "Reagan and the Neokitsch Aesthetic," in Sidney Blumenthal and Thomas Byrne, eds., *The Reagan Legacy* (New York: Pantheon Books, 1988): 263.

14. Wills, *Reagan's America*: 5.

15. Lawrence Grossberg, *Dancing in Spite of Myself: Essays on Popular Culture* (Durham, NC: Duke University Press, 1997): 192.

16. Harvey J. Kaye, *The Powers of the Past: Reflections on the Crisis and the Promise of History* (New York: Harvester Wheatsheaf, 1991): 99.

17. Grossberg, *Dancing in Spite of Myself*: 281.

18. Cited in Wallace, *Mickey Mouse History*: 255.

19. Lawrence Grossberg, *We Gotta Get out of This Place: Popular Conservatism and Popular Culture* (New York: Routledge, 1992): 277.

20. This term was coined by Paul Erickson and is cited by Wallace in *Mickey Mouse History*: 264. For a consideration of *The Cosby Show* and *The Wonder Years*, see, respectively, June M. Frazer and Timothy C. Frazer, "'Father Knows Best' and 'The Cosby Show': Nostalgia and the Sitcom Tradition," *Journal of Popular Culture*, 27, no. 3 (1993): 163–174; and Jerry Herron, "Homer Simpson's Eyes and the Culture of Late Nostalgia," *Representations,* 43 (Summer 1993): 1–26.

21. See Jim Cullen, *The Art of Democracy: A Concise History of Popular Culture in the United States* (New York: Monthly Review Press, 1996): 259–269.

22. See Cheryl Russell, *The Master Trend: How the Baby-Boom Generation is Remaking America* (Reading, MA: Perseus Books, 1993); and Susan Mitchell, *American Attitudes: Who Thinks What about the Issues that Shape our Lives* (Ithaca, NY: New Strategists Publications, 1998).

23. "Interview with Ron Neeson" (27 April 1998) <www.flightalk.com>.

24. Press release, "Nostalgia Good-tv Launches Fall Season with New Variety, Sports and Personality Programs" (27 April 1998) <www.goodtv.com>.

25. "NBG investor relations" (27 April 1998) <www.nbgradio.com>.

26. See Phil Williams, "Feeding off the Past: The Evolution of the Television Re-run," *Journal of Popular Film and Television,* 21, no. 4 (1994): 162–175.

27. Lynn Spigel, "From the Dark Ages to the Golden Age: Women's Memories and Television Reruns," *Screen,* 36, no. 1 (1995): 18.

28. Soliciting an older target audience in the nostalgia market, American Movie Classics had reached a highly respectable 29 million subscribers in 1991. Figures for the top cable networks in 1991 can be found in Janet Wasko, *Hollywood in the Information Age* (Cambridge: Polity, 1994): 87.

29. Collins, *Architectures of Excess*: 3.

30. Bernard Hollard, "New Nostalgia on Record," *Herald Tribune,* 4 June 1997: 12.

31. Richard Cook, "Nostalgia," *Gramophone* (August 1997): 102–104.

32. See Jim Cullen, *The Art of Democracy*: 269–274.

33. Douglas Gomery, *Shared Pleasures: A History of Movie Presentation in the United States* (Madison, WI: University of Wisconsin Press, 1992): 276–293.

34. For an economic and industrial consideration of the impact of home video on the movie business, see Gomery, *Shared Pleasures,* and Thomas Schatz, "The New Hollywood," in Jim Collins, Hilary Radner and Ava Preacher Collins, eds., *Film Theory Goes to the Movies* (New York: Routledge, 1993): 8–36. On the impact of video more generally, see Sean Cubitt, *Timeshift: On Video Culture* (London: Routledge, 1991).

35. A further byproduct of the video revolution has been that of the camcorder, a "technology of memory" that has revitalized the market in *home* movies. The first camcorder became available in the mid-1980s. By the mid-1990s, estimates put the total number of camcorders owned worldwide at 40 million, with 14 million owned in America. Technically, they contribute to a culture where storing and reliving the past has become more possible than ever before.

36. "U.S. Dept. of Retro Warns: We May Be Running out of Past" (7 November 1997) <www.theonion.com>.

37. My thanks to Rudi Franchi for explaining some of the trends in selling nostalgia, both in conversation on 5 December 1996 and through e-mail on 17 December 1997.

38. See Samuel, *Theatres of Memory*: 83–118.

39. See Susan Hayward, *French National Cinema* (London: Routledge, 1993); and Robert C. Reimer and Carol J. Reimer, *Nazi-Retro Film: How German Cinema Remembers the Past"* (New York: Twayne, 1992).

40. Samuel, *Theatres of Memory*; Umberto Eco, "Innovation and Repetition: Between Modern and Post-Modern Aesthetics," *Diogenes,* 114, no. 4 (1985): 161–184.

41. Collins, *Architectures of Excess*: 157–185.

42. Graham, "History, Nostalgia": 354.

43. Linda Hutcheon, *A Poetics of Postmodernism: History, Theory, Fiction* (London: Routledge, 1988): 89.

44. Kaja Silverman, "Fragments of a Feminist Discourse," in Tania Modleski, ed., *Studies in Entertainment: Critical Approaches to Mass Culture* (Bloomington, IN: Indiana University Press, 1986): 150.

45. For a consideration of the heritage industry in the United States, Britain, and Ireland, see, respectively, Kammen, *Mystic Chords of Memory*; Robert Hewison, *The Heritage Industry: Britain in a Climate of Decline* (London: Methuen, 1987); and David Brett, *The Construction of Heritage* (Cork: Cork University Press, 1996).

46. M. Christine Boyer, *The City of Collective Memory: Its Historical Imagery and Architectural Entertainments* (Cambridge, MA: MIT Press, 1994): 407.

47. Found on the Internet (Yahoo browser) under the heading of "bygone" (24 November 1997).

48. Edward Bruner, "Abraham Lincoln as Authentic Reproduction: A Critique of Postmodernism," *American Anthropologist*, 96, no. 2 (1994): 394–415.

49. Barbara Kirschenblatt-Gimblett, *Destination Culture: Tourism, Museums and Heritage* (Berkeley, CA: University of California Press, 1998): 149.

50. Kirschenblatt-Gimblett, *Destination Culture*: 131–176.

51. Jim Collins, "Genericity in the Nineties: Eclectic Irony and New Sincerity," in Jim Collins, Hilary Radner, and Ava Preacher Collins, eds. *Film Theory Goes to the Movies* (New York: Routledge, 1993): 242–263.

52. For useful summaries of the debates surrounding postmodern history, see Alan Munslow, *Deconstructing History* (London: Routledge, 1997); and Keith Jenkins, ed., *The Postmodern History Reader* (London: Routledge, 1997). The American "memory wars" that emerged in the late 1980s and early 1990s were, in part, driven by a destabilized sense of "knowledge" about the past. History and memory were embroiled in political debates that eschewed univocal and moved toward multivocal conceptions of the past.

53. Janice Radway, "What's in a Name? Presidential Address to the American Studies Association, 20 November, 1998," *American Quarterly*, 51, no. 1 (1999): 1–32. Radway argues that "The very notion of the U.S. nation and the very conception of American nationalism must now be understood as relational concepts, that is, as objects and/or figures constructed precisely in and through a set of hierarchical relationships with groups, communities and nations defined somehow as other, alien, or outside." Radway suggests that American nationalism is neither autonomously defined nor internally homogenous; America is not a self-contained entity but is "brought into being through relations of dominance and oppression."

54. Radway, "What's in a Name?": 12.

55. It is not insignificant that Radway's comments were part of a presidential address given to the American Studies Association in 1998. If the idea of a uniform, geographically determined national identity has been challenged—what can be seen as the result of a combination of deconstructive, decentering effects in social, cultural, and economic life—so too have the forms of knowledge-production that have given national culture a specific conceptual legitimacy. Responding to political transformations in American life and society in the last few decades, the paradigmatic frameworks of American Studies have, themselves, begun to scrutinize and revise a host of disciplinary assumptions about national mythology and meaning. Donald Pease has described this in terms of a crisis in the "field imaginary," or "disciplinary unconscious," of American Studies. He finds a shift in the orientation of the field, moving from a concept of "America" as a cultural, expressive unity toward a focus on dissent, dissensus, and the relationship between culture and politics. See Donald E. Pease,

"New Americanists: Revisionist Interventions into the Canon," *Boundary,* 2, 17, no. 1 (1990): 1–37; Amy Kaplan and Donald E. Pease, eds., *Cultures of United States Imperialism* (Durham, NC: Duke University Press, 1993).

56. Radway, "What's in a Name?": 8.

II

MONOCHROME MEMORY

3

Picturing History:
Time's Past in the Present

The use of black and white is rare these days; by its contrast from the norm, it draws our attention automatically. It is also reminiscent of the past—the only way life used to be remembered on film and television, or in photographs. In some way, black and white both speaks for a reverence for the past and re-creates it, brings the mind back to a slower, more studied pace.

Roger Rosenblatt, *Time* correspondent[1]

In 1995, the Hubble Space Telescope sent back to astronomers at the University of Arizona a series of vivid color images of the Eagle Nebula, a dense formation of interstellar gas and dust the likes of which cradle newborn stars. The pictures were of clouds ten trillion kilometers high, momentously captured as the intense ultraviolet radiation spewing from nuclear fires at the center of forming stars turned the clouds into pillars so rich that the breathtaking beauty of the images more than equaled their scientific value. These pictures were of cosmic phenomena 7,000 light-years from earth. As evidence that our perceptual universe, in every sense of the word, is defined by the representational powers of color technology, the Hubble's "cosmic close-ups" are a clear case in point. Our world is rendered and received in high-resolution color, almost always on television, overwhelmingly in photography and film, increasingly in printouts and photocopies. Color has become a standard representational form and hence the visual norm. If so, what can be said of the popularity and proliferation since the late 1980s of the black-and-white image?

The resurgence of monochrome in American and European visual markets during the 1980s and 1990s was most obvious within advertising and the poster industry, but the black-and-white image also developed a new kudos within photojournalism, as well as in genres like music video. Black and white is, of course, one of many styles in a rapacious image world that grasps for attention and insinuates the latest "look" within particular regimes of taste. For IKEA, the home superstore that commands 12 percent of the world market in print sales (8 to 10 million annually), black and white is just one of several styles used in the profitable business of selling picture frames. Monochrome or Monet? IKEA have the prints and the frames to suit. Andrew Anthony suggests that our design choices are invariably shaped by the combined strategies of home improvement wholesalers and publishers, creating "an unyielding middlebrow orthodoxy of appropriate consumer art."[2] Black and white is a particular look, a specific atmosphere, one of many stylistic alternatives. While the relationship between corporate distribution and consumer demand is a complex one that cannot be reduced to the conspiratorial taste-mongering argued by Anthony, neither can the popularity of the monochrome image be divorced from the context of its selling and commercial circulation.

Despite its relative place in the tremendous marketplace for prints and images, black and white became a defining style in the mid- to late 1980s. This was captured in two images that developed a certain iconic status within Britain and America. The first was a kitsch portrait of a toned and topless male cradling an infant; taken by Spencer Rowell in 1986 and titled "L'Enfant," the moody black-and-white photo-poster became an instant best-seller, capturing "new-man" tenderness in agreeably muscle-bound form. The second image was of two lovers kissing in a Paris street. Taken by Robert Doisneau in 1950, "Le Baiser de l'Hôtel de Ville" was initially part of reportage for *Life* magazine, a human interest story about Parisian springtime romance. Its second life began in 1986, when the image was sold around the world through the poster industries growing out of New York, London, and Paris. Peter Hamilton estimates that the image sold over a million copies between 1985 and 1995. While he relates its success within France to nostalgia for a sense of stable nationhood challenged by urban decay, social disorder, and pressing questions of immigration, this does not account for its larger international appeal.[3] Indeed, the Doisneau image must be set in relation to a developing market for monochrome, incorporating the work of photographers as diverse as Robert Mapplethorpe and Edward Steichen, Gertrude Kasebier and Herb Ritts.

By the early 1990s, both the Doisneau kiss and the Rowell cradle had surpassed their iconic moment. This was finally marked by postscript revelations that Doisneau's lovers were in fact models paid to kiss in a staged embrace, and that the male model used by Rowell was a sex addict who claimed he'd slept with over 3,000 women.[4] The way in which these images, taken forty years apart, became two of *the* monochrome photographs of the late 1980s can no doubt prove various things about particular gender values and cultural nostalgias of the time, not to say the way in which texts from past and present circulate seamlessly together. In visual terms, however, they might also be seen to index a growing market for "black and whiteness." This term refers less to the representational content of an image than to the expediency and function of black and white as a "nonrepresentational sign." Richard Dyer develops this concept, suggesting that qualities like color, texture, movement, rhythm, and melody, while abstract and with a less obvious relation to reality, still embody feeling. In this way, they can be linked to culturally and historically determined sensibilities.[5] One of the central questions in part II of this book is the nature of black-and-white "feeling" and the relevance and bearing of its deployment in the mass media during the 1990s.

Within any single image, black and white is one of several perceptive, rhetorical, tonal, and iconic codes that produce overall meaning.[6] The connotative value of black and white will itself be dependent on the presentational medium, the context of consumption, and the generic conventions that any filmic or photographic image is bound to work within. In short, there is no singular "meaning" to monochrome as a stylistic code. It can be used to suggest intellectual abstraction, artistic integrity, documentary realism, archival evidence, fashion chic, and film classicism, depending on the nature of a text's production and reception. Black and white can have various connotations, often simultaneously. For example, Madonna's music documentary *Truth or Dare* (1991) uses black and white to get "behind the scenes." Monochrome is juxtaposed with color to enhance distinctions between room/stage, person/showperson, real life/spectacle. Black and white is an expedient documentary aesthetic. However, it also invokes, intertextually, and in examples drawn from Madonna's own work, fashion photography (Madonna's erotic portfolio taken by Herb Ritts, *Sex*), music video (exemplified in "Vogue" and "Justify My Love"), and nostalgia (Madonna's Marilyn Monroe persona for the filmed Blond Ambition tour). The meanings of monochrome are multiple; black-and-white "feeling" is not a stable or fixed quality.

Acknowledging this fact, there are perhaps two connotations that have become central to the visual effect and signifying character of "black and whiteness." These are what might be called monochrome's "meta-abstractions." In different ways, the black-and-white image in contemporary visual culture has become associated with *authenticity* and *time*. In a sense, there is nothing new in this. The entire history of the (black-and-white) photographic image has been framed within discursive manifestations of these two themes. Miles Orvell suggests that, at the beginning of the twentieth century, photographic discourse focused upon the power of the machine to verify fact and reality within a developing "culture of authenticity." Within both art and documentary photography—Steilgitz and Strand to Evans and Lange—the camera became "a powerful instrument of revelation changing our sense of the world by its power to shock the sensibilities and move the viewer emotionally."[7] Photography became the mechanical synthesis of science and art; the black-and-white image was conceived as the authentic rendering of a more intense perceptual reality. Susan Sontag suggests that the history of photography could be recapitulated as the struggle between two imperatives—those of beautification and of truth-telling.[8] These imperatives have different histories, but they are joined by a discourse of authenticity that has long framed and maintained the power of photography to capture lived reality almost transparently.

The camera image was, of course, black and white by necessity until the middle of the century. Monochrome developed a mutually defining relationship with color as technologies advanced during this time, however. Conventions of use, in the movies particularly, further established black and white as an idiom of realism and veracity, compared with color, which became associated with genres of spectacle and show. Color's early generic range included the musical, the comedy, the adventure story, the cartoon, the fantasy, and the historical epic. Within the aesthetic regimes of Hollywood, it was monochrome that remained linked to ideologies of realism and cultural verisimilitude. This continued to be so until the introduction in 1954 of Eastmancolor, a technology that suddenly made color movies easier and far less expensive to make. By enabling color recordings and prints to be made on conventional black-and-white cameras and print machines, Eastmancolor was less cumbersome and less costly than Technicolor, with its special cameras and film. From 1955, 50 percent of Hollywood films were made in color, and within a decade, television's chromatic transition would normalize color within general viewing sensibilities. By 1965, black and white was no longer, to quote Stanley Cavell, the "mode in which our lives are convincingly portrayed."[9] NBC began its major shift to network color in this year, and between 1965 and 1967, network news programs began to broadcast color newsfilm. In terms of the US production of color feature films, between 1966 and 1970 output rose from 54 percent to 94 percent. Despite this dramatic decline in the use of monochrome, the artistic and documentary properties of black and white retained an aesthetic value. There remains to this day in photographic theory and practice a sense that color is artificial—"a coating applied later on to the original truth of the black-and-white photograph."[10] Through conventions of use and its more general place in the early history of the camera image, black and white became, and remains, a quintessential aesthetic of the authentic.

It was from the mid-1960s that monochrome fully developed connotations of memory and time, cinematically expressed by the sepia nostalgia at the beginning of *Bonnie and Clyde* (1967) and *Butch Cassidy and the Sundance Kid* (1969), as well as in the black-and-white atmospherics of *The Last Picture Show* (1971). When color became the norm, black and white was progressively distinguished as a style from a different era. Photography may be an intrinsic technology of memory, but monochrome has grown as a particular style code of the (remembered) past. Like art deco script and Super-8 film, black and white has developed a quality of visual pastness. Unlike art deco and Super-8, however, monochrome refers to no particular decade, movement, or country. It is neither of the European 1920s nor the American 1950s. Instead, it has come to represent a more general, geographically indeterminate sense of temporality. Roger Rosenblatt writes that black and white "speaks a reverence for the past and recreates it." One might argue that monochrome signifies time and timelessness.[11]

The monochrome past has sold very well since the mid-1980s, catalogued and displayed in a largely indiscriminate fashion by the poster industry. From Native American portraits by Edward Curtis to the migrant scenes of Dorothea Lange, whether a Stieglitz steerage or Brassaï's Paris, content is less significant than monochrome's time(less) style. Sixty percent of the profits of Magnum, the photo agency established by Henri Cartier-Bresson, are now drawn from sales of its black-and-white back catalogue. Raphael Samuel dates the so-called "discovery of old photographs" to the late 1960s. This marked the combination of a developing taste for images of the past generated by collectors, dealers, and museum curators, by the new significance of memory in advertising and fashion, and by a heightened sense of the visual with the eclipse of the radio.[12] The black-and-white past has been a collectible style for at least three decades. From the mid-1980s, however, it experienced a renaissance in commercial terms in both American and European markets. Set in the context of a growing and widespread preoccupation with memory and heritage, the popularity of monochrome can also be related to the increasing production of digital and media-based imagery. With the development of computer-based technologies and the new sophistication of color processing helping to embed the flow of color simulacra in our image world, monochrome assumed a heightened significance in punctuating the norms of visual reception.

To the broad question of why a society requires certain images at particular times, the answer for black and white can perhaps be found in its ability to arrest meaning within, and suggest something outside, an image culture of rapid simulation and relentless color stimuli.

In the image culture of the 1990s, black and white assumed the capacity of simulating slowness in a climate of speed, evoking time in a culture of space, of suggesting authenticity in a world of simulation and pastiche. While linked to the image-governed world of postmodernity, monochrome is set apart; it is an aesthetic born of the past and distinguishable from the dominant field of color representation. Monochrome is one of many available codes in contemporary visual media, but it can somehow appear to transcend the image culture in which it is produced. While arrayed as a style code at the postmodern cultural surface, the black-and-white image is able to produce an effect of depth and time. It is this visual quality that was used in the 1990s to accentuate the figurative gravity and authenticity of particular corporate and cultural representations.

David Harvey suggests that images of permanence in political and commercial culture represent "the fleeting, superficial, and illusory means whereby an individualistic society of transients sets forth its nostalgia for common values."[13] If monochrome is one such image of permanence, it has succored authority in a volatile global marketplace based on the impression of depth, continuity, and time. In examining a discourse of "black and whiteness" in the 1990s, my analysis in part II is synchronic rather than diachronic. I am not trying to narrate the history of the black-and-white image in cultural production or explain the meaning of monochrome in every possible use. I want in this chapter, and in the chapters that follow, to examine how monochrome has been taken up in the tacit negotiation of national identity. This is examined through media forms linked by their relation to specific institutional/critical networks of power. The corporate bodies that gird the "dominant media" to which I refer can be conceived in terms of a power configuration deriving from the entertainment, computer, and communication industries. This is important to note if one is to grasp, following Stuart Hall, "the shadow, the imprint, the trace" of a text's (i.e., monochrome's) relation to specific institutional positionalities. In a moment when governing narratives of national identity and memory had come under particular, and intensified, strain, "black and whiteness" became a strategic style used to arrest meaning within, and stabilize identity against, the vicissitudes of an increasingly decentered world.[14]

My theoretical interest in this chapter is the means by which black and white was used in *Time* magazine during the 1990s to give the American present a temporal and potentially nostalgic aura. If monochrome is an idiom of the past, it has the capacity to convey the present *as* a past, complete with a sense of narrativized historical form. When the visual pastness of monochrome in *Time* magazine combines with a powerful journalistic impulse to make sense of the world, black and white can help to configure subjects with historical gravitas. If monochrome is able to give issues and events the distance and authority of time, it has the potential for legitimation, giving archival aura to people and politics, cultures and corporations. During the 1990s, monochrome was used to transform news facts into chronicled history; black and white helped construct a sense of historicized national meaning in a cultural moment when the sureties of that meaning, in the past and for the present, seemed more than ever in flux.

If a news magazine like *Time* performs an ideological function helping to explain the meaning of a country to itself, black and white provides a way of framing news with documentary gravitas, of highlighting specific news information as historical. Walter Isaacson, managing editor of *Time*, explained in 1998 that the magazine aims to "provide the common ground of information and knowledge that all informed folks should share and enjoy sharing."[15] In the 1990s, the black-and-white image was instrumental in creating a shared sense of historical meaning; it helped to articulate what Andrew Ross has called *Time* magazine's "theme park view of the national essence."[16] *Time* magazine is, of course, not the only contemporary magazine to use black-and-white photography. In an information economy where current and future news production (and the production of images of history) rests overwhelmingly with televisual and electronic media, the black-and-white photograph has been fetishized in more general terms within print forms such as the broadsheet supplement and the weekly newsmagazine.[17] When the monochrome photograph appears, it is often used to suggest and position the journalistic gravity of print-based media, encoding stories with authenticity and the cultural weight of documentary photojournalism. *Time* is not exceptional in its use of black and white, but it does provide a salient case study in breaching questions about the way that monochrome has been used in the dominant media to aestheticize American memory and identity. The genesis and expedience of black and white is different in each media form that I treat in part II. In each case, however, the visual pastness of monochrome has been used to legitimate an archival sense of history/memory in a climate where historical meanings and cultural memories have become less coherent, more contingent, and subject to what Lawrence Grossberg has called postmodernity's "dissolution of the 'anchoring effect.'"[18]

TIME'S CHANGE

There was an interesting reversal in *Time* magazine during the 1990s. Once, technological and economic necessity had meant that *Time* was entirely black and white apart from its cover, a selection of advertisements, and those stories deemed "special," all of which appeared in color. Ever since the magazine turned full color in 1989, however, the advertisements and "special" stories have begun to be printed in black and white. There was a transfer of visual signification. If color was at one time the carrier of impact and meaning, black and white usurped this role. Of course, black and white has impact, because it is the contrast from the norm, a quality that color once enjoyed. Its currency in *Time* and *Newsweek* grew steadily during the 1990s, however, to the extent that it became a visual commonplace. This stylistic renaissance must be understood in relation to strategic factors within magazine publishing, but it can also be measured in terms of monochrome's signifying capital and political functionality. Black and white gives a picture status beyond that of being "news"—it suggests that an image has cultural significance in the broad construction of historical identity. If color reports, monochrome chronicles.

The use of color in the print media increased dramatically during the 1980s, made possible by new technologies of desktop publishing. In 1979, 12 percent of American newspapers used color in some form. By 1983, this had risen to 53 percent, and by 1990, 97 percent of American dailies were using color technology. The first full-color newspaper was *USA Today*. Beginning in 1982, the paper was accused of a lack of seriousness within the newspaper industry, reflecting aesthetic conventions in the print media that reserve monochrome for "real" news and color for spectacle and celebration. It was only in 1993 that the *New York Times* introduced color into sections other than its magazine, cautiously beginning with the *New York Times Book Review*. Color photography was used regularly on the front page of the news section from 1998 on—the same year that *The Washington Post* made its transition to color. The normalization of color within general aesthetic sensibilities moved many papers to new color formats. This was no small venture considering that a printing plant for a major newspaper can cost upwards of $300 million. It was the importance of advertising revenue, however, that made color capacity a real imperative for news organizations. A test by the Newspaper Advertising Bureau, reported by the *New York Times* in 1993, found that color ads produced 43 percent more sales than black and white.[19] Without color, newspapers would struggle to compete with promotional media like film and television. It was in this context that *Time* magazine appealed to advertisers within its own pages. Portraying a pastel-colored penguin, a 1989 advertisement was captioned: "When we say no more black and white, we mean it." Promoting itself as the first international news magazine to be published in color around the world (the domestic issue went full color in 1985), the ad explained that "This extra touch of color makes us a livelier and more appealing medium for your advertisements, as well as for our readers."[20] Within three years, aesthetic tastes would change, and the penguin would look its old self again: black and white was back in style.

The resurgence of black and white in *Time* was influenced by the turn to monochrome among advertisers themselves. It must also be seen in the context of *Time*'s redesign in 1992, the first since Walter Bernard and Rudy Hoglund systematized the style and typeface in 1977. The early 1990s were a period of recession in magazine publishing. At *Time,* ad revenue was down by 20 percent in 1991. This went along with significant staff reductions and a management shakeup at parent company Time-Warner. A year of analysis ensued at *Time,* strategy sessions addressing its own mission and the role of the news magazine generally. The redesign of *Newsweek* in the late 1980s had, in particular, served to close the gap between the two magazines and to challenge the dominance of *Time.* Stylistically inferior to *Newsweek*'s new layout, and accused of having abandoned news stories for celebrity features, the *Time* redesign responded to its depressed market performance by roping off a specific media and entertainment section and giving more space to longer in-depth news articles. In his position as managing editor, Henry Muller said at the time: "The priority was to define what a news magazine would be in the era of instant communication."[21] Facing increasing competition in the market for news and information, *Time* carved a niche for stories on general subjects like scientology and evil and gave current affairs extended feature-length coverage.

The black-and-white news photograph returned in the context of new editorial commitments to the market specificity of magazine journalism. Monochrome drew upon traditions of photojournalism that were being increasingly replaced in a media culture of soundbite over substance, where news editors have less time and space for lengthy photographic features. Black and white also distinguished *Time* in a magazine market that had become saturated with glossy Technicolor since new technologies of engraving made full-color formats economically viable in the late 1980s. Monochrome carried a suggestion of depth and seriousness, and it became popular in news magazines around 1992, when *Newsweek* ran a story on Sarajevo using black-and-white photographs by Tom Stoddard.[22] It was P. F. Bentley's portraits of Clinton's 1992 presidential campaign that helped pioneer its recent use in *Time*. This was by no means an explicit managerial strategy. While monochrome was first used in *Time* under the management of Henry Muller, Bentley had to force the initial decision by shooting mundane campaign material in color, keeping black and white for the more provocative shots. According to Bentley, the use of monochrome in *Time* was helped by a less skeptical view of black and white's aesthetic merits on the part of a new managing editor, Walter Isaacson. He comments that "Walter is into the 'exclusive' aspect of this (monochrome), savvy on public relations, and a newsman from way back."[23] Monochrome was never a calculated visual strategy at *Time*; it emerged in the context of particular stylistic and managerial transformations at the magazine in the early 1990s.

Bentley suggests that black and white is a means of "getting back to 'real' photojournalism." This is echoed in the preface to a book collection of his campaign photographs, *Clinton: Portrait of Victory* (1993). Roger Rosenblatt writes the introduction, explaining: "If color is the new journalism of photography, in which the photographer's presence is always loudly proclaimed, black and white is the old journalism, in which the photographer disappears, and things speak for themselves."[24] A quality of authenticity is ascribed to monochrome. It is part of a tradition of photojournalism that is able—and supposedly denied by the rapid flow and headline repetitions of CNN—to "probe the inner life of things." Getting back to "real" photojournalism is a sentiment expressed by many who lament the technological and market transformations that have shaped the image-world in which we live. The former editor of *The Guardian*, Peter Preston, writes: "The world is full of pictures; but they aren't the pictures that set the adrenaline of photo-journalists coursing. They illustrate, they soothe, they flatter, they fill acres of space. But they have no independent life of their own."[25] Black and white invokes a tradition and plays upon a notion of photographic authenticity. This is significant in a time when new capacities of digital alteration, together with practical changes like the decreasing role of the staff photographer, have transformed both the place of the photojournalist *and* the status of the news photograph.

The visual coding of "authenticity" in *Time* occurred in the same moment that computer manipulation was undermining the truth status of the photographic image. *Time* was embroiled in controversy in 1995, when a cover shot of O. J. Simpson was found to have been digitally altered and Simpson's face darkened. This not only raised questions about the suspect racial implications, it also made the representational authenticity of the photographic image a subject for public debate. This points to a rather intriguing cultural "coincidence" that developed in the early 1990s, whereby the capacity for digitally manipulating photography emerged in roughly the same period that black and white became a popular visual style. The undermining of photographic authenticity through computer technology, typified in the *Time* case, was met with a certain *reaffirmation* of photographic authenticity through popular aesthetics. Of course, black and white can be digitally altered like color, but it seems, nevertheless, to provide a more assured sense of veracity.[26] It is hard to say whether the black-and-white image compensates for a felt lack of authenticity in visual culture or is, instead, one of many visual styles marketing authenticity as a look. Miles Orvell suggests that the new postmodernist sensibility "has clearly gone beyond worrying about imitation and authenticity, though it is everywhere concerned with it."[27] The popularity of the black-and-white image is perhaps an aesthetic example of this "concern."

To summarize my points so far: the resurgence of monochrome in *Time* during the 1990s was the result of several economic and cultural factors. It relates to questions about the status of the news magazine, in particular the need to reestablish a journalistic niche in a ferocious market for information; it emerged through particular personalities like P. F. Bentley and Walter Isaacson, who favor "the old journalism"; it was sanctified and sustained by black and white's developing cachet in the taste regimes of media and commercial culture; and it can be situated in a cultural moment where photographic authenticity itself was being challenged by new digital technologies. What needs to be examined, having established certain contextual elements, is the *signifying function* of black and white in *Time*. In 1998, Walter Isaacson characterized *Time* as a news magazine by stating: "Through narrative and personality, analysis and synthesis, we try to make a complex world more coherent. The ultimate goal is to help make sure that the chaotic tumble of progress does not outpace our moral processing power."[28] I want to ask how black and white operates visually in this context: how, in particular, it intercedes in decisions about, and articulations of, moral and historical "coherence."

There is no formal policy concerning the use of black and white in *Time*. It is not a question of black and white being cheaper to print, for monochrome photographs are processed in color to achieve sharper image resolution. Black and white is not a question of economy; it is used instead for particular visual connotations. What makes this interesting from a cultural perspective is the pattern of its stylistic deployment. Since 1992, monochrome has been used to represent stories ranging from the Bosnian war to the rise of the Christian coalition. The black-and-white photographs of American political life by P. F. Bentley and Diana Walker, special correspondents for *Time*, are commonly used. The question that must be asked is: What, if anything, unites these subjects? What status are stories given by their monochrome representation?

Michele Stephenson, picture editor for the domestic issue of *Time*, explains that black and white is used for a documentary effect.[29] It creates a sense of unobtrusiveness and of being "behind the scenes," but it can also provide an archival and retrospective aura. While breaking news will almost certainly be shot in color, black and white is used to suggest qualities of introspection and poignancy. Henry Luce, founder of *Time*, said that "everything in *Time* should be titillating, or epic or supercurtly factual."[30] As a visual idiom, black and white leans toward an epic factuality—*monochrome documents and chronicles*. Stories in black and white are visually codified in a way that can provide them with historical significance. Victor Burgin suggests that the news photograph helps to transform the raw continuum of historical flux into the product of news. With black and white, we might reverse the terms—the monochrome photograph helps to transform the raw continuum of news flux into the product of history.[31]

Paul Durrant, picture editor of *Time Atlantic,* estimates that 96 percent of images used in *Time* are purchased from agencies. These tend to be in color. The rest of the images will be taken by contract photographers like Bentley and Diana Walker, who are guaranteed a certain amount of work each year. Specialties often develop among the contract photographers, and this can lead to monochrome appearing by default rather than by design. One cannot read cultural significance into every single use of monochrome by *Time.* This said, black and white *has* been used in some very particular ways. A certain amount of space was reserved during the 1990s for photojournalistic essays that followed in the hallowed traditions of Magnum. James Nachtway, himself a Magnum photographer, published various photo-essays dealing with conflict and warfare such as in Bosnia and Afghanistan. *Time* also published photo-essays by Anthony Saua, extracted from his ten-year project documenting the death of Communism. While these are significant in showing the scope of monochrome's visual presence in *Time,* I am more interested in the way that black and white has been used to create aesthetic effects conducive to particular kinds of story. These tend to be features that claim to get "inside" the subject and / or stories that *deal with memory.*

The equation between monochrome and memory can be observed in various kinds of story use, from obituaries to historical features. Two consecutive cover shots of Princess Diana in the weeks following her fatal car accident give this some illustration. On 8 September 1997, *Time* used a color portrait of Diana—a striking image of a smiling princess at a formal occasion.[32] The cover draws attention to Diana's brilliant blue eyes, perfect white teeth, and shining diamond earrings, but also to the words "Special Report" written boldly at the top of the page. This is breaking news. The cover of the next issue, on 15 September, is a black-and-white portrait of Diana, soft-focus and taken in a studio as a fashion portrait. Although clearly staged, it conveys a more "private" figure than the color photograph that showed her smiling openly for crowds and paparazzi. It is unusual for *Time* to use successive covers so similar in style, but the issues were sold in different ways. While the first was a "special report," the second had the more discreet "commemorative issue" written inside the word TIME. A character of remembrance was continued inside the magazine, where the death of Mother Teresa was also covered in black and white. For a news magazine, the coincidence of both women dying in the same year gave rich texture for journalistic meditations on youth and age, beauty and wisdom, "civic sainthood" and the "genuine article." The commemorative issue was reflective, poignant, and as a consequence, unsurprisingly liberal in its use of black and white. It became the best-selling issue of *Time* in the magazine's entire history, selling 1,183,758 copies.[33]

I am interested in the way in which cultural memory has underpinned the use of black and white in *Time*. More specifically, I want to consider how monochrome memory has given particular stories about American life a pregnant historical import. Marita Sturken writes that "cultural memory is a means through which definitions of the nation and 'Americanness' are simultaneously established, questioned and refigured."[34] Black-and-white images perhaps contribute to this negotiation of nation and "Americanness" by documenting issues and events in narratives of historical memory. If past events gain meaning by their existence in history, one could also say that present events are given meaning by their identification *as* history. The visual differentiation between chronicle (monochrome) and report (color) is the platform for editorial decisions about cultural meaning, about subjects that should be framed as more than reported news. I want now to examine three examples that focus, respectively, on social, political, and cultural life. These are all cover stories that use black and white on the actual cover page and reveal particular stakes in *Time*'s construction of chronicled history.

CHRONICLE OF A HISTORY FORETOLD

The 1990s were a period of cultural identity crisis for the United States, or at least a time when rhetoric of crisis seemed especially prevalent. One of the governing metaphors of the early 1990s, describing a wide series of anxieties, debates, and distempers about the question of identity and the legacy of the 1960s was that of "the culture war." Associated most specifically with controversies in education surrounding curricular revision, affirmative action, and speech codes, the culture war became a term that described a range of issues concerned with multiculturalism and the politics of identity. While the origins of the academic culture war can be traced back through the 1980s and its genesis in the 1990s can be set in relation to the end of the cold war, economic dislocations, globalization, demographic changes, philosophical currents, and long-standing identity debates, the culture war came most forcefully to public attention through the news magazine.[35] It was a cover story by *Newsweek* (24 December 1991) that brought the equation of multiculturalism, "political correctness," and left-wing "thought police" to full media fruition. Troubled by the so-called "politicization of the academy," editorials in *New York, The New Republic, The Chicago Tribune, Newsweek,* and *Time* spoke throughout 1991 of a "new intolerance" within universities and in cultural life more generally.[36] America was said to be suffering from a new kind of totalitarianism, or "McCarthyism of the Left." It was in this context, amidst media debate about left-wing tyrannies and cultural fragmentation, that *Time* ran a cover in 1991 with the question, "Who are we?"

The cover coincided with the 4th of July holiday. It was in bright pastels and showed cartoon figures of various American ethnic groups, marching to flute and drum with the stars and stripes snapping behind them. The cover was captioned: "American kids are getting a new—and divisive—view of Thomas Jefferson, Thanksgiving and the Fourth of July" (8 July 1991). The feature essay by Paul Gray developed the theme of division, chastising multiculturalism for its "regressive orthodoxies" and for exalting "racial and ethnic pride at the expense of social cohesion."[37] With an air of judicious consideration, measuring the benefits of multiculturalism with its more profound dangers, the principle of diversity with the need for shared values, the *Time* feature revealed what Michael Bérubé has called the "foundational slippage" in (many liberal) critiques of multiculturalism. This is the conflation of "common culture" and "common society," collapsing the two so that any reconsideration of the former can seem like an attack on the principle of the latter.[38]

It is worth developing this point, for it provides the background to a monochrome *Time* cover that, in May 1992, almost a year after the issue on multiculturalism, posed *"e pluribus unum"* as a question (see Figure 3.1). This cover echoed the title of the final chapter of Arthur Schlesinger Jr.'s best-selling book, *The Disuniting of America*: *Reflections on a Multicultural Society*. In this 1991 polemic, Schlesinger is troubled by the waning status of *e pluribus unum* in a country wracked by division. He writes that "The multiethnic dogma abandons historic purposes, replacing assimilation by fragmentation, integration by separatism. It belittles *unum* and glorifies *pluribus*." Underwriting the argument of *Disuniting* is the fear that America's cultural and political heritage is being compromised by a new "cult of ethnicity." Schlesinger is at pains to maintain principles of inheritance, legacy and tradition, defending a challenged "American Creed." If, as he argues, an ethnic upsurge "threatens to become a counter revolution against the original theory of America as 'one people,' a common culture, a single nation," multiculturalism is seen as a challenge of no small proportion.[39] With it rests the integrity of American identity and the communal bonds of the republic. "The historic idea of a unifying America is now in peril," writes Schlesinger. His "reflections" on a multicultural society are a defense of this "historic idea," both in education and through the teaching of history. His polemic against "disuniting" draws upon the force and authority of history, understood as pedagogical practice and unifying cultural experience.

Schlesinger is part of a much larger debate about education and knowledge, which I cannot explore here. It is perhaps enough to say

Figure 3.1 The Two Americas: *E Pluribus Unum?*
(Black-and-white cover of *Time*, 18 May 1992.)
Courtesy of Didier Ruef / Time / Rex.

that what Bérubé defines as his "weak liberalism"—namely, the accom-modation of multiculturalism with a hypothetical center as opposed to a broad institutional transformation *of* the center—distinguished *Time*'s early coverage of multiculturalism. It was befitting that Schles-inger should write a one-page article in the *Time* edition on multicultur-alism. His short essay developed several key themes from *Disuniting*, in particular the argument of a shifting balance from *unum* to *pluribus* and the dangers of multicultural separatism. Directing his concern at Afro-centrism, Schlesinger wrote that "if separatist tendencies go unchecked, the result can only be the fragmentation, resegregation and tribalization of American life."[40] The idea of fragmentation, together with the canard of political correctness, became a dominant feature of culture-war rheto-ric and would underwrite *Time*'s anxious question, "Who are we?" Todd Gitlin suggests that "such a question, asked so insistently, answers itself: we are a people who don't know who we are."[41] Within seven months, fragmentation would be joined by another adjective in the growing vocabulary of cultural crisis, that of "fraying."

The word was deployed by *Time* columnist and art critic Robert Hughes, who rehearsed the argument of his best-selling book, *Culture of Complaint: The Fraying of America* (1993) in a 1992 article that went by the shortened title "The Fraying of America." Influenced by Schlesinger, Hughes characterized "a society obsessed with therapies and filled with distrust of formal politics, skeptical of authority, and prey to superstition, its political language corroded by fake pity and euphemism."[42] Hughes is more concerned with the waning powers of an effective left than is Schlesinger, but there is equal dismay at the beleaguered status of *e pluribus unum* in a culture of grievance and increasing factionalism. Hughes suggests that multiculturalists want "cultural separatism within the larger whole of America. They want to Balkanize culture." While much could be said about the liberal critique of multiculturalism in the writings of Schlesinger and Hughes, I want to understand them contextually leading up to a particular black-and-white *Time* cover that showed a young black male sitting thoughtfully under the Statue of Liberty, with the headline "The Two Americas: *E Pluribus Unum*?"

For almost a year, *Time* had been discussing tribalization and the dangers of ethnic fragmentation. This was given an unforeseen resonance, however, when the politics of racial and ethnic identity suddenly moved from the realm of education to the rioting streets of Los Angeles. "There is no guarantee that the United States's long test of trying to live together will not end in fragmentation and collapse, with groups gathered around the firelight, waiting for the attack at dawn," Paul Gray had written a year before the riots in his essay on multiculturalism.[43] With the acquittal of the police officers who beat Rodney King, the language of firelight fear and dawn attacks became all too acute. Of course, the LA riots were not so much an expression of some militant form of multiculturalism, but rather a specific response to the failure of judicial procedure and the dumbfounding clarity of black disenfranchisement in the face of white power. With the beating of white truck driver Reginald Denny, the riots broadened in significance further still. The media portrayed race war: what *Time* would headline "the fire this time." Suddenly, the anxious question "Who are we?" no longer seemed the heart of the matter. It had been replaced on the cover of *Time* by the urgent plea of Rodney King: "Can we all get along?"

The LA riots were first reported in *Time* on 11 May 1992, in a cover story using color photography. The cover image showed police officers running in formation toward a blazing fire, captioned with the quotation from Rodney King. The cover of the following week's issue appeared in monochrome, "The Two Americas" written in bold black typeface. If the aesthetic shift of the Diana covers marked a movement from report to commemoration, a different transformation was achieved in the coverage of the LA riots. In this case, black and white did not commemorate the riots but framed them in historical terms. In monochrome, controversial stories can be given significance by locating their place in historical narrative. Lance Morrow, a senior writer for *Time*, suggests that a founding principle of the magazine was, and remains, the sorting of the world into stories, turning "the news into saga, comedy, melodrama."[44] Describing the "epic" voice of *Time*, Morrow suggests that in the early history of the magazine this was characterized by a "disciplined, moral understanding of history, an adult's steady gaze." There is something of this legacy of disciplined moral storytelling in *Time*'s treatment of the LA riots. Although the *Time* cover may question *e pluribus unum*, the cover works visually to authenticate the issue of race relations in broad historical terms. Monochrome gives postriot race relations a stabilizing historical dimension, helping to counter the language of anarchy and social breakdown that first accompanied volcanic eruptions of racial discontent.

The monochrome issue of *Time* tries to assimilate the experience of the riots and rationalize the violence. Inside the magazine are a series of reflections and postmortems on the riots, discussing the "Lessons of Los Angeles" and "The Two Ways to Play the Politics of Race." Various political implications are assessed, and the whole occurrence is framed as a sociopolitical catalyst—if an unsettling one—in the historical saga of American race relations. Placing the riots in a party-political context, their bearing on the 1992 presidential election is discussed. Significantly, Bush and Clinton are seen "battling to control the memories of Los Angeles." The riots quickly become an event to be remembered, a cautionary explosion, a lesson to be learned. By using black and white on its cover, *Time* brings the riots into a retrospective and memorial framework; the magazine attempts to contextualize the racial politics of the LA riots by posing them in historical terms, at least as a historical dilemma.

The riots moved racial and ethnic politics from the culture war over education, where Schlesinger entered the fray, to a more literal and disturbing kind of violence. In the volatile aftermath, *Time* saw fit to question *e pluribus unum*. With racial conflict breaking out in several of America's major cities, a swift historical perspective became pressing for a news magazine trying "to make a complex world more coherent." The use of monochrome in *Time* helped to locate the riots within a discourse of historical identity. Black and white became a visual means of transforming racial conflict from news (with its sense of presentness and unpredictability) into chronicle (with the implication of continuity and historical meaning). Black and white turned the question of social division from headline into history. Visually, it placed the riots within a

particular interpretative context that rationalized their historical significance, stabilized their meaning, and in some sense contained their potency as "news."

Time magazine has a circulation of 4.1 million, making it America's
twelfth-largest magazine. On average, each copy is read by five people,
meaning that it reaches about 12.5 percent of the nation's population.[45]
While *Time* may no longer be the flagship of the nation's middle-class
ideology, the magazine's synthesis and "storyfication" of news and
world events retains a pointed cultural authority. "The vestibule of this
new millennium continues to have intruders that *Time* tries to wrestle
into moral and historical context," wrote Walter Isaacson in an editorial
celebrating the magazine's seventy-fifth anniversary in 1998. Outlining
the values of the magazine, inherited from Henry Luce, Isaacson describes *Time*'s most enduring belief as "a fundamental optimism" and "a
faith in humanity's capacity for common sense." Isaacson states:

Our goal is to be a touchstone for this common sense. Rather than strike a
pose of pessimism about all values, we must hew to certain basic ones, such
as doing what's best for our kids. Rather than view individual rights as being
at odds with a compassionate sense of community, we must understand that
America's historic magic has been creating a social fabric that is strong
because it weaves these two strands together.[46]

Isaacson is aware and refreshingly unapologetic about *Time*'s ideological
commitments, or what he calls "prejudices." What is significant, however, is the example he draws upon to make his case for common sense.
Once again the language of historic magic and social fabric returns. The
fraying of America's social fabric was a perennial concern in the 1990s, a
fear that the plural tapestry of the nation was being vandalized by those
seeking to transform culture (as well as theorize culture) into separatist
threads. Visually and rhetorically, investments were made in *Time* to
restore a stabilizing historic dimension when identity debates—whether
in schools or in the streets—became volatile and fraught or seemed to
contravene the received wisdoms of consensual nationhood.

Monochrome linked the violence of the LA riots to the status of
American historical identity; it placed the event within larger debates
that warned against fragmentation and put a value on America's plural
tradition. Later in the year, six months after the Rodney King riots, *Time*
ran a black-and-white cover that achieved a different historical effect.
Poised for electoral victory, a black-and-white special feature taken by P.
F. Bentley traced Bill Clinton's presidential campaign, from sax playing
on the Arsenio Hall show to closed-door meetings with Jesse Jackson.
This did not stabilize the election so much as codify it with a sense of
nostalgia in and for the present. Sometimes, according to the way that

Figure 3.2 Bill Clinton's Long March.
(Black-and-white cover of *Time*, 2 November 1992.)
Courtesy of P. F. Bentley / Time / Rex.

Time presents a feature story and the discursive matrix that surrounds a subject matter, a monochrome picture may help to construct the present as a future memory *being lived*, as an authentic past *in creation*. I would understand many of Bentley's political images in this way. The second cover image I want to consider shows Bill Clinton addressing a crowd, a close-up documentary shot looking upwards at his face (2 November 1992). The caption that joins the black-and-white image reads: "Bill Clinton's Long March: The inside story of the making of his campaign for the presidency. Will he prevail?" (Figure 3.2).

As a concept applied to magazine discourse, nostalgia for the present describes an express configuration of memory, chronicle, and cultural meaning, a feeling of the workings of time for events that have yet to unfold. As an experience of time, it involves moving backwards to the past and forwards to the future in a simultaneous gesture, grasping the present as a cogent period with historical form. Essentially, the present is understood in terms of it being a future past; it is given the wholeness and aura that retrospection and the passage of time can provide *before* the passage of time has actually taken place. The nostalgia in question is anticipatory: we look forward to the future in order to look back on the present being lived, complete with shape and a sense of its archival place in historical narrative. Flaubert believed that pleasure is found first in anticipation, later in memory. Nostalgia for the present finds the two collapsing so that pleasure is to be found in the very *anticipation* of memory.

The black-and-white cover shot of the Clinton campaign illustrates nostalgia in and for the political present. It has two modes of authenticity. Firstly, it emphasizes "the inside story." The monochrome cover-shot is taken upwards of Clinton's face and shoulders as he speaks to someone outside the frame. It is not a conventional press image but documentary in style. The cover promises personal and political authenticity in a milieu known for its pursuit of controlled photogenia and the carefully managed photo opportunity. Despite the fact that photography can never exist in a transparent or unmediated relation to reality, monochrome is often seen as a transparent medium and not as a particular visual effect.[47] P. F. Bentley himself rather naively remarks on the authenticity of black and white by saying that "when you see a black-and-white photograph you are drawn only to its contents—there is nothing to hide behind."[48] Black and white is given a value of authenticity, something reinforced by photographic composition and the textual anchoring of captions.

The second mark of authenticity is historical in orientation. The cover is not simply about Clinton the man but the man's potential influence on American history, his so-called "long march." To understand any image, one must relate it to a series of intersecting discourses that produce meaning. Bentley's monochrome shots should be understood in the context of the nostalgia that defined Clinton's very campaign, from the bus trip across the Midwest to the dissemination of the photo of a young Clinton shaking the hand of President Kennedy. Clinton's candidacy was based partly on the question of his political authenticity, as to whether he could return the zest to American life once achieved by, or remembered in, Kennedy. This became a mark of *Time*'s own construction of Clinton's election identity. Lance Morrow wrote: "For years, Americans have been in a vague mourning for something they sensed they had lost somewhere."[49] Nostalgia was an expedient mode for Clinton and a tenor of *Time* reporting. This perhaps made the use of black and white more appropriate for P. F. Bentley. He explains that he based his images on those taken of Kennedy in the early 1960s by Jacques Lowe. By using black and white, Bentley made the 1992 election immediately archival; it conveyed the here and now as history that could one day be remembered itself—although it seemed ironic by the end of the decade—as an authentic beginning of a new golden age.

When interviewed about the photographs he took of the 1992 Clinton campaign, Bentley said: "First and foremost when you're taking photos for history, black and white is archival. Color is not and deteriorates over time. I would like these images to be seen long after we are both dead so there is a record of what happened during this era."[50] In a world that experiences such a fast turnover of images, stories, and news events in the visual media, it has become hard to elicit the "significance" of any one in particular. In the case of Bentley's photojournalism, black and white codes a particular historical significance. The documentary function of black and white should not be underplayed. The photo-essay inside the "Long March" issue has the style of a diary. Monochrome photographs show Clinton in solitary moments (jogging alone), in private exchanges with his friends and wife (talking to Al Gore on the campaign bus, playing table tennis with Hillary), and in public moments, where we see Clinton watching others (the back of Clinton's head as he fronts a media barrage). The adjoining captions create a diary sequence: "Labor Day," "Press Conference," "Comeback Kid," "Campaign Snapshots," "Us on a Bus," "Teamwork," "The Third Debate," "The Last Lap." The sense is of an intimate rather than intimated record of events.

The feature is *not simply* an "inside story," however. Describing one of Bentley's campaign shots where Clinton is seen addressing a crowd, Roger Rosenblatt writes: "Could they not be a political audience of the 1940s or 1950s, of almost any era really? One begins to dream back into the entire history of presidential campaigns, the history of American politics itself. . . ."[51] Black and white has a clear documentary function, but monochrome also creates a feeling of tradition and time. This is interesting in a culture that at the beginning of the 1990s was being diagnosed by E. J. Dionne as one suffering from chronic political disaffection and a veritable crisis in its democratic and public tradition. Dionne exhibits similar liberal anxieties about threatened unity as that witnessed in the writings of Schlesinger ("disuniting of America"), Hughes ("fraying of America") and Todd Gitlin ("twilight of common dreams"). Dionne writes that "our common citizenship no longer fosters a sense of community or common purpose."[52] Rather than focus his criticism directly on multiculturalism, his causal explanation for "the fragmentation of American society" resides in the failure of the American political system to respond to America's restive majority.

In his best-selling *Why Americans Hate Politics* (1991), Dionne argues that politicians are engaging in symbolic rather than substantive politics and that citizens are being turned away from "a deliberative, democratic public life" by false issues and false political choices. The number of eligible voters going to the polls in U.S. presidential elections is notoriously small, at roughly 50 percent. For midterm congressional elections this figure is in the region of 35 percent. In Dionne's account at the beginning of the 1990s, America was suffering from a "flight from public life." This was principally caused by the "phony polarization around the issues of the 1960s" that were serving to paralyze meaningful (that is to say anything but cultural) politics. Dionne evinces a clear antagonism to the issues associated with the culture war, and his talk of political debate "getting back to basics" reveals a somewhat familiar brand of weak, even reactionary, liberalism. *Why Americans Hate Politics* is a polemical work, as one might expect. There is something in Dionne's observation about a new seriousness demanded from politicians in the early 1990s, however, that might help explain the utility of black and white in *Time*'s coverage of the 1992 presidential election.

In his 1992 afterword, Dionne suggests that the 1990s offer "an unusual opportunity to solve problems by accepting the insights that both the left and right have offered in the last three decades . . . we can preserve the gains of the 1960s while recognizing the mistakes of that era."[53] He feels optimistic about the creation of a new political center and the generation of a concomitant political seriousness. While questions must be asked about the kind of politics he condemns as phony and unserious—largely, the politics of race, class, sexuality, and gender—Dionne suggests that the 1990s could mark a "new era of reform" developing from a more conciliatory relationship between liberalism and conservatism. This pre-Gingrich, preimpeachment vision is at odds with the partisan politics witnessed during the Clinton presidency, but it distinguishes the tone of historical possibility that came with the 1992 election. The monochrome *Time* issue dealing with "Bill Clinton's Long March" was concerned most immediately with Clinton's "textbook" presidential campaign. Black and white also gave the campaign a historical dimension, however. How had Clinton come this far? Would he prevail? Describing the broad support a Clinton presidency might receive in the polls, *Time* said (in a color news report in the same issue): "After one of the toughest and most serpentine campaigns in memory, Clinton would have a running start in setting the country on a new course after 12 years of Republican rule."[54] The 1992 election marked a political watershed; America was set for "a new course." Black and white framed this political anticipation in historical, memorial, and potentially nostalgic terms. *Time* inscribed the American political system with significance and possibility in a period when the voting public seemed disengaged or—to quote Warren Beatty's film about 1990s politics, *Bulworth* (1998)—"unaroused."

Black and white is first and foremost a documentary aesthetic. Understood within a signifying regime that differentiates news from chronicle, however, monochrome can also function as a visual signature of history and historical meaning. If so, one might ask why a conspicuously "historical" event like the 1998/1999 impeachment proceedings against Bill Clinton was never covered in monochrome. There are perhaps two main reasons for the impeachment saga being figured as "news" and not as "history." First, because of its fervent unpredictability and constant newsworthiness, and second, because reporting the issue, rather than documenting it, enabled the affair to be contextualized as a political convulsion instead of a dramatic and destabilizing historical trauma. Whereas the LA riots needed to be stabilized in historical terms, the historical import of the Lewinsky scandal, in particular the impeachment proceedings, was a political embarrassment that was downplayed visually. One might say that the Lewinsky scandal lacked the air of profundity and grandeur equated semiotically with black and white. The basic point to make here is that monochrome functions in accordance with cultural discourses that create *or deny* historical significance according to the complex balance of interests and identities at stake.

The relationship between monochrome and memory, and the creation of nostalgia in and for the present, is not exclusive to particular historical personalities or to major historical themes. A black-and-white cover (18 August 1997) depicting the man at the helm of Apple computers, Steve Jobs, talking on the phone with Bill Gates of Microsoft illustrates the deemed cultural significance of a financial deal between the two companies (Figure 3.3). The image shows Jobs dressed casually in black, crouching on a stage while listening or speaking into his mobile phone. There is a sense of documentary and of the inside story. The text on the cover includes the caption: "Exclusive: Inside the Apple-Microsoft Deal." The deal involves the financial bailout of struggling Apple by the much stronger Microsoft. The larger historical meaning is brought out on the cover by a quotation from Steve Jobs that reads: "Bill, thank you. The world's a better place." Indicative of the way that communication and information technology has been taken up centrally (at least in the United States) within globalized visions of the corporate and cultural future, it provides a suggestive final cover image to examine.

The larger discourse of cyberspace in American culture is significant if one is to appreciate why *Time* may have chosen monochrome as a suitable aesthetic for an otherwise mundane business story. *Time* has developed a particular, even rather devotional, interest in things cyber. *Time* was one of the first magazines to go online in the 1990s (with *Time Daily* in 1994), and parent company Time-Warner made considerable investments in multimedia projects throughout the decade, notably in its Path-

Figure 3.3   "Bill, thank you. The world's a better place."
(Black-and-white cover of *Time*, 18 August 1997.)
Courtesy of Diana Walker / Time / Rex.

finder supersite. Cyberspace represents challenges to, and possibilities
for, print journalism. Electronic journalism, and the technologies that
make it practicable, are tied to the very future of *Time* as a print magazine. As CEO of Time-Warner—and long before the momentous buyout
of Time-Warner by America Online in January 2000—Gerald Levin remarked: "I think we'll engage the consumer in the digital domain in a
way that forces new forms of publishing and moviemaking and music-
making and shopping and whatever."[55] In its coverage of cyberspace,
Time has continually framed the digital revolution in historical terms,
often establishing an expository relationship with digital culture in order to position and invigorate its own print voice.

In one pregnant example, *Time* ran a special issue in spring 1995 with
the cover headline, "Welcome to Cyberspace." The issue featured a wide
range of articles and features on cyberspace, relating it to education,
business, technology, behavior, misbehavior, the workplace, aging, gov-

ernment, and the press. Throughout the magazine, advertisements relentlessly promoted companies like Siemens, Apple, Nokia, and also *Time* itself. The magazine took an opportunity to make various claims about its own relationship with, and its capacity to explain developments within, cyberspace. Using the tag line, "Understanding comes with TIME," one advertisement unequivocally stated: "Telecommunications. Cyberspace. The Internet. Ironically, you can keep up with them by reading words printed on actual paper." This was typical of *Time* magazine's attempt in the 1990s to craft a distinct relationship with the computer age, of recurrently selling its own virtues as a print magazine that not only understood but could also explicate the technological significance and historical relevance of cyberspace. The visual gravity ascribed to the Apple-Microsoft story was partly a reflection of *Time*'s journalistic stake in information technology and, by turns, the computer industry.

While cyberspace for *Time* is an issue linked to the status of the news magazine, it has also become the locus for stories about American business life and, in broader terms, generative of questions about national identity. Computer technology has been largely pioneered in America, it has defined the language of the Internet as American, and it has produced one of the richest men in the world in Bill Gates. Cyberspace has become a new source for the discursive constitution of American triumph and anxiety. Computers are not simply a burgeoning industry; they constitute a technology that has been discussed in cultural terms that range from utopianism (global villages and electronic democracies) to apocalypse (virus terrorism, Internet pornography, and "Y2K" anxiety). Cyberspace is linked to a sense of America's prospective future, the United States leading the way in realizing the promise of micro technology or suffering from its worst excesses. In the Apple-Microsoft feature, black and white is a visual index of cultural meaning. Monochrome is rarely, if ever, used to cover simple business stories. If it is, historical gravitas is promptly established. If the deal between Apple and Microsoft made "the world a better place," black and white drew upon and helped mark the import of Apple's survival. In this particular case, the significance of the deal had less to do with the impact of computers per se than with the status of free and competitive trade in the neoliberal marketplace.

The use of monochrome in the Apple story must finally be understood in terms of the actual companies involved. The computer industry has seen prolonged corporate struggles waged to control the burgeoning PC market. No conflict has kept attentions rapt like that between Apple and Microsoft. Not only do the companies sell different technologies, they also market different attitudes *toward* technology (something I discuss in chapter 4). The reconciliation of Gates and Jobs was no casual matter. It joined two of the most charismatic and bold corporate foes of the computer industry. In business terms, the deal between them was "historic," for it joined what had previously seemed like the irreconcilable enemies of the industry. Black and white gave the deal its archival due. Indeed, the Apple–Microsoft alliance was understood with a particular nostalgia in and for the present, a new accent on business relations and on developing technological prospects. In a news magazine shaping and shaped by the larger discourse of cyberspace in American culture, monochrome codified the deal as a news exclusive with corporate, as well as cultural, significance.

CULTURAL MEANING AND MAGAZINE MEMORY

In the representational economy of *Time* magazine during the 1990s, the visual differentiation between chronicle and report became a platform for editorial decisions about cultural meaning, about the subjects that should be framed as more than reported news. In terms of the LA riots, black and white was used to give the violence a stabilizing historical dimension. With Clinton's 1992 election and in the business deal between Apple and Microsoft, monochrome helped create a documentary feel but also one of "memorable" history. In broad terms, the black-and-white image was used in *Time* magazine to create different kinds of temporal and authenticity effect. In constructions of the "inside story," monochrome appealed to an idea of documentary authenticity, bound in the verities of "real photojournalism." In this construction, *Time* did not report news so much as witness events. In constructions of the chronicle, monochrome appealed to a different kind of *historical* authenticity. In this case, black and white appealed less to the unmediated authority of the witness than to the unmitigated authority of the archive. In both instances, monochrome helped provide a visual gravity and depth of meaning that could penetrate and seemingly transcend the color norms of journalistic report.

In relating the photographic image to social and political history, critics invariably, and perhaps understandably, focus upon representational content. James Guimond, for example, locates American documentary photography within a dialectic of the "American Dream," showing how images throughout the twentieth century have expressed, challenged and projected versions of a specific American reality.[56] Underexamined in much of this kind of cultural history is the nonrepresentational significance of the photographic image and its contribution to visual meaning. Black and white has performed cultural work in *Time* by transforming the flow of reportable news into something archival, historical, temporal. This process can be seen in political terms. Black and white provides a method of deciding upon, and visually framing, the constituents of shared history; monochrome bestows a status of chronicle upon stories that support particular stakes in the form and definition of national meaning.

In the examples I have chosen, black and white gives a stabilizing historical dimension to negotiations of ethnic and racial difference, specifically in the face of multicultural "fragmentation"; it gives a legitimating historical pedigree to the U.S. political and electoral process in a time of deepening public skepticism about politicians and political authority; and it gives a promissory historical significance to computer technology, an industry in which Time-Warner has a commercial stake and for which *Time* magazine has worked to refine the cultural meanings. Walter Isaacson writes of *Time* playing "the storyteller who comes to your front porch with the color and insights that turn facts into coherent narratives."[57] What Isaacson fails to acknowledge here is that sometimes, and rarely without significance, the storyteller comes not with color but with monochrome; black and white functioned in the 1990s by turning news facts into the "coherent narratives" of chronicled history. At a time when confidence in American historical identity was becoming less secure and more confused—caused by changing expectations in the domestic sphere, together with a need to create a new global role—monochrome helped to articulate and affirm the constituents of historicized national meaning.

How can the currency of black and white in *Time* be summarized? Set in the context of contemporary theories of memory, one view might see the use of black and white as a pure simulation of authenticity, the mark of a culture grasping for a sense of significance and history denied by the rapid pace of change in late capitalist society. Pierre Nora talks of modern culture's hyperrealization of the past due to definitive estrangement from it. He writes that "modern memory is, above all, archival. It relies entirely upon the materiality of the trace, the immediacy of the recording, *the visibility of the image*" (italics added).[58] The indiscriminate production of archives is, he goes on to say, an expression of "the terrorism of historicized memory." Perhaps black and white contributes to this archival imperative, the need to create a sense of memory in the face of uncertainty in the present and the breakdown of memorial consciousness. Pursuing his theory that "our society is torn from its memory by the scale of its transformations but all the more obsessed with understanding itself historically," Nora might see the use of black and white in *Time* as an example of the proliferation of attempts by the media to create nonevents as "anticipated commemorations of themselves."[59]

While provocative, Nora underestimates the cultural work performed by representational modes. He laments the passing of "true" or "spontaneous" memory, replaced by its contemporary inscription in sites, or *lieux de mémoire*. Black and white, in this scheme, would be an example of the prosthesis memory that Nora ascribes to an anxious and amnesiac modern culture. Through its visual coding of chronicle, however, monochrome is not simply a scaffold of memorial prop but a visual agent for particular hegemonic formations of national identity. In a full-color magazine like *Time*, black and white inscribes an image with qualities that set it apart from color. A. Robert Lee writes that in America the camera has always offered "a quick visual fix appropriate to a nation doing its historic business at high speed."[60] In a culture of rapid and profligate image making, and in a time when constructions of national identity have become increasingly destabilized, monochrome can visually mark that which should be *considered* historic business. In the pages of *Time* during the 1990s, black and white functioned as a particular kind of nostalgia mode; it performed chromatic work in the inscription of chronicled national meaning.

NOTES

1. Roger Rosenblatt, "Prologue: In Black and White," in P. F. Bentley, *Clinton: Portrait of Victory* (New York: Warner Books, 1993): 9.

2. Andrew Anthony, "There's One Good Thing about the Nineties," *Observer Review*, 14 July 1998: 5.

3. Peter Hamilton, "France and Frenchness in Post-War Humanist Photography," in Stuart Hall, ed., *Representations: Cultural Representations and Signifying Practices* (London: Sage, 1997): 75–150.

4. "Le Baiser de L'Hôtel de Ville" acquired notoriety in 1994 when a married couple took Doisneau to court, suggesting that he had photographed them decades before without consent. This led to the public "admission" that models had been used in the famous "*baiser*" image, although this fact had never been a secret. The male model used in Rowell's "L'Enfant" became the subject of various British tabloid features in 1997, notably Sarah Chalmers, "Confessions of a New Age Man," *Daily Mail*, 3 April 1997: 39.

5. Richard Dyer, *Only Entertainment* (London: Routledge, 1992).

6. For a semiotic perspective on the production of photographic meaning, see Victor Burgin, ed., *Thinking Photography* (London: Macmillan, 1982); and Roland Barthes, *Image Music Text*, trans., Stephen Heath (London: Fontana, 1977).

7. Miles Orvell, *The Real Thing: Imitation and Authenticity in American Culture 1880–1940* (Chapel Hill, NC: North Carolina University Press, 1989): 239. For a more specifically gender-oriented perspective on the practice of photography at the beginning of the century, see Judith Fryer Davidov, *Women's Camera Work: Self/Body/Other in American Visual Culture* (Durham, NC: Duke University Press, 1998). Davidov is concerned not simply with photographic revelation but with strategies of claiming agency and representing otherness.

8. Susan Sontag, *On Photography* (London: Penguin, 1979): 86.

9. Stanley Cavell, *The World Viewed: Reflections on the Ontology of Film* (New York: Viking Press, 1971): 94. A good treatment of the history and ideology of color in (American) cinema can be found in Steve Neale, *Cinema and Technology: Image, Sound, Colour* (London: Macmillan, 1985). See also Gorham A. Kindem, "Hollywood's Con-

version to Color: The Technological, Economic and Aesthetic Factors," *Journal of the University Film Association*, 31, no. 2 (1979): 29–36.

10. Roland Barthes, *Camera Lucida,* trans. Richard Howard (London: Vintage, 1993): 81.

11. For a thoughtful examination of Super-8 as a particularly American nostalgia code within consumer culture, see Grace Elizabeth Hale and Beth Loffreda, "Clocks For Seeing: Technologies of Memory, Popular Aesthetics and the Home Movie," *Radical History Review*, 66 (Fall 1996): 163–171. For a discussion of art deco, see Fredric Jameson, *Signatures of the Visible* (New York: Routledge, 1990).

12. Raphael Samuel, *Theatres of Memory: Past and Present in Contemporary Culture* (London: Verso, 1994).

13. David Harvey, *The Condition of Postmodernity* (Oxford: Blackwell, 1989): 288.

14. For a discussion of the "crisis of the grand-governing narratives" in Britain and America since the 1960s, see Harvey J. Kaye, *The Powers of the Past: Reflections on the Crisis and the Promise of History* (New York: Harvester Wheatsheaf, 1991).

15. Walter Isaacson, "Luce's Values—Then and Now," *Time*, 9 March 1998: 103.

16. Andrew Ross, *No Respect: Intellectuals and Popular Culture* (New York: Routledge, 1989): 8.

17. For perspectives on the relationship between history and television, see Marcia Landy, ed., *The Historical Film: History and Memory in Media*, part 4 (London: The Athlone Press, 2001): 269–329.

18. Lawrence Grossberg, *Dancing in Spite of Myself: Essays on Popular Culture* (Durham, NC: Duke University Press, 1997): 191–252.

19. William Glaberson, "Newspapers Adoption of Color Nearly Complete," *New York Times*, 31 May 1993: 41.

20. *Time*, 5 June 1989: 1.

21. Cited in Deirdre Carmody, "One More Time: Magazine is Reborn," *New York Times*, 13 April 1992: 1.

22. Paul Durrant (Picture editor of *Time Atlantic*), telephone interview, 25 March 1997.

23. P. F. Bentley, e-mail interview, 28 April 1997.

24. Rosenblatt, "Preface: In Black and White": 12.

25. Peter Preston, "The Last Picture Show," *Guardian Weekend*, 28 November 1998: 28.

26. On the issue of computer manipulation, see Fred Ritchen, "Photojournalism in the Age of Computers," in Carol Squiers, ed., *The Critical Image: Essays on Contemporary Photography* (London: Lawrence and Wishart, 1990): 28–37.

27. Orvell, *The Real Thing*: xxv.

28. Isaacson, "Luce's Values—Then and Now": 104.

29. Michele Stephenson, telephone interview, 24 March 1997.

30. Cited in Lance Morrow, "The Time of Our Lives," *Time*, 9 March 1998: 27.

31. Victor Burgin, "Looking at Photographs," in Burgin, *Thinking Photography*: 144. It is important not to lose sight of the practicality of monochrome to picture editors. The archival quality of the black-and-white photograph enables it to be reused in different feature stories months and years apart. Of course, color can also be reused in this way, but the association of color with breaking news does not give it the same license for portfolio and retrospection. Black and white may represent a specific news moment, but it can also frame it within a broad scheme of chronicled history. When Newt Gingrich was made *Time* "Man of the Year" in 1995, it was accompanied by a nineteen-page monochrome photo-feature by P. F. Bentley (25 December 1995). Most

of the images were taken on Capitol Hill: Gingrich in meetings, making speeches, having his hair cut. The only image of Gingrich-at-play was a rather unflattering picture of him gingerly kissing his wife while standing in the surf on a California beach. This image was reused three years later when Gingrich resigned as leader of the House of Representatives. Initially, it had formed part of a character study, assessing the "master of the House." The second time around, the photo was part of a retrospective, detailing the "fall of the House of Newt" (16 November 1998). Both features took historical stock of Gingrich's influence on American politics, and the archival quality of black and white meant that the picture was serviceable in each case.

32. All of my references are to that of *Time Atlantic*. While there are certain differences in style, content, and layout between the domestic and the international editions of the magazine, enough overlap exists between them not to interfere with my treatment of black and white. For a consideration of *Time Atlantic* as an international edition, see Paul Grainge, "Global Media and the Ambiguities of Resonant Americanization," *American Studies International*, 39, no. 3 (2001): 4–24.

33. This figure is cited in *Time*, 9 March 1998: 97. Indicative of the global fascination with Princess Diana, the next-best-selling issue is the Diana special report, having sold 802,838 copies.

34. Marita Sturken, *Tangled Memories: The Vietnam War, the AIDS Epidemic and the Politics of Remembering* (Berkeley, CA: University of California Press, 1997): 13.

35. On the causes of the culture war, see Todd Gitlin, *The Twilight of Common Dreams: Why America is Wracked by Culture Wars* (New York: Henry Holt, 1995).

36. For a good summary of the media treatment of political correctness at the beginning of the 1990s, see Jim Neilson, "The Great PC Scare: Tyrannies of the Left, Rhetoric of the Right," in Jeffrey Williams, ed., *PC Wars: Politics and Theory in the Academy* (New York: Routledge, 1995): 60–89.

37. Paul Gray, "Whose America?" *Time*, 8 July 1991: 23–27.

38. Michael Bérubé, *Public Access: Literary Theory and American Cultural Politics* (London: Verso, 1994): 225–241.

39. Arthur Schlesinger Jr., *The Disuniting of America: Reflections on a Multicultural Society* (New York: W. W. Norton, 1991): 43.

40. Arthur Schlesinger Jr., "The Cult of Ethnicity, Good and Bad," *Time*, 8 July 1991: 28.

41. Gitlin, *The Twilight of Common Dreams*: 44.

42. Robert Hughes, "The Fraying of America," *Time*, 3 February 1992: 84.

43. Gray, "Whose America?": 24.

44. Morrow, "The Time of Our Lives": 27.

45. "Papering the Nation," *Time*, 9 March 1998: 99.

46. Isaacson, "Luce's Values—Then and Now": 104.

47. See Burgin, *Thinking Photography*, and John Tagg, *The Burden of Representation: Essays on Photographies and Histories* (London: Macmillan, 1988).

48. P. F. Bentley, email interview, 28 April 1997.

49. Lance Morrow, "Man of the Year: The Torch Is Passed," *Time*, 4 January 1992: 27.

50. P. F. Bentley, email interview, 28 April 1997.

51. Rosenblatt, "Prologue: In Black and White": 9.

52. E. J. Dionne Jr., *Why Americans Hate Politics* (New York: Touchstone, 1991): 18.

53. Dionne, *Why Americans Hate Politics*: 368.

54. Laurence I. Bennett, "It's Not Quite Over," *Time*, 2 November 1992: 32.

55. Cited in Elise O'Shaughnessy, "The New Establishment," *Vanity Fair* (September 1994): 240.

56. James Guimond, *American Photography and the American Dream* (Chapel Hill, NC: North Carolina University Press, 1991).

57. Isaacson, "Luce's Values—Then and Now": 104.

58. Pierre Nora, "Between Memory and History: Les Lieux de Mémoire," trans., Marc Roudebush, *Representations*, 26 (Spring 1989): 13.

59. Nora, "Between Memory and History": 22. Nora's theory is applied specifically to France, but his distinction between "sites of memory" and "environments of memory" has been applied to other cultural—in particular American—paradigms. See Genevieve Fabre and Robert O'Meally, eds., *History and Memory in African-American Culture* (New York: Oxford University Press, 1994).

60. A. Robert Lee, "Shooting America: American Images: Photography 1945–1980," *Journal of American Studies*, 20, no. 2 (1986): 294.

4

Advertising the Archive:
Nostalgia and the (Post)national Imaginary

To understand "black-and-whiteness" as a visual discourse in the 1990s, it is necessary to consider the use and expedience of monochrome across a range of mediums and from different institutional positions; one must examine the status and function of black and white *intertextually*. The "meaning" of the black-and-white image is never contained within any single medium, but is informed by its use across the cultural terrain in different texts and contexts, from the news magazine to the adverts that appear *in* the news magazine. This chapter is concerned with the black-and-white image as it was used in the global strategies of corporate advertising during the 1990s. More precisely, it explores how the reconstitution of American national identity has taken place in the context of black-and-white brand campaigns by Apple and The Gap.

In theorizing the emergence of a "global cultural economy," Arjun Appadurai relates a postmodern commodity sensibility based on nostalgia to a "complex transnational construction of imaginary landscapes."[1] He is concerned with the cultural flows that move between and across national boundaries in a newly globalized world and comments on the possibility of "nostalgia without memory." This locates the Jamesonian nostalgia mode, understood as a form of pastiche, in a culture of world image systems. Appadurai suggests that "The past is not a land to return to in a simple politics of memory. It has become a synchronic warehouse of cultural scenarios."[2] One consequence of the past existing in this way, as a cultural style within advanced global capitalism, is the possibility for people around the world to consume images that belong to a cultural past that has no relation to their own. With images circulating in a newly heterogeneous and transnational public sphere, Appadurai suggests that nostalgia can be experienced for a past that has never been lost in any culturally specific or referential sense.

Appadurai is one of a growing number of critics who theorize globalization as an interactive sociocultural process. In his argument, this entails a substantial weakening of national communities and the creation of a decentered transnational global system. The imagination is central to this system; Appadurai argues that a new kind of deterritorialized community is created, or imagined, in a world of global image flows and electronic mediation. Imagined national communities have been replaced, one might say, by imagined worlds. In Appadurai's argument, this is a portentous sign, an indication of the end of the nation-state and the emergence of a complex and borderless global economy. Although sharing many critical sympathies with Appadurai, Frederick Buell is more cautionary, believing that globalization is "still substantially managed by the official mind of nations and by transnational, as well as national, entrepreneurial mentalities."[3] While inclined to see globalization in cultural terms that go beyond theories that understand it as a narrative of capitalist penetration and integration, Buell examines the status of "nationalist postnationalism." More specifically, he looks at a process that in the 1990s saw the "reconstitution of American national identity for postnational circumstances."

David Harvey writes that "Advertising and media images have come to play a very much more integrative role in cultural practices and assume a much greater importance in the growth dynamics of capitalism."[4] If images promote structures of desire and inform economies of taste, they can also legitimate forms of authority and power. Focusing on Apple's award-winning "Think different" campaign, I want to show how, while serving specific business needs, brand advertising has also functioned culturally in the negotiation of nation. Critically, this chapter provides a case study of global promotion, placed in the context of debates about postmodern nostalgia and, from the vantage point of globalization theory, set in relation to what Buell has described as the "reconstitution of U.S. cultural nationalism in an interesting postnational form."[5]

BACK TO THE FUTURE

In August 1993, Pablo Picasso, Muhammad Ali, and Amelia Earhart were among twelve celebrities whose black-and-white portraits appeared in *Time*, *Newsweek*, and *The New Yorker*. They were part of an advertising initiative by The Gap to sell its khakis. The so-called "Who wore khakis?" campaign lasted for six weeks and used a series of origi-

nal monochrome photographs of cultural figures, including Arthur
Miller, James Dean, Gene Kelley, Chet Baker, Ava Gardner, Norma Jean,
Miles Davis, Rock Hudson, and Jack Kerouac. They were all pictured
wearing khaki trousers. They were not wearing Gap khakis, but this was
hardly the point. In the bottom corner of each portrait was the distinctive
Gap logo and the assurance that Picasso—or whoever—"wore khakis."
Association was enough.

In September 1997, Picasso, Ali, and Earhart were back again. They
appeared once more in black and white, this time selling the corporate
philosophy of Apple computers. The global "Think different" campaign
by Apple used over forty individuals, including Albert Einstein, Ma-
hatma Gandhi, Rosa Parks, Ted Turner, Buzz Aldrin, Thomas Edison,
Jim Henson, Bob Dylan, Richard Branson, and Martha Graham. Monochrome portraits of a diverse pantheon of "heroes" and mavericks appeared around the world in news magazines, on billboards, wrapped
around forms of public transport, and pasted imposingly onto hoardings
and walls (Figures 4.1–4.4). The campaign was an ambitious marketing
strategy aimed at reinvigorating the flagging fortunes of the Apple
brand. It was no doubt pleasing to agents of The Gap that Picasso and
Earhart were still seen wearing their khaki pants.

While Gap lauded "legendary writers, actors, adventurers with style,"
the ad agency TBWA Chiat Day created for Apple a paean to "the crazy
ones . . . the ones who see things differently." Both companies sought
to construct a tradition for the particular values associated with their
brand; archival celebrity portraits gave a historical pedigree to their
respective versions of corporate *esprit*. For Gap, monochrome "legends"
galvanized its selling of the fashion classic. The "Think different" campaign was less product-driven than geared toward a symbolic reclaiming of company values. Misguided investments, quality control mishaps,
poor inventory management, and unfocused marketing had, by the mid-
1990s, caused a defection of Apple customers to the Windows/Intel
platform. Between 1993 and 1997, Apple's market share dropped from
12.1 percent to 3.5 percent. In 1997, losses totaled $1.5 billion, leading
Business Week to proclaim gravely the "death of an icon." Drastic meas-
ures were required to prevent calamity, and, inspired by the return of
Steve Jobs as interim CEO in July 1997, this led to a new communications
strategy. "Think different" heralded a branding blitzkrieg that tried to
reestablish connections between computer technology and the creative
individual, values that had defined Apple ever since it launched the
Mac in 1984. Versions of individuality were central to both campaigns.
Mobilizing a concept of individualism participates in a long advertising
tradition whereby the consumption of standardized and mass-produced
goods is figured as an expression of unique selfhood. What made the
two campaigns (visually) arresting in the context of 1990s advertising

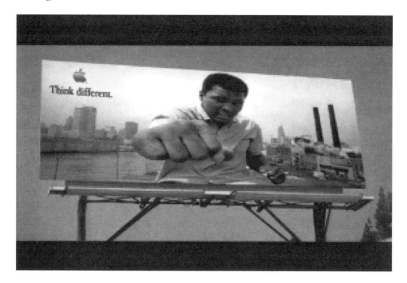

Figure 4.1   Muhammad Ali billboard (Apple screengrab, 16 March 1998.
http://www.apple.com/pr/photos/ads/AlibillboardLgHi.jpg).

was their specific appeal to—and coding of consumer individuality
through—an archival, black-and-white, nostalgia.

John Berger suggests that "publicity is, in essence, nostalgic. It has to
sell the past to the future. It cannot itself supply the standards of its own
claims. And so all references to quality are bound to be retrospective and
traditional."[6] The nostalgic past has shaped commercial imagery at various points in the history of American advertising.[7] The appeal to an
authentic past in corporate promotion is nothing new. Within recent
consumer literature, however, several theories have been used to explain the *proliferation* of nostalgic themes within contemporary advertising. While Barbara Stern suggests that promotional nostalgia responds
to "the double whammy of an aging population confronting a century in
its final years,"[8] Andrew Wernick provides a different perspective, relating nostalgia in contemporary advertising to a "sea-change in values."
He speaks of a "phase-shift in capitalist culture" where the progressive
future has lost its ideological force and "the arrow of time has been
reversed."[9] This is a more suggestive explanation for the popularity of
the past in contemporary advertising, moving away from Stern's rather
simplistic assumptions about the nostalgic experience within personal
and historical life cycles. Nostalgia, in Wernick's case, is set in a cultural
moment where the past has developed a particular discursive power
and where memory has become a new locus of both cultural identity and
commercial style.

Writing about the imbrication of heritage and tradition in contemporary taste regimes, Jim Collins suggests that "temporality has become perhaps the most significant priority in the determination of style values in the nineties."[10] Both the Apple and Gap campaigns can be seen in relation to this particular taste economy. Specifically, they drew upon a tradition of hip consumerism—what Thomas Frank relates to the idea of cultural and creative rebellion used within advertising codes of the 1960s—and linked it visually to the capital (and memory) of cultural celebrity. The temporal locutions and monochrome memories of the Apple and Gap campaigns are, of course, stylistic effects within a vast promotional repertoire. They may in this way be deployed or discarded according to the changing dictates of corporate imaging. For both companies, the black-and-white campaigns were superseded in the late 1990s by promotions where products and logos (in color) were offset by clinical white backdrops. Monochrome memory is a variable style in corporate promotion, but it was expedient to Apple and Gap in the 1990s in framing a heritage of commodified hip.

In general terms, monochrome experienced a resurgence in brand advertising during the 1980s and 1990s by global multinationals such as Nike, Coca-Cola, and Calvin Klein. With engorged advertising expenditures helping to create what Naomi Klein labels a "new branded world," monochrome became a strategic promotional mode, used both for its connotations of time and its association with artistry and style.[11] In the fashion industry, in particular, black and white was used as a signature of designer legitimacy and high-street chic, advertising anything from the chiaroscuro elegance of Giorgio Armani to the sport/street styles of Adidas. Monochrome was also taken up within the more explicit "memory ad," however. According to Judith Williamson, these are advertisements that create a specific narrative of memory that locate the subject within a temporal story.[12] Whether in black-and-white ads for Patek Philippe watches ("Begin your own tradition") or H. Samuel jewelry ("Give her a Christmas gift she'll *never* forget,") monochrome was used to heighten the symbolic quality of goods that are bought and given as objects and tokens of memory. The temporal and authenticity effects of black and white were utilized in a number of ways to accentuate the exclusive and/or symbolic status of particular brand goods during the 1990s, including the brand identities of Apple and Gap.

A promotional mode of nostalgia is, in some sense, consistent with each company's image, for both corporations have staked their origins and identity in values derived from, and remembered in, the hip 1960s. With its genesis in 1960s San Francisco and its reference to the "generation gap," the clothing retailer originally tapped countercultural values of simplicity and personal authenticity. These have since informed the concept of Gap style, of enduring fashion "basics" that contrast with the fickle and overdesigned fads of the larger clothing industry. Apple has also built its reputation on values of independence and simplicity. Ever since the famous "1984" commercial—a television ad devised by Chiat Day and directed by Ridley Scott, which saw a young woman smash the looming screen image of a figurative "big brother"—Apple has positioned itself as a voice of innovation and individuality in a world of lumbering technological conformity. If, as Thomas Frank suggests, hip has become the basis of a pervasive commodity logic where products exist "to facilitate our rebellion against the soul-deadening world of products,"[13] Apple and Gap framed this rationale—invoking rebellion as an imperative for brand loyalty—within narratives of corporate/cultural tradition.

The Gap developed a promotional currency in the 1990s based on the fashion "classic," referring specifically to the khaki and denim wares that have become the mainstay of Gap's fashion pedigree. Offering "the perfect balance between updated classics and seasonal styles," a host of celebrity individuals, from the boxer Evander Holyfield to the singer Anthony Kiedis, were used in the 1990s to endorse Gap fashion. The 1993 "Who wore khakis?" campaign was a *historical* figuration of Gap's more general promotional vocabulary. American cultural "legends" such as Chet Baker and Humphrey Bogart were able to provide an alternative set of individuals through whom Gap could market its brand language of personal authenticity. In so doing, the campaign catered to a slightly different, somewhat older, target audience. Monochrome signified designer style but gave a mytho-historical dimension to its selling of individualism and the fashion (khaki) classic. There was no similar promotional context or generic precedent for the black-and-white Apple campaign; "Think different" was distinct within computer/Apple promotion for its archival and overtly temporal structure. If advertising has increasingly become not simply a matter of persuading consumers to buy particular goods, but, as Pasi Falk argues, a battle for recognition in a complex, intertextual mediascape—a semiotic terrain where advertising is just one category in a wide range of experiential media products— "Think different" used the archival celebrity portrait to create a historical aura vital to the rebranding of Apple's corporate identity.[14] It is this campaign that I want to consider in some detail.

In 1998, a list composed by *Advertising Age* of the 200 biggest brands in America placed Apple 169th, between Nicorette chewing gum and Huggies disposable diapers.[15] This was indicative of the sagging fortunes of a company that was losing its hold in a market that, during the 1980s, it had significantly helped to create. The Apple Mac revolutionized personal computing. More expensive and with fewer applications than IBM machines, the Mac pioneered the graphic user interface. This introduced a visual element into the computer market that would shape user-friendly principles and standardize graphic icons and pull-down menus. The Mac was not, in itself, the making of Apple. The breakthrough came in 1985 with laser printing. This capitalized on Apple's graphic capacities with a printing system that became known as "what you see is what you get." Replacing primitive Dot Matrix printers, Apple's technological emphasis on graphic simplicity and printing clarity helped to pioneer desktop publishing. The Apple brand developed a reputation for accessibility and creativity. Although posting its first quarterly losses in 1985, Apple's stock increased in value through the 1980s and early 1990s, reaching a high in March 1991.

From 1993, both stock prices and market share began to slip. This was the result of a combination of factors. Prominent among them was an increasing number of PCs entering the marketplace, all using the Windows system developed by Microsoft. Windows enabled the graphic simplicity pioneered by Apple to be used on DOS-based machines. This led Apple to sue Microsoft in 1988 for copyright infringement, a battle that took nearly a decade to resolve and saw the launch of Windows 3.1 and Windows 95 in the process. The fortunes of Apple were hit by developments in a fierce PC market but were also the result of strategic blunders and fraught boardroom politics that ultimately led to the return of Steve Jobs. Many consider Jobs to be *the* Apple visionary; he was the cofounder whose force of personality had inspired innovation, animosity, and success. Jobs had left the company in 1985 after a bitter dispute with the Apple board of executives. His return was therefore rich in symbolism. He brought with him something of Apple's past, a dynamism and charisma that could, it was hoped, restore faith in the brand and repel the specter of Bill Gates. *Time* put the situation like this: "Understand, the idea of Jobs returning to Apple is something akin to that of Luke Skywalker returning to fight what, until last week, cultists regarded as the evil empire."[16] The arch-enemy of Apple has long been that of Microsoft. The first decision Jobs made at the helm of Apple, however, was not to challenge Microsoft but to strike an alliance, a corporate "meet the Apple-Gates." Resolving old grudges with his nemesis, Jobs formed a strategic relationship that would secure Apple's prospects of immediate survival. This came in the form of stock investment by Microsoft, a payment of $150 million by Gates to settle the issue of patent authority, and the agreement by Microsoft to publish Mac software into the next century. This was a "rescue" package that saved Apple from collapse but also served Microsoft very well, both financially through investment and legally in the company's fight against a mounting antitrust suit (this was the deal addressed in the *Time* cover issue discussed in chapter 3).

Shoring up the structural difficulties of Apple was Jobs's immediate priority. This had meaning only insofar as Apple could reinvigorate its

Figure 4.2 Albert Einstein billboard (Apple screengrab, 16 March 1998. http://www.apple.com/pr/photos/ads/EinsteinBillboardLgHi.jpg).

market profile, however. Stopping the rot had to be followed by serious repair work on the ailing brand identity. In 1997, Jobs sacked Apple's advertising agency, BBDO, and appointed TBWA Chiat Day. The agency was given responsibility for implementing a $60 million brand campaign that would position Apple more distinctly in a global market anticipating the "second digital revolution" of the Internet. With dominant sales in education and desktop publishing, Apple sought to extend principles of simplicity and creativity that would attract new consumers and refresh the loyalties of established converts. The result was the black-and-white "Think different" campaign.

The new brand advertising was launched on 28 September 1997, with a television commercial that was aired twice during the network premier of *Toy Story*. In a neat stroke of synergy, this was a film made by Pixar, the animation company owned by Steve Jobs. The commercial was in black and white, showing fast-cut footage of cultural figures from the twentieth century, including Einstein, John Lennon, Thomas Edison, Martha Graham, Martin Luther King, Gandhi, Picasso, Ted Turner, and many others. The actor Robert Duvall read a voice-over, reciting an ode to "the crazy ones," a poem that celebrated "the ones who see things differently." The television advertisement was soon followed by a flood of black-and-white images in the print media. On posters and billboards, on bus shelters and in airports, the "Think different" message went global, carried forth by a roster of celebrity mavericks, archival emissaries of Apple's new market bite.

Strategically, "Think different" established an attitude; it identified the "distinct sensibility" of the Mac user. A combination of creativity and independence of thought were the values that, Apple hoped, would distinguish its product in a world market dominated by the Windows-operated PC. Steve Jobs said that "Think Different celebrates the soul of the Apple brand . . . that creative people with passion can change the world for the better."[17] It was necessary to transform Apple's difference in the computer market—an integrated system of software and hardware with its own applications and support servicing—from a potential liability into a positive virtue. All the time that Apple seemed to be in jeopardy, new consumers would be deterred, made anxious by the prospect of buying a computer that had no future. By associating Apple's difference with a certain character of mind, however, a renegade spirit in the tradition of Muhammad Ali and Martin Luther King, Apple could stand for something more than risk. The new brand campaign focused on the achievement and genius that *comes from risk*—a tactical sleight that turned beleaguered market share into a matter of creative independence. The Mac user was identified with those who are "not fond of rules" and have "no respect for the status quo." Apple defined itself against the PC norm in such a way that buying Apple became a statement of character in tune with a rich legacy of modern cultural heroes.

Creativity has been integral to Apple's brand image since the launch of the Mac in 1984, and creativity was a powerful value in reasserting Apple's brand identity in the global marketplace. It was something that could appeal, in the words of Apple's worldwide head of advertising, Allen Olivo, to "people who don't care so much about what a computer does as what they can do with a computer."[18] This reversed a trend in Apple advertising that had, since the early 1990s, either focused upon corporate rivalry—expounding the difference between Apple computing and the mere cosmetic benefits of Microsoft—or developed profile through product placements in films like *Mission Impossible* and *Independence Day*. No clear marketing message emerged through these strategies, however. "Think different" was an attempt to renew focus on Apple's users and key markets, including the prospective market opened up by the Internet. By celebrating a selection of widely admired "misfits," "rebels," and "troublemakers," the suggestion in "Think different" was that Apple exemplified and, at the same time, enabled the creative energy of historical innovators. By establishing a tradition of revolutionary free thinkers, Apple sought to locate itself within, and sell its wares upon, a history of maverick creativity.

This market strategy was seen within the company as a philosophical homecoming. In 1996, the summary paragraph of any Apple press release described the company as a "recognized innovator in the information industry and leader in multimedia technologies, [creating] powerful solutions based on easy-to-use personal computers, servers, peripherals, software, personal digital assistants and Internet content." By 1997, the tone had changed, becoming less descriptive and more promissory. Apple proclaimed that it was *"recommitted to its original mission*—to bring the best personal computing products and supports to students, educators, designers, scientists, engineers, businesspersons and consumers" (italics added). The "Think different" campaign signaled a return, a symbolic reclaiming of the values that launched Apple in the 1980s. Allen Olivo said that "Think different" expounds "exactly the same message as when we launched the Mac back in 1984. If you look at the '1984' commercial, it's about one individual taking control of the situation and saying, "I can change things."[19] The archival pastness of "Think different" symbolized, in part, a strategic nostalgia for Apple's early brand values, reestablishing connections between technology and creative individuality. This relationship was something that had been lost, according to Olivo, when Apple started marketing itself as "a computer box company rather than a creative, thinking company." Apple's new communication strategy was based on the construction of a corporate, as well as a cultural, sense of the historical past. "Think different" used the aura of tradition to galvanize a maverick company soul and to suggest a return by Apple to its founding principles. In so doing, Apple appealed to a "uniquely defined group of people whom we understand on an emotional level." As a campaign, "Think different" addressed a target audience of established and first-time computer users ranging from young "twenty-somethings" to middle-aged baby-boomers: a stratum of consumers, in the domestic, educational and desktop markets seeking easy-to-use, not to say chic, Internet technologies.

Steve Jobs once said that the great thing about the Mac was that the people who designed it were musicians, poets, artists, zoologists, and historians, who also happened to be the best computer scientists in the world. The Apple "revolution" of the 1980s saw technical invention riding a crest of idealism, a utopian, some might say "hippy," vision of new technological possibility. The Apple family were the informally dressed, creatively unorthodox flower-children of the computer industry, compared with the corporate Goliath of IBM and, later, the Machiavellian maestros of Microsoft. The "Think different" campaign drew upon the admixture of creativity and empowerment that had originally fired the Apple brand; it literally pictured the poets, artists, and musicians whom Jobs associated with the Mac, and with Apple's (hip) negation of conformity. Before becoming a member of Apple's executive board in 1997, Lawrence Ellison, the chief of software giant Oracle, commented that "Apple is the only true life-style brand in the computer industry. It's the only company people feel passionate about."[20] "Think different" sought to capitalize on this, to reinvigorate the brand philosophy that had done so much to inspire Apple's loyal following. Some market analysts saw a risk in trying to sell computer hardware through "lifestyle" advertising, the contextualization of commodity advertising in market strategies that attempt, at some level, to transgress the commercial realm. The campaign was only the first part of a larger strategy, however. Indeed, "Think different" cannot be seen apart from the $100 million campaign used in 1998 to promote the futuristic iMac.

The iMac campaign focused on a particular product and became the biggest marketing launch in Apple's history. With its striking blue shell, the iMac was aimed at a consumer market wanting speed, simplicity, and, most importantly, access to the Internet. Steve Jobs explained that "iMac does for Internet computing what the original Macintosh did for personal computing. Macintosh let anyone use a computer and iMac lets anyone get on the Internet quickly and easily."[21] Memories of the Mac were invoked to sell the capacities, and market significance, of the iMac. The iMac was new, innovative, and by Apple's own definition, part of a company tradition. Television advertising for the iMac premiered on the Wonderful World of Disney. Beginning in August, ads also ran on Seinfeld, News Radio, and cable shows like South Park and Larry King. A twelve-page insert was distributed in magazines like *Time, Newsweek, Business Week, People, Sports Illustrated*, and *Rolling Stone*. The advertising was in two principal colors—white and blue—displaying the machine with the discreet "Think different" logo in the corner. This chromatic effect continued the visual simplicity of Apple marketing. The white background offset the translucent blue of the machine, creating a sense of purity and freshness. The iMac was bracing and cool, removed from the stale designs of Apple's rivals. As one ad put it: "Sorry, no beige."

One of the selling features of the iMac was design, in particular its color. Andrew Ross suggests that the design aesthetic of much information technology has not been distinguished by the high progressive futurism that influenced the machine age. He writes: "The casing designs for information hardware have retained the chunky, robotic iconography of office equipment, and have not generally sought to simulate the physical sensation of unidirectional speed."[22] The iMac was not entirely different in this regard, but it was certainly less austere. The new Apple machine was self-confessedly "chic, not geek." Ross suggests that the selling of the information age has rested both on the promise of hidden delights and on the threat of being left behind. The iMac's delights were fairly well displayed. The *San Francisco Chronicle* reported that "Apple followers and first-time buyers are gobbling up the machine because of its space-age look and appeal as an Internet terminal."[23] The iMac was the best-selling computer in the United States during August, the month of its launch, and it pushed Apple's market share back up to 13.5 percent. If black and white gave the Apple brand a soul, color gave the new Apple machine a spirit. When Apple introduced the iMac in five new colors in January 1999—a choice of strawberry, lime, blueberry, tangerine, and grape, together with the original Bondi blue—Steve Jobs said: "What's your favorite color? is going to become one of the most important questions for PC consumers."[24] Ideas of taste were organized and reorganized through shifts in chromatic advertising; black and-white gave the company an authority and quality based on tradition, while color gave the new Apple product a compelling sense of innovation, style, and fun. It was difficult to judge how lasting the iMac's appeal would be in the fiercely competitive computer market, but early signs were promising. Apple sold 278,000 machines in the first six weeks of the iMac launch. Within three months it had become the fastest-selling computer in Apple's history, winning a host of design awards into the bargain. These included *Business Week*'s "Best new product of 1998," *Newsweek*'s "Best Design of 1998," and *Time*'s "Machine of the Year."

The iMac and the "Think different" ads ran simultaneously at the end of 1998, selling the monochrome past and the color future with a common admonition *to think* (from the proverbial "Think different" to the more philosophical "I think, therefore iMac"). People from the past and machines of the future were the basis of a broad image strategy used to reposition Apple. It was, at once, archival and anticipatory, based on tradition and innovation. A visual nostalgia was used in combination with a cool futurism, authenticating the brand name with marketing that moved backwards and forwards in time. Lifestyle values and corporate soul mean very little in the computer industry without (the marketing of) genuine technological difference. With the return of Steve Jobs, however, selling a soul and marketing a machine became a mutually reinforcing task.

Within Apple's global advertising strategy, a new, and rationalized, product line came to emblematize a maverick creativity that was associated with the company tradition and that belonged to a larger history of rebel innovation. The monochrome "Think different" campaign established a broadly cultural, and implied a specifically corporate, sense of heritage. The past was the authenticating cornerstone of Apple's new future, and the campaign served a necessary function in repositioning the Apple brand as stylish, innovative, and different. As an aesthetic, black and white was *visually* different within computer advertising. Of course, the "meaning" of any advertising campaign does not exist, and cannot be examined, in isolation from the visual and commercial culture in which it circulates. "Think different" must be understood in relation to other campaigns, not only in terms of Apple's own iMac promotion or, intertextually, with other black-and-white media products / advertising campaigns, but against rivals like Microsoft and Intel. Both of these companies have figured brand identities based on the future (Intel's spacemen) and the empowering possibilities of the present (the Micro-soft logo, "where do you want to go today?"). What distinguished Apple in the general marketing of information technology was a quite unusual recourse to the historical archive. "Think different" sold not the future or the possibilities of the present, but a heritage of cultural rebellion. Tho-mas Frank suggests that there are "few things more beloved of our mass media than the figure of the cultural rebel, the defiant individualist resisting the mandates of machine civilization."[25] In reinvigorating the value, or "intellectual property," of the Apple brand name, "Think dif-ferent" inventively *sold* machine civilization through an archival history of defiant individualists.[26]

The "Think different" campaign is the complex result of contemporary taste values and specific market strategies. It has a promotional context and commercial genesis, and should not be used metaphorically to draw sweeping conclusions about global advertising, postmodern historicity, or anything else. The articulation of cultural heritage in the campaign does warrant attention, however. "Think different" gathered an eclectic mix of cultural icons and gave them patrimonial value. "You can praise them, disagree with them, quote them, disbelieve them, glorify or vilify them. About the only thing you can't do is ignore them. Because they change things." So went the ode to the "crazy ones." Apple's brand advertising, vital to its more direct product-oriented marketing, devel-oped a concept of heritage based on the unorthodoxy of purposefully diverse cultural icons. Steve Jobs said: "The 'think different' campaign set out to honor our heroes."[27] This begs two immediate questions: who exactly are "our" heroes, and what does it mean for these "heroes" to be used in a black-and-white campaign selling computers in the global marketplace? I want now to look more closely at the question of nostal-gia and the construction of heritage—*our* heritage—in the "Think differ-ent" campaign.

(POST)NATIONAL NOSTALGIA

My own first exposure to the "Think different" campaign was in Copenhagen. A giant monochrome poster of Alfred Hitchcock appeared one morning, draped from a building at Rädhuspladsen, the central town square. Another poster, possibly 30 feet in length, hung beside it. Instead of one single image, it had three separate black-and-white por-traits, Einstein among them. In the corner of each poster was a colored apple and the words "Think different." They remained in the town square for several weeks, something of a relief, certainly a contrast, from the hypnotic neon dazzle of the corporate slogans and business logos that blinked relentlessly from the electronic ad space enclosing Rädhus-pladsen. I had two other encounters with the campaign: once on television with Robert Duvall's earnest recital of "the crazy ones," the second time in Copenhagen airport. My parting image of Denmark after a three-month stay was orchestrated by the ad folks of TBWA Chiat Day. Eight equally spaced black-and-white portraits hung beside each other, dangling above the length of the check-in counter. Jim Henson, Gandhi, and Amelia Earhart were among the individuals pictured. I recognized most of them, but two escaped me; I later discovered the mysteries to be Martha Graham and Thomas Edison.

While anecdotal, my experience may suggest something significant about the Apple campaign. Simply put, it didn't require recognition of each and every individual. It established, instead, a principle of commonality *between* individuals. "Think different" was not about any single person, but about the invented tradition to which they all belonged. To the *New York Times*, the interpellation of disparate icons within the promotional strategies of a multinational corporation like Apple made the campaign seem "audacious."[28] "Think different" made unlikely, if not opaque, connections between people who were identified quite simply as "the round pegs in the square holes." The Apple campaign was seen around the world, its version of maverick heritage consumed by West and East alike. Certain disputes emerged from the representational politics involved. In Hong Kong, for example, Apple bowed to Chinese pressure to withdraw a monochrome "Think different" image of the Dalai Lama. The endorsement of maverick political "individualism" may have been safe using images of Gandhi and Martin Luther King, but not for those who remain central to ongoing, and unresolved, ideological disputes. For less political reasons, Apple was refused permission by the family of Jacques Cousteau to use an image of the celebrated diver. With the iMac unable to perform under the sea, Cousteau was a hero that Apple could surely do without.

As these disputes might suggest, the representational content of the campaign is not without cultural significance. However, issues of representation cannot be seen apart from the nonrepresentational effects of "Think different." By this I am referring to the campaign's "black-and-whiteness." Black and white is an idiom that can mark but, in the same instance, flatten time. Monochrome suggests temporality but is often described as "timeless." By draining the historical, chromatic specificity of an image, black and white is able to create an aura of temporality. Images are *of* time but not always specifically *in* time. Black and white was serviceable to Apple by creating a terrain of tradition in which individuals with no discernible connection could be summarily linked; monochrome established a visual relationship between people brought together in a hypothetical commonality—exemplars of a brand value. In accounting for the visual aesthetic of "Think different," I would suggest that monochrome helped to bring the Apple mavericks into a realm or

Figure 4.3   Gandhi billboard (Apple screengrab, 16 March 1998.
http://www.apple.com/pr/photos/ads/GandhiBillboardLgHi.jpg).

economy of *affective nostalgia*. The nostalgia of the campaign was not
rooted in a sentimental regard for any specific memory or cultural history. It was, instead, free-floating and abstract. It did not stop and rest
with any one individual, any special place or moment. It ranged across
the surface of time and fame, creating a particular, or potential, "nostalgia without memory." Writing of the new global system, David Morley
and Kevin Robins suggest that "what corporate maneuvers and machinations are seeking to bring into existence is a global media space and
market."[29] If transnational advertising has become part of a process of
"standardizing everything into a common global mode," the Apple
campaign sought to create a common global heritage based on a cumulation of individuals, set within an aesthetic of the archive.

As a global advertising campaign, "Think different" can be characterized in two ways. First, it exemplifies what Arjun Appadurai has called
"the fetishism of the consumer." He writes: "Global advertising is the
key technology for the worldwide dissemination of a plethora of creative, and culturally well-chosen, ideas of consumer agency. These images of agency are increasingly distortions of a world of merchandising
so subtle that the consumer is consistently helped to believe that he is or
she is an actor, where in fact he or she is at best a chooser."[30] Based on a
concept of maverick individualism, "Think different" frames unconven-
tionality as a consumerist value. Narratives of agency are rooted in
market-based ideas of creative freedom, expressed in both the choice
and use of goods linked to a specific brand. Second, the campaign fig-

ures an imagined postnational past. In marketing terms, this is practical in giving "Think different" global reach. It is defined by its visuality (rather than textuality) and uses a large number of international icons; the campaign is a demonstration of multinational efforts to overcome the borders of national community and address the prospective "global" consumer.

This "address" was evidenced in the very dissemination of the campaign. While the print campaign was largely carried in international magazines like *Time, Business Week, Rolling Stone*, and *Wired* and located within "non-places of global deterritorialization"[31] such as airports, the television campaign aired during internationally syndicated cable shows like South Park and Seinfeld and during major network premieres. These forms of print and televisual advertising—suggestive, in themselves, of Apple's youthfully hip and, also, professionally mainstream target audience—accompanied massive billboard campaigns that saw giant "Think different" posters appear in metropolitan city centers from Houston to Helsinki, from Atlanta to Hong Kong.[32] One might say that "Think different" was located within global space; it addressed passengers, pedestrians, commuters, and consumers within the circuits of transnational capital and international media flow. Nigel Turner, vice-president of marketing for Apple Europe, said that "Think different" was conceived as a global campaign from the very beginning. It was centralized through the advertising channel of TBWA Chiat Day and did not bend or adapt to local markets. (By comparison, previous Apple marketing used different ad agencies in trying to cater to local markets. To many Apple insiders, this made the company message rather piecemeal and lacking in cohesion.) Turner said: "the world has moved on these days and those companies which have global brands must manage them on a global basis."[33] Transforming itself from a computer box to an Internet company, Apple deployed a synchronous world campaign that, in some sense, was commensurate with the form and discourse of global connectivity associated with the cultural (and economic) prospects of the Internet.

As a market, the Internet has become linked to the promise of international information flow. While critics have shown that the structure and basis of our current global economy can trace a history that far predates the recent (usually post–cold war) markers that are often taken to designate the "global era,"[34] it is only more recently that a *discourse* of globalism has taken hold within strategies of transnational corporate promotion. (This was typified in 1992 by the launch of Time-Warner's new corporate motto, "the world is our audience.") With patterns of social interaction and information flow increasingly occurring across national borders and with communications at the center of current global restructuring, Annabelle Sreberny-Mohammadi suggests that "large corporations have not been slow to recognize the positive public value attached to the notion of 'globalization' as a unifying process of recognition of a common humanity, and coolly to adopt it for their own purposes."[35] Apple's "Think different" campaign can be seen in this context. While previous Apple campaigns, such as "1984," functioned in the global marketplace, "Think different" was forged with principles of global commonality in mind: it developed an "ecumenical fantasy" rooted in a shared heritage ("our heroes") of free-thinking "difference."[36]

"Think different" addressed a global audience. Ideologically, however, it was rooted in the values of America. This is significant if one is to trace, from a broadly cultural perspective and in the context of media representation, the way that national identities can and do reconstruct themselves in the transnational sphere. The Apple campaign is an example of what might be called *nationally nuanced* transnationalism; the campaign's international figuration of heritage was organized around an implicit idea of American national genius. With a statistical preponderance of American "heroes" in the campaign, and tapping the association of cyberspace as something that derives from, and is being scientifically propelled by, American technological initiative, Apple helped construct a maverick inheritance of a particular kind. (The fact that the textual tag, "Think different," remained in English/American around the world gave this cultural disposal some shape, perhaps linked in kind to the adoption of American as the universal language of computer technology and the Internet.)

I do not want to suggest that the campaign was received uncritically, or uniformly, around the globe. Indeed, a different kind of analysis might look more closely at the reception of the Apple campaign in specific local contexts. One should be careful not to overdetermine the popular "meaning" of "Think different" as a market campaign; its cultural decoding will depend on numerous contextual factors (those of nation, generation, class, gender, occupational culture) that relate to, and bear upon, Apple's—and, indeed, America's—status and presence in the global marketplace. While acknowledging the critical salience of audience-response, my conceptual emphasis is on the discursive context of the campaign's production. In this regard, I would argue that "Think different" can be seen in the context of attempts in the dominant media to articulate a reconfigured sense of American national identity. The campaign was, in Frederick Buell's terms, part of a process of reconstituting "U.S. culture within the disorganizing forces of current globalization."[37]

Buell maps a shift in American globalist discourse during the 1990s. He suggests that while globalization initially produced a set of anxieties about lost national foundations, the movement of the "global economy" into mainstream discourse gradually turned the global into the basis for a new national "recovery narrative." This involved a reinvention of national culture, accomplished by the Clinton presidency but also helped by "neoliberal politics, corporate policy and public relations, the media, and even a variety of the newer intellectual and social movements."[38] One of the main sites through which this reconstituted national culture came to be articulated was that of the information industry. While U.S.-based corporations have long dominated world positions in the market for information-based commodities (generating over 50 percent of global revenues), it was in the 1990s that the global information economy garnered a particular discursive weight. If, as Edward Comor contends, "American private and public sector interests have come to recognize that future U.S. hegemonic capacities depend on the internationalization of liberal ideals and consumerist practices," the information and communication industries became a prime site of ideological investment.[39] Computer technologies, in particular, were central to a global information revolution that America was both seen, and positioned, helping powerfully to shape.

Buell suggests that during the 1990s the democratic and interactive possibilities of cyberspace were celebrated in libertarian ideological terms in much of the corporate culture based in and around the computer industry. Apple was no different in this regard. The "Think different" campaign established a global history of free thinkers and creative innovators; its libertarianism was expressed through recourse to a corporate-cultural maverick heritage. Apple strategists were, of course, hoping to capitalize on the global capacities of the Internet with the iMac. It was therefore apposite that Apple's maverick past should be figuratively borderless. Using "heroes" from France, Britain, Germany, India, America, and Spain, "Think different" had a polycultural dimension. There was never any real doubt about the gravitational center of the cultural heritage at stake, however. "Think different" expressed a legacy that was nominally global but clearly American. Apple purveyed a cultural inheritance that reinforced the ideological position of America at the center of the wired global system. Buell writes: "The information industry would be a crucial place for the corporate restructuring of American identity."[40] By developing the concept of the "maverick"—a term that integrates American individualist and anti-institutional traditions—Apple stitched together a postnational heritage using a distinctly American fabric.

By focusing briefly on the global cultural economy, I want to highlight certain ways in which the Apple campaign helped construct national, as well as corporate, identity. This possibility is something that has been underexamined by commentators who concentrate upon, and then lament, the campaign's ahistoricism. To its critics, the randomness of "Think different" is the main point of issue—namely the means by which Apple devoured the contextual specificity and cultural significance of its various "crazy ones." A *New York Times* article said: "Apart from their accomplishments, what the 20 or so famous figures have in common—and their relationship if any to computers—is unclear."[41] Writing in *Time*, Salman Rushdie was particularly critical of Gandhi's image being used, suggesting that his "thoughts don't really count in this new incarnation. What counts is that he is considered to be 'on message,' in line with the corporate philosophy of Apple."[42]

The Apple and the Gap campaigns both illustrate the commercial appropriation of personality and the means by which historical images circulate in contemporary visual culture. To Fredric Jameson, this kind of corporate rummaging through the iconic past, where archival photographs form the basis of contemporary brand campaigns, is indicative of postmodernism's "crisis of historicity," of the inability in contemporary life to imagine the past as radically different. Jameson suggests: "Nostalgia art gives us the image of various generations of the past as fashion-plate images, which entertain no determinable ideological relationship to other moments of time: they are not the outcome of anything, nor the antecedents of our present; they are simply images."[43] Judged in these terms, the Apple campaign would illustrate how the past is now compressed within an overwhelming and depthless present. History is used in the campaign as a store-house of images, a selection of texts that seem to function randomly, with little or no sense of connection between them beyond the relationship established by Apple. There is something postmodern about Apple's sense of the past: the way that images from different times, of different generations, circulate seamlessly in the selling of a brand identity. And yet, the lament for "genuine historicity" does not do justice to the way that advertisers incorporate what Andrew Wernick calls surrounding "moods, codes and cross-currents" into the semiotic and rhetorical basis of their market campaigns.[44] I would suggest that the "Think different" campaign structures a principle of heritage the cultural significance of which cannot be reduced to postmodern historicist crisis, but which must be seen in terms of the dominant reconfiguration of American national identity at home and abroad.

It is here that we might want to focus briefly on the representational content of the campaign. The individuals who carry Apple's "Think different" message are diverse but not random or indiscriminate. Different kinds of heritage are figured along overlapping racial, gender, generational, and professional axes. This helps create a canon of distinguishable heroes. These include black heroes (Martin Luther King, Muhammad Ali, Rosa Parks), female heroes (Amelia Earhart, Maria Callas, Martha Graham, Rosa Parks), political heroes (Gandhi, Martin Luther King), entrepreneurial heroes (Ted Turner, Richard Branson), modernist heroes (Pablo Picasso, Albert Einstein, Alfred Hitchcock,

Figure 4.4 Rosa Parks billboard (Apple screengrab, 16 March 1998.
http://www.apple.com/pr/photos/ads/Rosa ParksLgHi.jpeg).

Frank Lloyd Wright), postmodernist heroes (Jerry Seinfeld), scientific
heroes (Thomas Edison, Albert Einstein), national heroes (Buzz Aldrin),
countercultural heroes (John Lennon, Bob Dylan), and many more configurations between them. Apple provides an over-history that accom-
modates a plethora of historical figures within a basic framework of
maverick individualism. The underlying corporate aim of this, as I have
said, is to foster notions of consumer agency based upon narratives of
creative choice and achievement.

Apple's sense of tradition gestures toward diversity. The "crazy ones"
are male and female, black and white; there are representatives from
high and popular culture, art and science, politics and commerce.
"Think different" creates a tableau of tradition through which multiple
histories emerge and play off of one another. A "Think different" advertisement in *Wired* can illustrate the point. It carried a page of nine small
monochrome portraits, symmetrically organized in three x three columns, so that the ad appeared like this:[45]

PICASSO	EINSTEIN	GANDHI
HENSON	GRAHAM	ALDRIN
ALI	HITCHCOCK	EARHART

The top row depicts three non-American icons from the early decades
of the twentieth century—Picasso, Einstein, and Gandhi. Depending on

how the eye moves from one picture to the next across and down the columns, however, many unlikely histories can be made. Pablo Picasso, Jim Henson, and Muhammad Ali in one, Amelia Earhart, Buzz Aldrin, and Gandhi in another. Apple presents the maverick past as varied and without hierarchy. In this sense, it reflects the steady breakdown of barriers between high and popular culture, and the challenge to older prescriptions of cultural inheritance that have taken place in American society in the last few decades. In some sense, the campaign adopts multiculturalism as an exportable, (post)national identity, supporting Frederick Buell's contention that multiculturalism had become by the late 1990s "a new, powerful official culture for the United States in a global world."[46]

In her work on global media and local culture, Ien Ang suggests that people who live in a media-saturated culture have to be active in their response to the overdose of contemporary images in order to produce any kind of meaning from them.[47] Reciprocally, advertising must engage with the values, norms, goals, and dreams of those to whom it is addressed. Drawing upon the international capital of cultural celebrity, the Apple campaign created a pregnant space for consumers to connect and project linkages between a diverse range of cultural, political, and scientific icons. The campaign relied on the visual literacy and interpretive skill of a sophisticated consumer audience that would respond to the particular fusion of advertising and art discourse (in this case, black-and-white portrait photography), and that could also find connections between the Apple icons. While inviting a degree of associative free-play in the latter case, it would be wrong to suggest that "Think different" was entirely without an organizing frame of reference. Indeed, narrative links had to be forged between icons who were contextually corralled in Apple's rhetoric of craziness and difference but that have also, in each case, become heavily embedded within the capitalist marketplace. The images of certain individuals, like Picasso and Einstein, have become floating signifiers, constantly sold and reprocessed in contemporary visual media to support a host of corporate and cultural meanings. Others, like Richard Branson and Ted Turner, literally help to maintain the basis of multinational capitalism upon which Apple clearly depends. Bob Dylan has by now been fully incorporated within establishment histories, and Jim Henson and Jerry Seinfeld both made fortunes selling their products to corporations like Disney and NBC. While the "crazy ones" may have been controversial in their own time, their maverick messages have been neutralized through the cultural refashioning of their iconoclasm. "Think different" thought about difference only if, and insofar as, the particular rebels used by Apple were culturally sanctioned. The campaign was designed to elicit a narrative of rebellion, but within the discursive confines of legitimated insurrection.

Focusing especially on educational, creative, and home users in the international PC market, "Think different" established a flexible heritage that sanctified the autonomous individual as maverick/consumer. Unlike previous Apple campaigns that carried detailed technological claims about the speed of its Pentium chip, or that negatively advertised rivals like Microsoft, "Think different" helped to weld together a transnational consumption community based on the semblance of a shared past. Different audiences may, of course, read into the campaign different kinds of meaning, the likes of which may be highly resistant and critical. While Salman Rushdie laments Gandhi's incorporation within a campaign that largely figures America as the maker and custodian of history, the rejection of Cousteau as an Apple icon may suggest a certain anxiety about the cooptive Americanization of national heroes. Advertising messages are never stable, secure, or consistently successful. However, on the evidence of Apple's market performance after the "Think different" campaign and the attendant iMac launch (its global market share rising from 3.5 in 1997 to 13.5 percent in 1998), there is reason to believe that "Think different" successfully appealed to its target audience of young professional computer/Internet consumers. This appeal was not only based on the campaign's use of cultural celebrity and its economy of visual nostalgia, but also perhaps on its absorption of what Avery Gordon and Christopher Newfield have called (in the context of America) an "assimilationist grip on a multicultural ideal that is rapidly being adopted by the state, the corporation, the military, the arts council, the university."[48]

To situate "Think different" in the cultural and discursive context of the late 1990s, one might relate and compare it with the figuration of heritage in the earlier Gap promotion. Unlike Apple, the Gap campaign utilized the past to sell a focused generational nostalgia. "Who wore khakis?" specified the identity of the individual as set within a particular historical period. All of the figures—Humphrey Bogart, Jack Kerouac, Sammy Davis Jr., Arthur Miller, Norma Jean, Rock Hudson, James Dean, and Ernest Hemingway—reached the pinnacle of their fame before the 1960s. In each monochrome portrait it was made clear who, exactly, "wore khakis." The individuals had significance in their own right; the campaign developed a more obvious nostalgia for the cultural "legends" of America's past.[49] In marketing terms, the campaign appealed to an older target audience, developing an *icon*-ography that tapped a particular generational nostalgia, or at least sold the idea of a specific American generation. In promoting a fashion "classic," Gap appealed to a sense of classic—which in this context meant pre-1960s—America.

"Think different" was broader in scope; it ranged across place and time and was both transnational and multicultural. It is tempting to use the two campaigns to mark a cultural shift in the corporate construction of American identity during the 1990s. The Gap campaign appeared in 1993 and the Apple campaign in 1997. This was roughly the time that saw the discursive transition outlined by Frederick Buell, a rhetoric of endangered national foundations and traditions giving way to a national "recovery narrative" set within a global context. While selling different products and engaging different ideas of "America," neither the Apple nor the Gap campaign can be entirely divorced from the cultural climate in which they both evolved. One might argue that the discursive transition from a sense of having lost "authentic" America to the reconstitution of "America" in global terms had a contextual (if never a causal) bearing on the two campaigns. The Gap campaign appealed fundamentally to a pre-1960s nostalgia. This, of course, distinguished much of the prevailing culture war rhetoric of the time, with battles fought over the legacy of the 1960s and the compromised nature of American tradition. "Think different" emerged when these debates had all but run their course. The late 1990s, rather than bearing witness to cultural anxiety about the loss of tradition and the clouding of "authentic" American identity, saw an investment in a more globalized and multicultural form of nationhood. The Apple campaign inscribed brand values through the articulation of a plural (post)national past. It was perhaps this that gave "Think different" the cultural appeal that deepened its claim for, and helped it win, the 1998 Emmy for Outstanding Commercial.

"Think different" must be understood, primarily, in the context of American business culture and in terms of the beleaguered state of the Apple brand at the end of the 1990s. I would argue that its promotional and visual strategies reveal certain taste values and cultural tendencies within 1990s image culture, however. "Think different" was part of, but at the same time seemingly beyond, contemporary promotion. It was lifestyle advertising based upon the transcendent virtues of cultural heritage. Drawing specifically on the market niche for black-and-white celebrity portraits—monochrome images ministering to a "youthful and culturally dissident" public, according to Raphael Samuel, who dates the entrance of black and white in the shopping-mall poster-shop market to the mid-1980s[50]—the Apple campaign married a concept of tradition with modern style values. The articulation of heritage in the campaign was responsive to contemporary notions of taste, but it was also contributive to cultural constructions of (post)national identity. By using the aura of the archive, Apple claimed a "tradition" that, while transparently invented, positioned Apple and America at the technological and ideological center of the global information revolution. Apple classified a tradition of innovation through recourse to the "multicultural" maverick. Heroism was judged in American terms and, drawing upon a principle of diversity, used a large majority of American examples. Monochrome memory and the celebrity icon became the basis for a brand campaign that established a global heritage of common heroes whom Apple *and* America were seen to inherit and embody, and whose spirit and legacy they would mutually carry forth.

John Tomlinson has stressed the importance of thinking about globalization in its cultural dimension. He suggests that "the huge transformative processes of our time that globalization describes cannot be properly understood until they are grasped through the conceptual vocabulary of culture."[51] By considering a particular case of brand advertising, this chapter has been concerned with the impact of globalization on American culture, or, more specifically, its impact on corporate constructions of American national identity. While international media and transnational capitalism may be driven more by market opportunity than by national identity in today's global economy, there remains an internal tension between the neoliberal global marketplace and a residual, and patriotic, attachment to the idea of national culture. According to Frederick Buell, the reframing of globalist discourse that took place in American culture during the 1990s led, crucially, to the articulation of a new national identity—one "that is, much more transparently than ever before, produced with global forces and a global audience in mind."[52] Strategically conceived in terms of global marketing, "Think different" can be seen in this context. Tailoring a past that could overcome national boundaries, but that also retained America as the main symbolic and ideological locus, the aestheticization of heritage in the Apple campaign is one example of how U.S. national culture is being *representationally* restructured for a postnational world.

As with *Time* magazine's picturing of history in the 1990s, the black-and-white image became an expedient visual mode for Apple. In a climate where "culture" and "identity" have become based far less on fundamental, or agreed-upon, essences than upon the contingent and moving play of global and ethnic differences, the temporal and authenticity effects of black and white have helped to contribute to media articulations of coherent cultural memory. Both *Time* magazine and Apple marketing utilized black and white to aestheticize the archival legitimacy of particular histories and versions of heritage.[53] In each case, this came to intercede with questions about, and constructions of, American cultural nationalism. I have so far been concerned in part II with the articulation of history/heritage as it has taken place in print form. If monochrome appeals to a transcending permanence found, or rather figured, within the historical archive, Apple and *Time* drew upon the visual aura of the black-and-white photograph to aestheticize determinants of national and postnational memory. In chapters 5 and 6 I consider the moving image at the beginning of the 1990s. This was a period when culture war discourse instilled a more protectionist mode in the attempt to stabilize and preserve the chords of American memory. In outlining the specific interests served in the aestheticization of national memory, it is important to anchor the discourse of "black-and-whiteness" to more politicized contexts of negotiated meaning. No consideration of memory politics in the mass media can, in this vein, overlook Hollywood film.

NOTES

1. Arjun Appadurai, "Disjuncture and Difference in the Global Cultural Economy," *Public Culture,* 2, no. 2 (1990): 4.
2. Appadurai, "Disjuncture and Difference."
3. Frederick Buell, "Nationalist Postnationalism: Globalist Discourse in Contemporary American Culture," *American Quarterly,* 50, no. 3 (1998): 551.
4. David Harvey, *The Condition of Postmodernity* (Oxford: Blackwell, 1989): 287.
5. Buell, "Nationalist Postnationalism": 551.
6. John Berger, *Ways of Seeing* (London: BBC and Penguin, 1972): 139.
7. Jackson Lears and Michael Kammen both point to the conflict between nostalgia and progress in nineteenth-century commercial culture. The past was commonly invoked, but usually to ground a sense of modern improvement. It was not until the Depression that progressive idioms were seriously challenged by the value attached to tradition. Lears suggests that it was in the 1930s that "advertisers began an unprecedented effort to associate their products with the past." The rediscovery of folkish imagery and the validation of heritage was a response to economic crisis, a new "pseudotraditionalism" creating a mythic version of the American past that could, it was hoped, restabilize confidence in modern business. See Jackson Lears, *Fables of Abundance: A Cultural History of Advertising in America* (New York: Basic Books, 1994): 383; and Michael Kammen, *In the Past Lane: Historical Perspectives on American Culture* (New York: Oxford University Press, 1997): 125–142.
8. Barbara B. Stern, "Nostalgia in Advertising Text: Romancing the Past," *Advances in Consumer Research,* 19 (1992): 388. See also Barbara B. Stern, "Historical and Personal Nostalgia in Advertising Text: The Fin de siècle Effect," *Journal of Advertising Studies,* 21, no. 2 (1992): 11–22; and William J. Havlena and Susan L. Holak, "'The Good Old Days': Observations on Nostalgia and Its Role in Consumer Behavior," *Advances in Consumer Research,* 18 (1991): 323–329.
9. Andrew Wernick, "Resort to Nostalgia: Mountains, Memories and Myths of Time," in Mica Nava, Andrew Blake, Iain MacRury, and Barry Richards, eds., *Buy This Book: Studies in Advertising and Consumption* (London: Routledge, 1997): 207–223.
10. Jim Collins, *Architectures of Excess: Cultural Life in the Information Age* (New York: Routledge, 1995): 158.
11. Naomi Klein, *No Logo* (London: Flamingo, 2000).
12. Judith Williamson, *Decoding Advertisements: Ideology and Meaning in Advertising* (London: Marian Boyers, 1978).
13. Thomas Frank, *The Conquest of Cool: Business Culture, Counterculture, and the Rise of Hip Consumption* (Chicago, IL: University of Chicago Press, 1997): 229.
14. Pasi Falk, "The Benetton–Toscani Affair: Testing the Limits of Conventional Advertising." In Nava et al., *Buy This Book*: 64–83.
15. Cited in Matt Toor, "Different Strokes," *MacUser,* 14, no. 8 (1998): 69. In measuring brand profile and size, *Advertising Age* focused upon the amount of money

companies from Coca-Cola to Sony spend on brand advertising each year; its list was not a measurement of company profit or annual turnover in the form and tradition of *Fortune 500*. Within the computer industry, the biggest investors in global advertising in 1998 were IBM ($500 million), Intel ($400 million), and Microsoft ($300 million). This compared with the more limited $100 million budget that Apple had at its disposal.

16. Cathy Booth, "Steve's Job: Restart Apple," *Time*, 18 August 1997: 35.

17. "Apple Launches Brand Advertising Campaign" (29 September 1997) <www.apple. com>.

18. Cited in Toor, "Different Strokes": 64.

19. Toor, "Different Strokes."

20. Cited in Booth, "Steve's Job": 38.

21. "Apple launches its Largest Marketing Campaign Ever for iMac" (13 August 1998) <www.apple.com>.

22. Andrew Ross, *Real Love: In Pursuit of Cultural Justice* (London: Routledge, 1998): 27.

23. "iMac Is Too Hot to Handle," *San Francisco Chronicle*, 8 September 1998: 6.

24. Press release, "iMac Given New Colors" (10 January 1999) <www.apppple.com>.

25. Frank, *The Conquest of Cool*: 227.

26. "Intellectual property" is a corporate and legal term for the hidden dimension, or "intangible asset," a company may own (specifically its brand name) that can produce higher quality earnings. For a discussion of brand identity from an industry perspective, see Paul Stobart, ed., *Brand Power* (London: Macmillan, 1994).

27. "Apple's Think Different Ad Wins Emmy for Outstanding Commercial" (31 August 1998) <www.apple.com>.

28. Stuart Elliot, "New Apple Ad Lifts Off from Disney's Land," *New York Times*, 29 September 1997: 13.

29. David Morley and Kevin Robins, *Spaces of Identity: Global Media, Electronic Landscapes and Cultural Boundaries* (London: Routledge, 1995): 15.

30. Appadurai, "Disjuncture and Difference": 16.

31. I take this phrase from John Tomlinson, *Globalization and Culture* (Cambridge: Polity Press, 1999).

32. On a point of comparison, the Gap "Who wore Khakis?" campaign relied on print mediums and inserts within magazines such as *Time*, *Newsweek* and the *New Yorker*. It has been hard to ascertain the exact means by which the campaign was globally disseminated but, from a British perspective, the Gap campaign seemed exclusive to billboards and magazines. It never appeared in airports, on television, or in many of the other contextual mediums and locations favored by Apple.

33. Cited in Toor, "Different Strokes": 69.

34. See, for example, Roland Robertson, *Globalization: Social Theory and Global Culture* (Sage: London, 1992); Anthony Giddens, *The Consequences of Modernity* (Stanford, CA: Stanford University Press, 1991).

35. Annabelle Sreberny-Mohammadi, "The Global and Local in International Communications." In James Curran and Michael Gurevitch, eds., *Mass Media and Society* (London: Arnold, 1996): 183.

36. For a discussion of ecumenical fantasies in global advertising, specifically those of Benetton and Coca-Cola, see Falk, "The Benetton–Toscani Effect": 73–75.

37. Buell, "Nationalist Postnationalism": 577.

38. Buell, "Nationalist Postnationalism": 552.

39. Edward A. Comor, "The Re-Tooling of American Hegemony: U.S. Foreign Communications Policy from Free Flow to Free Trade." In Annabelle Sreberny-Mohammadi et al., *Media in Global Context: A Reader* (London: Arnold, 1997): 195. Comor relates his analysis to initiatives in foreign communications policy directed by the American State. This is part of a broad argument about the nation state as a "mediator of globalization." He suggests that "Rather than its relative *decline*, I believe that what is underway is a shift in the *form* in which the nation state relates to transnational developments."

40. Buell, "Nationalist Postnationalism": 566.

41. Stuart Elliot, "New Apple Ad Lifts Off from Disney's Land," *New York Times*: 13.

42. Salman Rushdie, "Mohandas Gandhi," *Time*, 13 April 1998: 71.

43. Anders Stephanson, "Regarding Postmodernism," in Douglas Kellner, ed., *Postmodernism/Jameson/Critique* (Washington, DC: Maisonneuve Press, 1989): 60.

44. Andrew Wernick, *Promotional Culture: Advertising, Ideology and Symbolic Expression* (London: Sage, 1991): 45.

45. *Wired* (December 1997): inside cover.

46. Buell, "Nationalist Postnationalism": 563.

47. See Ien Ang, *Living Room Wars: Rethinking Media Audiences for a Postmodern World* (London: Routledge, 1996).

48. Avery F. Gordon and Christopher Newfield, eds., *Mapping Multiculturalism* (Minneapolis, MN: University of Minnesota Press, 1996): 109.

49. The one exception in terms of nationality was Picasso, although his international capital as *the* twentieth-century artist has given him a symbolic place in American, as well as European, cultural life.

50. Raphael Samuel, *Theatres of Memory: Past and Present in Contemporary Culture* (London: Verso, 1994): 353.

51. Tomlinson, *Globalization and Culture*: 1.

52. Buell, "Nationalist Postnationalism": 554.

53. In its own construction of cultural heritage, *Time* magazine ran a series of special issues in 1998 and 1999 estimating the "people" and "person" of the century. The selection of individuals in the *Time* 100 list could be as surprising as the "audacious" juxtapositions of the Apple campaign. *Time* placed together Hitler and Pope John Paul II, Le Corbusier and Coco Chanel, Walt Disney and Ray Kroc, Sigmund Freud and Robert Goddard. It was perhaps not surprising, considering their mutual interest in the construction of historic and heroic legacies, that on the back page of *Time*'s issue on "Builders and Titans" Apple should place an advertisement for the iMac. The ad was white, the computer was Bondi blue, and "Think different" was written in the top right-hand corner. Featured inside the magazine were figures such as Henry Ford, David Sarnoff, Louis B. Mayer, Walt Disney, Lucky Luciano, Ray Kroc, Estee Lauder, Akio Morita, and, perhaps inevitably, Bill Gates. Steve Jobs was given a two-column footnote after the Gates feature, saying that "he may not run the computer world, but he sure can make a dent." Apple used the *Time* issue to situate the iMac within a history of business innovation. In the context of the larger *Time* narrative, it was part and product of a culture where, as a congratulatory by-line put it, "capitalism not only won, it turned into a marvelous machine of prosperity, led by people who could take an idea and turn it into an industry" (*Time*, 7 December 1998). If Steve Jobs was the person and iMac the idea, the industry belonged to America. See Paul Grainge, "Remembering the American Century: Media Memory and the *Time* 100 List," *The International Journal of Cultural Studies*, 5, no. 2 (2002): 367–385.

5

Documenting Memory:
Remembering the Past in Hollywood Film

To suggest that a film is concerned with cultural memory assumes a particular relationship with the historical past. History and memory are by no means oppositional categories; they interact, overlap, and help construct each other. All "historical" films are in some sense concerned with cultural memory, whether the period piece and its historically decorative tableaux or the grandiloquent stagings of the past in movies that use history as a vehicle for genres like the action adventure and the romance.[1] These films differ in kind, however, from movies where the historical past is understood as contributive to, or at least exerting a contextual bearing on, contemporary life and its structures of belief. Marita Sturken writes that "cultural memory is a field of contested meanings in which Americans interact with cultural elements to produce concepts of the nation. . . ."[2] By this definition, films that are in some way "about" cultural memory participate in a dialogue that equates how we remember with who we are. The representation of the historical past is a question not just of atmosphere or decoration but of cultural identity.

Writing of particular transformations in American film since the 1970s, Robert Sklar suggests: "In the last quarter of the twentieth century, the cultural disunity of American society gave rise to a new concern, not with a traditional rhetoric of myths and dreams, but with historical memory."[3] If memory has become the new locus of a movie's cultural power, as Sklar suggests, this was notably evidenced in the 1990s, when major Hollywood films such as *Dances with Wolves* (1990),

JFK (1992), *Malcolm X* (1993), *Schindler's List* (1993), *Forrest Gump* (1994), *Amistad* (1997), and *Saving Private Ryan* (1998) came to articulate themes of American national memory. This chapter concentrates on two of these films—*Schindler's List* and *Forrest Gump*—and considers both their stylistic use of monochrome and more general intersection with the politics of memory in the climate of the early 1990s. Concentrating on the political stakes of documentary-based memory films, this chapter is concerned with the production of cinematic master memories and the political interests they serve; it considers how the attempt to galvanize a core national memory at the beginning of the 1990s was also often a question of defending a social formation that has long privileged the white, straight, middle-class male.

Liam Kennedy suggests that one consequence of the uncertainties and paranoias that characterized the early 1990s—from moral panics over crime, drugs, family values, and multiculturalism to the uncertain ending of the cold war and the requiem for the American Empire brought about by the challenge of Asian fiscal influence—was "that it (has) led to a growing recognition of whiteness as a social category and more particularly to white male selfhood as a fragile and besieged identity."[4] Linked to the disruption of ideological moorings, the early 1990s can be seen as a period when new relations between center and margins were generating a crisis of cultural and critical authority, acutely experienced by the white male. The debates gathered under rubrics such as "identity politics" and the "culture war" were symptomatic of the social, cultural, and economic changes that were beginning to question (or renew old questions about) the basis of hegemonic power in American life. Debates in the academy over canonicity and political correctness were just one expression of the struggles fought in the cultural sphere over the structures of privilege and (related) systems of knowledge that sustain and legitimize a governing order that has normalized whiteness, masculinity, and heterosexuality as dominant social categories.

Not only in education, similar struggles were being waged in the realm of popular culture; attempts were made in Hollywood film both to challenge and also *to restore* national mythologies and their invested relations of identity and power. Memory, in particular, became a field of negotiated meaning. If the academy was debating how, if, and in whose interest a culture remembers the past, similar issues of memory and identity were being figured cinematically. Thematically, *Schindler's List* and *Forrest Gump* may not seem like obvious films to compare on these grounds. One is a sober true-life tale of a Nazi war profiteer and his rescue of 1,200 Jews from certain death in Auschwitz, the other is a sanitized political allegory of the baby-boom generation, based around an idiot savant from the American South. Despite obvious differences in subject and style, however, there is much that can be seen to connect them (beyond the fact that both films swept the Oscars in consecutive years, including the prize for "best picture"). It is necessary at this stage to expound on these connections, establishing the terms of analysis.

A comparison between *Schindler's List* and *Forrest Gump* can arguably be made on four related grounds. On textual and discursive terms, these comparative factors include their mutual figuration of cultural master memories, their dependence on techniques and/or credentials of documentary, their demonstration of stylized nostalgia judged within the framework of contemporary "genericity," and their valorization of white masculinity as an agent of historical redemption. The monochrome effects of *Schindler's List* are the starting point for this chapter. However, the analysis of the film's (black-and-white) memory work can profit significantly by drawing it into relation with that of *Forrest Gump*. Echoing an essay on *Schindler's List* by Miriam Hanson, each film "demonstratively takes on a trauma of collective historical dimensions; and reworks this trauma in the name of memory and national identity, inscribed with particular notions of race, sexuality and family."[5]

Schindler's List and *Forrest Gump* are both self-conscious in foregrounding the issue of cultural memory. Concerned with trauma of quite different kinds, they each claim a technical and aesthetic pedigree in their representation of a past that is, or should be, remembered. Each must be seen in relation to specific kinds of memorial discourse. On release in 1993, *Schindler's List* was part of widespread fiftieth-year Holocaust commemorations that in America saw the opening of the Holocaust Memorial Museum on Washington Mall. At a time when "negationists" were denying that mass killings had ever taken place and living survivors who could refute the charge and explicate the horror were becoming numbered, Holocaust remembrance was a matter of apparent urgency. Both films deal in one way or another with the question of victims and the nature of survival. If one film remembers victims created by the genocidal rupture of the Holocaust, the other politicizes victims "created" by the social rupture of the 1960s. *Forrest Gump* can be set in the context of debates about the meaning, legacy, and memory of the 1960s. With the first baby-boom president in office and the film released several months before the Republican Congressional landslide in 1994, bringing with it Newt Gingrich's "Contract with America," *Gump* intervened, and was politically invoked, in attempts to define the significance of the 1960s. Both films developed a sense of incorporative memory. If, as Yosefa Loshitzky suggests, "*Schindler's List* attempts to provide the popular imagination with a master narrative about the Holocaust," *Forrest Gump* did the same for the generational experience of the baby-boom.[6] In the words of Martin Walker, it surged "beyond the sealed enclave of the cinema into the wider national discourse, to become a parable of the American condition."[7] With the accentuated cultural legitimacy that both films drew from their respective rush of Oscars, *Schindler* and *Gump* became veritable touchstones of remembrance.

If *Schindler's List* and *Forrest Gump* deal with a past marked by trauma—the Holocaust in one and the impact of divisive social turbulence in the other—the filmic reenactment of that past assumed a function of catharsis and healing, a process of endowing events with narrative coherence and redemptive closure. It is not insignificant that each film ends with a scene at a gravestone, accompanied by a sense of a new generation made possible by those now mourning or mourned. Freud would call this a process of "working through." By creating a narrative, or "construction," a sense of wholeness and coherence can be given to the past, countering the fragmentary nature of "screen memories" with their basis in wish and repression. In a primary sense, *Schindler's List* and *Forrest Gump* are comparable in that each film tells not *a* story but *the* story of events. They are both episodic in dealing with the past, containing the experience of the Holocaust and the baby-boom within a chronological and iconographic frame that moves from a discernible beginning to a tangible end. In their representational strategies, both films are iconic and intertextual, either discreetly subsuming other cinematic treatments of the Holocaust or explicitly "quoting" moments from America's recent cultural and media history. *Schindler* and *Gump* both work stylistically to incorporate familiar images and representations of the past within subsuming master memories. The status of each film *as* a master memory was at the time compounded by explicit denials on the part of each director regarding the perspectival, attenuated, or necessarily political nature of their respective memory narratives. Unlike *JFK*, which became riven with controversy about its historical (mis)interpretations—related to the perception of Oliver Stone's own conspiratorial obsessions—Spielberg and Robert Zemeckis sought to position their films in a way that forestalled accusations of directorial subjectivity. When filming *Schindler's List*, Spielberg said to his crew: "We're not making a film, we're making a document."[8] Meanwhile, Zemeckis said that his purpose in making *Forrest Gump* was "to present this (baby-boom) generation *without commenting on it*" (my italics).[9] If Spielberg relied on a concept of witnessing to authorize his representation of the Holocaust, Zemeckis played upon a suggestion of neutrality in mapping the contours of postwar America. The status of each film as a "master memory" is, of course, related to the way that they were taken up in public discourse and sanctified through industry prize-winning. At the outset, however, each film sought validation through an implied sense of historical objectivity and/or impartiality.

In representational terms, both films execute the same two-step in claiming the past as cultural (master) memory; the remembered past is structured as a narratively rounded and morally resolved parable while, at the same time, it is given the status of (or at least a relation to) documentary "reality." Their incorporative memory narratives play with codes of fiction and history, faction and historicity. They both create a sense of "documentary memory," a form of cultural remembrance that, while shaping the past for present needs, is authorized by the aura of recorded history. Examining Hollywood films' attempt in the 1990s to articulate narratives of nation through recourse to memory and the past, Robert Burgoyne writes of "current cinematic struggles to redefine the national text."[10] While cinematic negotiations of nation would seem to apply more accurately to *Forrest Gump* than to *Schindler's List*, both films use historical trauma to establish the basis of a nationally shared sense of memory and / or remembrance. They strive to articulate and fix a common past based on their reenactment and resolution of ruptured histories. Of particular interest are the techniques and terms on which their memory narratives are written and achieved. The two films are, of course, markedly different in style and focus. However, the difference between them may not seem quite as profound if their cinematic effects and terms of remembrance are understood in a particular way. Put simply, both engage modes of documentary memory, which, seen in terms of emergent (postmodern) genre categories, are nuanced by a stylized nostalgia. At some level, this corresponds with, and helps to condition, a more politicized nostalgia organized around the figuration of white male agency and authority—something that can be set in relation to contemporary discourses of identity in the early 1990s and to the "crisis" of white masculinity.

The documentary claims of *Schindler* and *Gump* are different in form. If *Schindler's List* was to be an artifactual "document" in its own right, *Forrest Gump* was described by Zemeckis as a "docu-fable." Insisting upon a documentary link between representations of the Holocaust and the actual event itself is common not simply among film-makers but also among novelists and playwrights. James Young suggests that while claims of documentary may reinforce the factual authority of the Holocaust, it can also create an ambiguity between fictional and factual elements, such that an author or director is relieved of certain obligations of historical accuracy while being able at the same time to exploit the documentary aura of real events, of true stories.[11] Relying on the scripting, sequencing, and dramatization of reality, documentary has never been a purely indexical form and has strong fictive elements. Robert A. Rosenstone has discussed this in the context of film, demonstrating the continuities between what he calls "history as drama" and "history as document."[12] Despite their similarities, documentary nevertheless differentiates itself from fiction by an appeal to some kind of truth, provenance, or what has been called "heightened epistemic authority."[13] *Schindler's List* sought to achieve this through various kinds of authenticity effect: geographically by using locations in Poland, through non-diegetic elements such as a coda that relates characters to real survivors, and stylistically by employing the documentary credentials of (hand-held) black-and-white cinematography—what Spielberg has likened to a "truth serum."

If the documentary claims of *Schindler's List* are intimately bound up with the status of the Holocaust and questions arising from the nature and limits of representation, those of *Forrest Gump* can be set in the context of a surge of documentary styles in mainstream and commercial culture from the late-1980s. Paul Arthur relates this to the development of home video and cable TV, to the success of nonfiction genres in the publishing industry, and to the promise of documentary addressing social issues with greater verisimilitude.[14] Documentary has become a cinematic, televisual, and marketing mode based on ideas of indexical reality but never bound by strictures that preclude overt fictionalizing. Typified by the proliferation of docudramas in the 1980s, the status of *Forrest Gump* as a "docu-fable" is symptomatic of the more general *hybridization* of generic forms in contemporary cultural production.

The documentary effects of *Schindler* and *Gump* reflect the poignant and parodic nature of their respective memory narratives. This difference in style must be set in relation to the subject matter at hand, but it is also a matter of genre; the mode of each film is indicative of its relative position in the terrain of contemporary film "genericity." At some level, the two films represent the difference between emergent genre formations that Jim Collins has labeled "new sincerity" and "eclectic irony."[15] Collins suggests that these genres have developed in response to the saturation of images in postmodern media culture. While eclectic irony greets new forms of textuality by recycling images in playful and hybrid combinations, the new sincerity rejects irony outright, favoring instead an imaginary age before the mediated character of contemporaneity. If the former relies heavily on cinematic quotation and textual referencing, the latter pursues a lost authenticity before the emergence of postmodern hybridity. In terms of their respective embrace/rejection of the mediated character of postmodernity, *Forrest Gump* and *Schindler's List* fit a broad description of these generic tendencies. While Robert Zemeckis, whose biggest hits came with the *Back to the Future* series, continued with an eclectic historical approach in *Gump*, Steven Spielberg marked his directorial coming-of-age with a film that proved his own "new sincerity."

The genres of new sincerity and eclectic irony help to think about the basis of documentary in *Schindler's List* and *Forrest Gump*: one strives for an unmediated representational authenticity and the other depends on the playful arrangement of mediated representations. However, the genre categories also help, in a different sense, to think about various kinds of (textually figured) nostalgia. Collins states that "Narrative action now operates at two levels simultaneously—in reference to character adventure and in reference to a text's adventures in the array of contemporary cultural production."[16] If character adventure in *Schindler* and *Gump* is given a certain documentary feel, the so-called "textual adventure" is defined in each movie by a mode of cinematic and/or stylized nostalgia. In *Schindler*, this remains implicit and is part of the film's more general authenticity claims, linked significantly to the film's use of black-and-white cinematography. To think of the Holocaust in terms of nostalgia is clearly perverse. However, if one concentrates more on the (monochrome) mode of *Schindler's List* than on its actual subject matter, there is perhaps a character of nostalgia for a previous cinematic moment. Critical opinion was quick to praise the film's cinematic achievement, a "masterpiece" within the larger canon of Spielberg frivolity. In its technical and aesthetic devices, *Schindler's List* was praised for its "superb editing," "starkly beautiful cinematography," "abundant virtuosity," and "harrowing authenticity."[17] The visuality of *Schindler's List*, most significantly its use of black and white, was deemed to create a sense of both documentary *and* cinematic authenticity. At some level, *Schindler* appeals to aesthetic and narrative conventions that invite nostalgia for an "authentic" film past, ostensibly based on classical Hollywood.

Forrest Gump is more explicit in its nostalgic effects; it actively courts nostalgia in the face of trauma that includes war, assassination, domestic violence, and fatal illness. Stylistically, the film is a paradigm of Fredric Jameson's "nostalgia mode." The past is realized through pop images and informational props, traversing decades of recent American history using what Robert Zemeckis calls "familiar icon imagery." The eclecticism of *Gump* can be found in its interplay of generic forms and cinematic quotation. It evokes everything from *Midnight Cowboy* to *Platoon*. Threading through the entire narrative is mediated (and in this film manipulated) archival footage, together with a soundtrack of emotive hits. *Forrest Gump* is very much a product of new media technology and that technology's capacity both for increasing the volume of visual imagery in cultural life and for digitally manipulating its character. If the memory narrative of *Schindler's List* is based on a concept of archival and cinematic authenticity, predating the eclectic signifying strategies of postmodern culture, that of *Forrest Gump* is defined by the playful negotiation of the array of signs that constitute its very textual character. In each case, and in different ways, the explicit documentary status of *Schindler* and *Gump* can be measured alongside an implicit mode of stylized nostalgia.

Jim Collins suggests that "eclectic irony" and "new sincerity" are different kinds of response to semiotic excess; they both work within a media-sophisticated culture that has enabled new forms of textuality to emerge. He writes: "Both types of genre have a meta-mythological dimension, in which the cultural terrain that must be mapped is a world already sedimented with layers of popular mythologies, some old, some recent, but all copresent and subject to rearticulation according to different ideological agendas."[18] Having aligned *Schindler* and *Gump* with tendencies in contemporary genre formation, one might ask what can be said of their comparative ideological agendas. It is, of course, impossible to provide any single or concrete response. Both films are wrapped in complex discursive conjunctions and enter particular cultural debates. *Schindler's List*, for example, can be measured in relation to enduring cultural and ethical questions about the representational status of the Shoah, the question of showing / not showing, the so-called "Americanization of the Holocaust," and the emergence of a cinematic discourse of Nazism that Saul Friedlander has defined in relation to "kitsch and death."[19] *Forrest Gump*, on the other hand, participates in a range of cultural discourses surrounding the status of the 1960s, the experience of the baby-boom, the loss of American innocence, and the nature of decency and "dumbing down." While there is no ideological denominator linking the two films, there is perhaps a common dimension between them that can be read in ideological terms. This, put simply, is their elevation of a redeeming and / or redeemed white "father." Although different in form, both *Schindler* and *Gump* create documentary-based, but morally resolved, memory narratives that give the power of historical redemption to their eponymous male protagonists.

Hollywood has long privileged the white male as hero and protagonist. It should not be surprising that two Hollywood films by major directors should give the past the form of a story, or center upon the white male as a moral and historical protagonist. However, the films must be situated in the cultural climate in which they were produced. The early 1990s were not only marked by a pervasive discourse of "fragmentation" and "amnesia"—raising the stakes of a consensual and documentable past—they were also defined by cultural struggles that transformed white masculinity into a troubled identity. Numerous critics have examined this, suggesting a series of causal explanations: the threatened role of "protector–provider" masculinity in the face of a downturn in real wages and an increase in job insecurity, the development of multiculturalism and the growing recognition of whiteness as a social category, debates in education about canonicity ("dead white males") and affirmative action, and the more general dissolution of national myths that have normalized white, male, middle-class heterosexual power.[20] In their construction of cultural master memories, both *Schindler* and *Gump* bear out Robert Sklar's suggestion that in 1990s film "the problem of historical memory appears as a variant of patriarchy's crisis: what we lack in the present, what they had in the past, were true father–leaders."[21] At some level, the textual mode of nostalgia in each film provides a stylistic frame for an affirmation of white male selfhood, nostalgic in kind.

Forrest Gump has been widely discussed as a film that works to homogenize American national identity in ways that nostalgically restore the authority of the white, male subject. While professedly apolitical, *Forrest Gump* is, in fact, a highly politicized revisioning of America's cultural past. For Thomas B. Byers, this has the express effect of "remembering" a particular historical subject. He suggests:

To an alarming degree, the beleaguered white, middle-class, baby-boomer father *is* America in the iconography of popular narratives such as *Forrest Gump* and other products of the New Hollywood. Indeed, this figurative identification, as compensation for the white male subject's cultural and political castration anxiety, is one key to the success both of these films and of the New Right ideology that has recently come to dominate American political discourse. To "remember what made America great" is to re-member the great white Father.[22]

At first, it would seem hard to fit *Schindler's List* into this particular scheme. The film bears no direct relation to the fashioning of American identity as witnessed in *Forrest Gump*; nor does it have any connection with the American middle-class, with the generational baby-boom, or with conspicuous tenets of New Right ideology. However, the film is not entirely removed from the cultural debates and discursive formations that locate *Gump*. Indeed, *Schindler's List* became a virtually sacrosanct text of cultural memory (at least within American public discourse) structured around the documentary "reality" of benevolent male authority. In both *Schindler* and *Gump*, reenacting the past gave rise to a form of historical coherence and moral closure based on the white male as savior, healer, redeemer.

I have so far established certain grounds of comparison between *Schindler's List* and *Forrest Gump* based on various cultural, textual, and discursive elements. The purpose of this lengthy introduction is to set up a discussion of their respective figurations of cinematic memory. By relating *Schindler*, and its stylistic devices, to *Forrest Gump*, I want to consider the way in which both films construct memory narratives that privilege, and congratulate, white masculinity. This chapter has two remaining sections. The first addresses the stylistic techniques of *Schindler's List* and *Forrest Gump*, considering the representational status of each film as—nostalgically nuanced—memory texts. This uses the black-and-white image as a basis of comparison, demonstrating the difference between genre forms organized around ideas of sincerity (authenticity) and eclecticism (irony). The second section looks more closely at the political stakes of the remembered past in *Schindler* and *Gump*, judged in terms of white male identity "crisis." It is here that, despite different generic orientations, the two films evidence similarities in certain of their ideological prescriptions and determinants of value. Expanding the discussion of monochrome memory by demonstrating the use of black and white in two very different "documentary" film texts, the chapter explores the specific political interests served in *Schindler* and *Gump* as incorporative (national) master memories.

DOCUMENTARY MEMORY

Gentlemen, in a hundred years still another colour film will portray the terrible days we are undergoing now. Do you want to play a role in that film which will let you live again in a hundred years? Every one of you has the opportunity today to choose the person he wishes to be in a hundred years. I can assure you that it will be a tremendous film, exciting and beautiful, and worth holding steady for. Don't give up! [Joseph Goebbels, 1945][23]

Joseph Goebbels could hardly have known that one of the most influential films about the "terrible days" of the Second World War—at least in terms of global distribution, media interest, and commercial success—would not be in color, as he assumed, but rather in black and white. *Schindler's List* is perhaps not what Goebbels had in mind when inviting Nazi rank and file to consider their chosen role for cinematic immortalization, but then history is hard to predict and the conditions of memory even more so.

   Schindler's List tells the story of a charismatic yet complex hero, a Nazi war profiteer called Oskar Schindler, who fulfills ambitions of wealth and luxury by establishing a metalware factory in Krakow, exploiting the war economy and cheap Jewish labor to make enormous personal profits. As the war continues, and his workforce is subject to greater threats from Nazi racial policy, exercised by Amon Goeth at the Plazsow labor camp, Schindler increasingly finds himself in a position of conscience. Gestures of comfort, aid, and individual rescue culminate in the purchase and transportation of 1,200 Jews from Poland to his home town in Czechoslovakia, saving them from the terrifying inevitability of Auschwitz. In this context, black-and-white cinematography serves the film in several ways. It is a documentary aesthetic and provides *Schindler's List* with a mode of unobtrusiveness, contributing to a supposed *witnessing* of events. At the same time, however, black and white takes on a character of remembrance through its association with visual representations of the Holocaust and through its elegiac contrast with color. We remember as we witness; we witness as we remember. On another level, monochrome locates *Schindler's List* within a concept of cinematic tradition, emulating the style of classical Hollywood and providing a visual cue for Steven Spielberg's new directorial seriousness. Cultural memory is figured in terms of the Holocaust *and* Hollywood. In all of these ways, the use of black-and-white cinematography makes *Schindler's List* a complex memory text; it creates a visual effect of witnessing *and* remembrance, of terror at the topic but nostalgia for its style.

The immediate effect of black and white—a point that has been made many times and in most reviews—is to create for the film a sense of documentary authenticity. *Schindler's List* drew upon a concept of authenticity in several different ways: the film was shot in original Polish locations, including Schindler's metalware factory (although not at Auschwitz, for which permission was denied by the World Jewish Congress on the grounds that it is a memorial to those who perished beyond its gates); the original *Schindlerjuden* were participants, some as consultants and many appearing in the film's coda; there was even a sense of the cast and crew undergoing a certain authenticity of experience, harrowed by the trauma of shooting a film so close to the original scene of events. Spielberg said afterward: "I'm recovering from this film. And my wife thinks the recovery is going to take a long time."[24] While filming, temperatures were bitter, there were publicized incidents of anti-Semitism directed at cast and crew, and many scenes were so harrowing that cameramen tried not to watch the events they were actually filming. Spielberg remarked that "every day was like waking up and going to hell." A character of documentary was integral to the filming of *Schindler's List*, and this was manifest in its stylistic techniques, notably the use of hand-held cameras that helped to create deliberate imperfections and, more generally, the use of black-and-white photography. Instead of the seamless, glossy, high-tech effects more usual to Hollywood (and Spielberg) productions, *Schindler's List* sought a restrained photojournalistic quality where the viewer is positioned to witness, not to watch. As cinematographer Janusz Kaminski himself comments: "The newsreel quality of the black and white seemed to fade the barriers of time, making (the footage) feel like an ongoing horror that I was witnessing firsthand."[25]

While associated with the documentary traditions of photojournalism, the black-and-white image retains a suggestive archival pastness. The vast majority of photographic and filmic images taken during the Second World War exist in black and white. Kaminski prepared for *Schindler's List* by studying photographs taken between 1920 and 1939 by Roman Vishniac of Jewish settlements in Poland. To Spielberg, the black-and-white image was representationally more "real" than color. As he said: "I think certainly color is real to the people who survived the Holocaust, but to people who are going to watch the story for the first time, I think black and white is going to be the real experience for them."[26] The effect of "witnessing" the Holocaust in *Schindler's List* is linked to mediated memory—or, rather, to the memory of images that dominate contemporary impressions of the Nazi genocide. From the outset, the documentary effect of *Schindler's List* works through, and in relation to, a sense of period "reality" shaped by the visual determinants of photographic memory. Its strategies of transparency are shaped by an archival familiarity that makes black and white the most appropriate mode of 1940s "realism."

If memory was central to the discourse surrounding *Schindler's List* when it opened in 1993, an explicit character of remembrance is established within the film through particular chromatic juxtapositions between color and black and white. In the film's color prologue and coda, and in moments where particular images appear in color, the contrast with monochrome gives the film a distinct memorial character. The prologue of *Schindler's List* shows the lighting of a Sabbath candle and a group of people listening to a man intone a Jewish prayer. As the flame of the candle expires, it creates wisps of smoke, providing a visual link between the contemporary observation of Judaism and a black-and-white image of a steam train's belching funnel. This image is significant not least for the reason that trains are used iconically throughout the film to symbolize the presence of death at the end of the tracks at Auschwitz. In a different visual shift, the coda moves from a black-and-white image of a line of people against the horizon as they walk toward the camera (the weak and dislocated *Schindlerjuden* beginning their journey of recovery at the war's end), to a color shot of a line of people against the horizon as they walk toward the camera (the real *Schindler-juden* gathering to pay their respects at Schindler's grave in Israel). These chromatic movements reinforce the connections between past and present in terms of cultural memory; Judaism cannot forget the Holocaust, the *Schindlerjuden* refuse to forget their savior.[27] The most significant use of color *within* the film's monochrome narrative is that of a Jewish child whose dress is shown red as she wanders, lost, during the liquidation of the ghetto in 1943. This signifies a decisive moment for Schindler, whose attention to the girl is symbolized by the visual effect. When he sees her red tunic later in the film, she is strewn with a pile of dead bodies, awaiting incineration. As a symbol of innocence, the colorized child is a turning point in the moral identity of Schindler; the red coat marks the individual memory of a life once observed, ending in anonymous death.[28] Color, in this case, brings out the elegiac character of the film, composed within and against the documentary and archival pastness of black and white.

The visual strategies of *Schindler's List* construct the film as document and memory, experience and elegy. Monochrome is instrumental in achieving these effects, but the use and significance of the black-and-white image cannot be explained in these terms alone. A sense of documentary authenticity and historical memory is matched with black and white's articulation of cinematic authenticity and Hollywood memory. It is impossible to divorce the function of black and white in *Schindler's List* from Steven Spielberg's directorial presence. *Schindler* was a new departure for a film-maker who has pioneered the spectacular—and, some would say, emotionally simplified—blockbuster. While several of his movies, such as *The Color Purple* (1986), *Amistad* (1997), and *Saving Private Ryan* (1998), have taken on weighty sociohistorical themes, Spielberg has identified *Schindler's List* as the film that first marked a movement away from the character of sentimentality that has defined much of his work. *Schindler's List* was never conceived as a box-office smash; gone are the caricature Nazis of the *Indiana Jones* series. At the time, the film was a departure both in style and mood for a director who, perhaps because of his cartoonish vision of the world, had been conspicuously ignored in the American Academy Awards. In one sense, the use of black and white in *Schindler's List* is linked to a seriousness generated by the very subject and the director's relationship to it as a Jew. Spielberg claimed that the film was intimately tied to a personal rediscovery, commenting: "I've never identified more as a Jew as I have in the process of researching and producing and directing this film."[29] In other terms, however, black and white was a self-conscious mark of Spielberg's new directorial maturity; it was part and proof of his—and in turn Hollywood's—capacity to treat serious themes in a serious style. As Leon Wieseltier argued in *The New Republic*: "What is at stake [in *Schindler's List*] is the honor of Hollywood."[30]

If the New Hollywood has been criticized for its outpouring of vacuous movie blockbusters, *Schindler's List* appeals to a form of cinematic authenticity associated with classical Hollywood. Reviewing *Schindler's List* in *The New Yorker*, Terrence Rafferty wrote that "few American movies since the silent era have had anything approaching this picture's narrative boldness, visual audacity, and emotional directness."[31] This was typical of critical response in the media press. *Schindler* was described as having a quality rarely witnessed in contemporary cinema; it was a "masterpiece" reminiscent of an era before the dominance of visceral and kinetic thrills. *Premiere* called it a "tribute to the heritage of black-and-white film."[32] Retreating from the signifying excess and spectacular effects of New Hollywood, *Schindler's List* appeals to a form of cinematic authenticity located in the past. Miriam Hansen argues that with *Schindler's List* Spielberg is trying to inscribe himself into American film history by referring pivotally to *Citizen Kane*. There are, she suggests, similarities of style between them in their low-key lighting, montage sequences, angles and compositions in frame, and self-conscious use of sound. She even likens Schindler to an inverted Kane, transforming as he does from a character of surface and presentation to one of moral depth and fortitude. All of this contributes to an aesthetic that fuses "modernist style, popular storytelling and an ethos of individual responsibility." Hansen demonstrates how *Schindler* gestures toward the day when films could reflect upon the "shocks and scars inflicted by modernity" while remaining accessible to the general public.[33] The essential point is that *Schindler's List* creates a filmic pastness that is concerned with, and refers to, Hollywood as well as the Holocaust.

Yosefa Loshitsky has examined how *Schindler's List* is both iconic and highly intertextual in its recreation of the cultural/cinematic past. Its referencing strategies depend on a particular kind of quotational practice that works invisibly so that stylistic transitions do not draw attention to themselves. First, the film incorporates images from other works on the Holocaust, from abandoned heaps of luggage (taken from Alain Resnais's *Night and Fog*) to the figure of a Pole symbolically pulling a finger across her throat (an image inspired by Claude Lanzmann's *Shoah*). Second, it quotes different kinds of black-and-white film style. *Schindler's List* is cast in a realist tradition, using a classical mode reminiscent of the 1940s and 1950s. Within this format are various cinematic conventions based on their use of monochrome. While interplays of light and shadow evoke film noir and the chiaroscuro lighting associated with Hollywood studio films, black-and-white street scenes of the Krakow ghetto are strongly reminiscent of Italian Neorealism and its depiction of life after the war. Loshitzky suggests that Spielberg's "use of black and white is indebted more to cinematic traditions associated with black and white than to any claim to truth. In fact, black-and-white cinematography today has more the aura of 'arty' glamour than a claim to formal authenticity."[34] If monochrome has a range of connotations that can produce different signifying effects in the same signifying moment, the black-and-white cinematography of *Schindler's List* is not simply a documentary aesthetic but can suggest a host of (nostalgically inscribed) cinematic memories.

There are vigorous debates, cultural and philosophical, concerning the representation of the Holocaust in literature, film, museums, and memorials. Can it be represented? How should it be represented? By and for whom? *Schindler's List* has been criticized by scholars and the likes of Claude Lanzmann for failing to respect the uniqueness of the Holocaust, for trying to represent events within conventional narrative forms, and for portraying Jews without giving any one the substance of character, and it has been praised for problematizing Nazi clichés and for dealing with the Holocaust in affective terms. Black and white is embroiled in these debates. For Leon Wieseltier, the particular use of monochrome in *Schindler's List* proves that Spielberg has not grasped the humility required of the subject; it is a mark of the film's "self-regarding" quality. He writes: "Renunciation of color is adduced a sign of its stringency; but the black and white of this film is riper than most color. The glints and gleams are smart. The edges of the frame are faded. The shadows are exquisite. The darkness of this film about darkness is, in sum, gorgeous."[35] This kind of objection reflects something of Saul Friedlander's concern that the reevocation of Nazism in the West has shifted from one of "subdued grief and endless meditation" to "voluptuous anguish and ravishing images."[36] In a different sense, the use of black and white has been praised for its visual gravity and mark of seriousness. Spielberg had to resist pressure from Universal to shoot a color version of the film for television release. Monochrome was an unusual, and in some sense brave, choice for a director striving for an effect of authenticity that may well have left audiences cold. For better or for worse, black and white advertised the film as different and significant. By transcending the color norms of Hollywood, black and white raised the status of *Schindler's List*; in aesthetic terms, it would become the cornerstone of a reverential discourse helping to sanctify the film as Hollywood's "statement" on the Holocaust, its ultimate, and incorporative, master memory.

The black-and-white image does not, on its own, confer the status of "master memory" on *Schindler's List*. This can be explained through a range of related factors, from the attempt by Spielberg to tell a representative story of human suffering and survival to the larger discourse of Holocaust remembrance in America that elevated the film to a position of educational authority. While it is just one stylistic feature in a film that can be discussed in many different ways, black and white is central to the cultural and cinematic authenticity claims of *Schindler's List*. The same can hardly be said of *Forrest Gump*, a film that also laid claim to a concept of documentary, that became another Hollywood master memory, and that emerged as the most lucrative and Oscar-laden film in the year following the release of *Schindler*. If black and white helped to legitimate *Schindler's List* as a memory text by locating both the action and the style of the film in a documentable and remembered past, *Forrest Gump* drew its effects, and established its status, in quite a different way. The black-and-white image was taken up playfully in ways that subverted the documentary and memorial authenticity of monochrome, renarrating American postwar history in more overtly fictive terms.

On release, *Forrest Gump* became a talking point and touchstone—a film that made sense of four decades of turmoil in American life and brought it to a tender resolution. Victims of the counterculture and Vietnam are joined in symbolic harmony, bitterness and divisions are salved, and hope is laid on an innocent generation neither knowing nor burdened by the traumas that once befell the nation. At the center is

Forrest Gump, an innocent himself, who, by literally witnessing events
that impressed a powerful, destructive turbulence into the slipstreams
of American society and culture, is able to redeem and heal the suffering
through his innate sensitivity, emotional honesty, and homespun wisdom. Gump sits calm and uncomprehending within the eye of a storm
that rips across the landscape of American life, killing presidents and
throwing society into violent conflict. Born in Alabama in the 1950s,
Forrest becomes an accidental hero of every shape and form: a football
all-star, Medal of Honor recipient, multimillionaire, philanthropist, and
celebrity cult. He meets three presidents, Elvis, and John Lennon, and
unwittingly he participates in both the notorious confrontation between
George Wallace and black desegregationists and the exposure of the
Watergate break-in. The film has two interweaving narratives, historical
and romantic. *Forrest Gump* is both an iconic journey through recent
decades of American history and a story about love and the family ideal.

If *Schindler's List* uses monochrome to achieve various cultural and
cinematic authenticity effects, this can be conceived under the generic
category of "new sincerity," what Jim Collins describes as the purposeful
evasion of "the media-saturated terrain of the present in pursuit of an
almost forgotten authenticity that avoids any sort of irony and eclecticism."[37] By contrast, *Forrest Gump* is based on the very qualities that
Schindler avoids. Characteristic of "eclectic irony," its production of pastness relies upon the recycling of media texts, from footage and music to
the filmic quotation and pastiche of cinematic genres. When Forrest
meets an army friend in New York who is crippled, alcoholic, and
disillusioned, having returned from Vietnam—reminiscent of Ron Kovic
in *Born on the Fourth of July* (1989)—we see Forrest pushing him in a
wheelchair to the song "Everybody's Talkin'." This, of course, is the
musical theme of *Midnight Cowboy*, a story about a cripple in New York
living a similar kind of metropolitan suffering and alienation. This is
typical of the way that *Forrest Gump* plays upon a shared filmic, as well
as historical, past. Trawling images and evocations that realize, in whatever way, an iconic sense of common memory, *Gump* replays and
rearticulates history through a range of textual traces, including that
of—black-and-white—documentary footage.

Forrest Gump draws specific attention to the mediated nature of history. The presence of television in the film is unstinting, and the status of
documentary is built up through the sustained presence of archival
footage, from the Zapruder film of the Kennedy assassination to the first
moonwalk and the resignation of Richard Nixon. Typically, the archival
images are taken from footage that has become deeply ingrained in the
visual iconography of American culture, and, in particular cases, it is
used to locate Gump as an agent and observer of "official" national
history. This is achieved through the digital insertion of Gump within

specific archival vignettes. In the course of the film, Forrest is introduced to Kennedy, Johnson, and Nixon, meets John Lennon, and watches the Wallace stand-off. In *Schindler's List*, the sense of documentary is achieved through chromatic and technical effects simulating a mode of indexicality; we are made to witness history being lived. In *Forrest Gump*, the status of documentary is based far more on the representation of history in the media; historical reality is evoked not through our witnessing events but via our familiarity with its archival character in the mass media. Both *Schindler's List* and *Forrest Gump* ground their narratives in historical "reality," but while the former claims a transparent relation with this reality, the latter manipulates it playfully to expedite a moral narrative of national reconciliation.

Black and white is one of many stylistic effects used in *Forrest Gump* to map an iconic, and affective, postwar terrain. Technically, decades are evoked through different film stock and color diffusions. The 1950s are given a softer grain than the hard texture of the 1960s, which are, in turn, different from the clean, sharper aspect of the 1980s. According to Don Burgess, director of photography, "Because the film jumps around so much we made a conscious effort to have the visual imagery telegraph exactly what zone you're in."[38] Integral to this "zoning" process is the use of archival footage and a soundtrack of period hits. Both help to implicate Forrest within the very fabric of American national and popular history; he becomes a cypher of cultural experience, an omnipresent shadow in the nation's common past. Just as Gump is placed, quite literally, in the historical archive, so the lyrics of period music often describe the diegetic events of the film itself: "California Dreamin'" when Forrest writes home from Vietnam, "Stoned Love" when Jenny, the film's countercultural emblem and Gump's childhood sweetheart, takes drugs, "Running on Empty" and "It Keeps You Running" when Forrest jogs across America.[39] Through a range of iconic and acoustic markers, *Forrest Gump* plays upon a shared sense of the past, explained and experientially distilled through a figure whose simple-minded decency can heal the pain and distemper of a bruised history. As a "docufable," the film draws upon the historical and cultural archive while, through the experience and narration of Gump, it paints the 1960s as a "fall" from which the nation must recover.

I have been concerned in this section with the techniques through which cultural memory is stylistically realized in two Hollywood "master memories" of the 1990s. Both *Schindler's List* and *Forrest Gump* lay claim to a particular kind of documentary memory; they are both concerned with the memory of, and meaning ascribed to, traumatic periods in the historical past. If one film reconstructs the past through poignant authenticity effects, the other is playful in its textual manipulation and pastiche of cultural genres. In different ways, and on certain terms, these documentary effects are inscribed with a character of nostalgia. In *Forrest Gump*, this is quite explicit; the film has a discernible and self-conscious "nostalgia mode" where periods of American history are given not significance but *feel*. In the Jamesonian sense, history becomes a scopic flow where the past is realized through pop image and textual pastiche. While *Schindler's List* is highly resistant to any concept of nostalgia, it, too, acquires a certain nostalgic effect through Spielberg's appeal to cinematic authenticity, based on the monochrome models of classical Hollywood.

In the next section, I consider how the documentary-based, but nostalgically nuanced, style of each film conditions a more politicized figuration of masculine authority. If each film became a "master memory" in the early 1990s—an incorporative, figuratively impartial visioning of the collectively remembered past—they both established a distinct relationship between historical victims and redeeming male protagonists. In the final part of this chapter, I consider how the different modes of documentary-nostalgia in *Schindler* and *Gump* correspond, at some level, with a narrative nostalgia for the benevolent white "father."

WHEN OSKAR MET FORREST

The first time we see Oskar Schindler in Spielberg's film, he is sitting at a table in a cabaret, immaculate and charismatic, framed by shadows and holding a cigarette with the deliberateness of a film star. The scene demonstrates Schindler's svelte charm, and every time the camera rests on him, it is with the chiaroscuro lighting of film noir. The tonal elegance of the cinematography matches that of Schindler's own self-styled panache. He is a picture postcard from classical Hollywood; the backlighting keeps his figure separate from the background, giving depth to the image, while lighting from above creates a sense of translucence and substance that Richard Dyer has linked to Hollywood conventions for presenting the (white) star.[40] In *Schindler's List*, Oskar is the agent and subject of the film. The narrative centers upon his emotional development and moral awakening; he transforms himself from a self-interested entrepreneur and unfaithful husband, willing to exploit Nazi connections and cheap Jewish labor to make enormous wartime profits, to a benevolent figure of redemption, committed both to his workforce and to his wife. Schindler is a laissez-faire Lothario but a character of integrity in the last instance. Spielberg's treatment of the Holocaust is figured, in part, as a narrative of male identity, of the charismatic masculinity captured in the form of Schindler and Amon Goeth.

Relating the memory narratives of *Schindler* and *Gump* to the "crisis" of white male identity in the early 1990s is, of course, not the only reading possible for either film.[41] However, it is an important one in judging the cultural stakes of two movies that received an elevated status at the beginning of the decade. The early 1990s were a period when questions were being asked about the status of victimhood and the nature of trauma. From sexual harassment in the workplace to affirmative action in education, from debates about recovered memory to the increased awareness of child abuse, the status of the victim was being discussed in both the courtroom and the mass media. Although at times appropriating the status of victim himself, the white male came under increasing scrutiny in cultural life, whether for his part in the creation of "hostile environments" and exclusive literary canons or for the past enslavement of blacks and the genocide of Native Americans. While a "cult of victimhood" was periodically diagnosed and dismissed as a worrying symptom of a new therapeutic ethos in American life—what Robert Hughes linked to an emergent "culture of complaint"—a fundamental stake in the politicized discourse of victimhood was the legitimacy of white, male, middle-class heterosexual power.[42]

Liam Kennedy suggests that the crisis of white masculinity was not only recognized by white males in the early 1990s but also successfully managed by them, notably in the way that liberal rhetoric recognized diversity but in ways that helped to reinvent and reassert the authority of white male identity. He writes: "The very rhetoric of crisis is one that has been franchised and mobilized by those incarnating it."[43] Concentrating on the way that Hollywood "has played a part in the ideological management of the visible crisis in white male authority," Kennedy examines the case of *Falling Down* (1992), a film that sought actively to dramatize white male anxieties while reinforcing the centrality of white male experience as the organizing, normative identity through which societal issues and problems are framed. With a similar interpretive framework, but using different filmic examples, Fred Pfeil examines a series of films that either inscribe their male protagonists in narratives of redemption and conversion—*Regarding Henry, City Slickers, Hook,* all in 1991—or that "cash in on the crisis of white masculinity by appealing to our ambivalence about what it should be or become—*Falling Down, In the Line of Fire* (1993), *Forrest Gump*.[44] The point to make here is that white male identity developed as an implied or, at times, explicit cinematic theme in the 1990s as Hollywood took on, and responded to, discourses shaped by identity politics.

Schindler's List is not concerned with white male identity in any obvious sense, as could be said of *Forrest Gump*. This does not mean to say, however, that the film has no relation whatsoever to contemporary discourses of identity. As James Young has shown, the Holocaust is remembered in different countries according to various national myths and political needs.[45] While Young concentrates on memorials, the same principle applies to media texts. For example, there is an argument that the emphasis on family and local community in the American docu-drama, *Holocaust*, which began in 1978, reflected contemporaneous debates about the status and breakdown of the nuclear family.[46] Likewise, *Schindler's List* can be set in relation to cultural debates about identity, memory, and trauma. The early 1990s were a period when the status of victimhood had become a contested badge in claims of cultural redress. *Schindler* helped suggest, and authenticate, an idea of Jewish historical victimization.[47] This was structured, however, around a relationship between historical victims and the oppressive *and redemptive* agency of patriarchal authority. *Schindler* concentrates not on the victims themselves, who are often represented in a pasteboard manner, but on their relation to charismatic masculine authority, neither innocent of callous and violent domination nor unable to undo its effects through virtuosity and "family" commitment. The meaning of the Holocaust in the film is not simply a question of remembering the dead. It is about survival and those who make it possible.

Quite simply, it is Oskar Schindler who makes it possible, and it is here that nostalgia in the black-and-white film style might be seen to figure and frame a more political nostalgia for the ravishing authority of the central male protagonist. In using narrative and aesthetic conventions associated with classical Hollywood, Miriam Hansen points to relationships in the film that are predicated on masculinist hierarchies of gender and sexuality and to the fact that larger problems are resolved through the formation of family. The nostalgic cinematic pastness of *Schindler's List* authenticates a certain style of nostalgic, masculine hero. In Schindler this becomes a mixture of the dashing bon vivant and the authoritative yet benevolent "father." Throughout the film, Schindler takes increasing responsibility for his workforce, growing from a distant patriarch into a more caring father-figure. He even renounces promiscuity and returns to his wife in the last third of the film. As the symbolic "father," Schindler frequently identifies his workforce as personal to him, disguising an emotional responsibility with a language of economic common sense. "I want *my* people," he explains to Goeth, negotiating the transportation of his Jewish workforce to Czechoslovakia. "Who are you? Moses?" Goeth replies. In many respects, Schindler *is* the figure of Moses, a patriarch leading his people to safety and freedom. There is even a symbolic sense of Christian virtue in the film, a powerful, hand-some, tall Christian redeemer set against physically small and puny Jewish victims. Throughout the film, Schindler's heroism is cast in terms of his power to act, to intervene, to save. Underlying the complexity of his character is a trajectory of patriarchal virtue that, in the climate of the early 1990s, can be seen in terms of, and is perhaps commensurate with, a discourse figured around the recoupment of male authority.

Schindler's List manages to avoid polarizing a scheme of good versus evil by making the two central male protagonists, Schindler and Goeth, similar in temperament. Oskar has come to Poland with the intention of making money. He indulges in a taste for good wine and beautiful women, and at the beginning of the film the fate of his Jewish workforce is largely a question of costly interruptions to his own factory's productivity. Amon Goeth has similar tastes in wine, women, and finery, and he is less fanatical about his position as Nazi commandant than he is burdened by its bureaucratic demands, demonstrating the fact that genocide was more routinized in its terror than openly sadistic. Schindler tries to account for Goeth's violence, suggesting to Itzack Stern, his Jewish accountant, that it is the war that brings out the worst in people and that he cannot enjoy the killing. He says: "In normal circumstances he wouldn't be like this. He'd be all right. There'd just be the good aspects of him, what . . . he's a wonderful crook, a man who likes good food, good wine, the ladies, making money . . ." Schindler and Goeth manage to slip the clichés of the good German and the Nazi villain by reflecting each other's basic preoccupations—or, rather, the temperaments they would have shared pre-Occupation. For all the seeming complexity of character, however, *Schindler's List* remains a story of heroes and villains, of moral agency in a battered world.

Schindler's energies flow in increasingly selfless and political channels as the film unfolds. Once his moral conscience and sense of responsibility have been awakened, Schindler is never blemished with doubts about his virtue. At his new factory in Czechoslovakia, he is a loyal husband in charge of a factory that purposefully makes defunct ammunition, and he goes bankrupt funding the safety of the *Schindlerjuden*. His moral virtue is finally established in a rather heavy-handed scene where Schindler breaks down, at not having saved more lives. It is at this moment that his Jewish workforce present him with a ring bearing the Talmudic inscription: "He who saves a life, saves the world entire." The *Schindlerjuden* give coherence to their experience by framing it within the moral wisdom of the Talmud. As such, they turn the events, and the film, into the form of a parable, the sense of which bespeaks of singular (male) heroism. This informs the color coda of *Schindler's List* in which the real *Schindlerjuden*, accompanied by the actors who played them, individually lay a stone on Schindler's grave in Israel. The factional status of the film comes together here with some force. A caption on the screen reads: "There are fewer than four thousand Jews left alive in Poland today." It is followed by another caption that reads: "There are more than six thousand descendants of Schindler Jews." Schindler not only redeemed 1,200 Jews, he provided for their regeneration. Even if the final caption remembers the six million Jews who died, the coda honors the memory of one Gentile, Schindler. He is the focus of the film's closure, Liam Neeson, the actor who played him, laying a rose upon a gravestone covered in stones.

There are many ways that one can discuss the "Americanization" of the Holocaust in *Schindler's List*. The film is, most obviously, a product of an American culture industry, and it works within Hollywood conventions that figure an epic narrative around a central protagonist who transforms the course of events. The film comes to a resolute closure, and, according to Sara R. Horowitz, it "reassures the audience of the rightness of the workings of history" by showing the survival of those who in some way earn it.[48] That the film is concerned with survivors at all is perhaps an indicative American Holocaust trope. *Schindler's List* concentrates on 1,200 who survived when six million perished. One of the most resonant details, however, revealing the film's cultural genesis, is in Spielberg's own dedication. While *Schindler's List* remembers the six million Jews, the film is dedicated to Steven Ross, chief executive of Time-Warner and a personal friend of Spielberg. Ross was a model for the portrayal of Schindler; Spielberg told Neeson to watch and learn from his mannerisms. This is not to draw any deep conclusion about the character in light of the fact. It simply suggests that *Schindler's List* was never based on characters and events in any strict documentary sense. From the outset, Spielberg had a particular model of paternal masculinity in mind for Schindler, drawn from a knowledge of Oskar, but also influenced by contemporary models and male identities. As portrayed by Spielberg, Schindler is a charismatic capitalist and benevolent father who, in a world unhinged by war and genocide, is figured heroically in the nostalgic monochrome tones of cinematic classicism.

Susan Jeffords has argued that representations of masculinity in mainstream Hollywood film changed during the 1990s. Her argument is couched in a starkly periodized framework where 1991 represents "the big switch," moving from hard-body action heroes—*Lethal Weapon, Rambo, The Terminator*—to sensitive, nurturing family-men—*Regarding Henry, City Slickers, The Terminator 2: Judgment Day*. Jeffords suggests that 1990s masculinity represents not a simple warming of the male heart, but a "wholesale social patterning" that shows men providing, in their role as father, for future generations.[49] One may be suspicious of the blanket claims she makes about restructured male identity, especially in light of the range of films that may complicate her theory, from *Basic Instinct* to *Pulp Fiction*. However, if her claims are read in a less schematic and determined fashion, they can be suggestive of particular kinds of negotiated identity in 1990s film. Indeed, both *Schindler* and *Gump* demonstrate tendencies in Hollywood film that Jeffords relates to "increasingly emotive displays of masculine sensitivities, traumas and burdens." In the case of Oskar and Forrest, both men undergo a process of emotional maturation, developing into father figures who provide for the future.

The relationship expressed in *Schindler's List* between historical victims and a redeeming male protagonist would perhaps have less cultural significance if it were not for the proximity of *Forrest Gump*. As touchstones of remembrance, sanctified by the American Academy, both films produce forms of historical coherence and moral closure based on the visioning of male saviors; they base documentary memory narratives upon the redemptive and regenerative virtues of men. In *Forrest Gump*, this is more explicitly related to American history; it enters debates about the status and significance of the 1960s and, implicitly, the crisis of white male identity. Stylistically, *Gump* creates a nostalgic currency of shared participation that is mobilized in particular, and highly politicized, ways. If monochrome engenders a mode of nostalgia in *Schindler*, framing a particular kind of "authentic" masculine hero, *Gump*'s strategies of pastiche locate Forrest in a lapsarian history that makes him the singular force of reconciliation. Analyzing the dual tendencies of *Forrest Gump* both to forget history (notably, the history of popular struggles undertaken by, and for, the rights of marginalized "others") and to rewrite history in patriarchal narratives of consensual nationhood, Thomas Byers suggests that the film's "nostalgia mode" helps to "clear the way for a renarration of the history of struggle that serves the most powerful of entrenched interests and carries a vicious edge under its carefully contrived demeanor of historical innocence."[50] *Forrest Gump* creates a terrain of pastness through a nostalgia mode of pop iconography. Within this recognizable and shared past stands Gump himself, a character whose decency, honesty, and clarity of vision represent the best hope for recovered harmony in the wake of the turbulence caused by the cultural struggles and social dislocations associated with the 1960s. As Robert Burgoyne writes: "With the slate 'wiped clean' of female presence, of racial others, and of social discord, the period can, in effect, be retrofitted to an emergent narrative of white male regeneration."[51]

Taking $100 million in its first three weeks and moving on to become the fifth-highest-grossing film of all time, with $270 million in domestic earnings, *Gump* was claimed by various political groups. The film was taken to "prove" both liberal and conservative value structures; it was, at once, a critique of racism, sexism, and child abuse and a defense of national integrity and family values. Appealing to the widest possible market, *Gump* was promotionally savvy in that it offered itself up for a conservative reading while also providing a view whereby conventional values appear to be satirized. For all its self-professed apoliticism, however, *Forrest Gump* is at heart a powerfully conservative film.[52] This can be measured in several ways, but endemic to it is a consensus view of

American history and national reconciliation based upon the authority of the white male and the marginalization of "others," notably the histories of feminism, African-American civil rights, and gay liberation. As Burgoyne continues, "the film associates the imagined community of nation with the saintly singularity of identity embodied in Gump."[53]

As narrator, Forrest Gump cannot understand historical and political conflict, only its effects. He experiences division and disruption without ever grasping the causal forces. This "enlightened" naiveté enables him to witness events with little or no capacity for social critique. At the level of historical narration, violent death is a denominator of the social turbulence that befalls America. Reference to individuals and icons like Elvis Presley, George Wallace, John and Robert Kennedy, John Lennon, Gerald Ford, and Ronald Reagan all reinforce premature death, assassination, or attempted assassination. Thomas Byers notes the astonishing absence of Martin Luther King and Malcolm X in *Gump*'s catalogue of assassinations. This is symptomatic, he suggests, of the victim status given to white men and the film's complex disavowal of white racism.[54] Death is never explained or set in context; it is simply an ongoing consequence of disharmony. In remembering little of the politics of the 1960s but everything about its turmoil, *Forrest Gump* centers the white male as a calming center of gravity without exploring how imperial white manhood may have been a cause of resistance and revolt. While the film gestures with some deliberateness toward sexual and racial oppression, it frequently becomes little more than a foil for Gump's own incomprehension, a means of disavowing the white male narrator from the processes of social power. Forrest is totally unable to understand or conceptualize oppression. He is a figure who did not need the 1960s to hone his sensitivity, and in consequence the period seems both disruptive and productive of undue turmoil. Protest was never the answer, simply the flowering of Gump-like decency.

Forrest Gump is a story of recovery and redemption for the victims created by the social and political turbulence of the 1960s. As Forrest at one point comments: "You've got to put the past behind you before you can move on." Through his inveterate place in the nation's collective past, and because of his ability through ignorance to transcend sociocultural division, Gump is given the symbolic power to reconcile victims of the baby-boom generation. The victims, in this case, are given a caricatured portrayal in the figures of Jenny and Lieutenant Dan. Both are realized less as people than as *types*; they each carry the weight of histories that define the 1960s—namely that of the counterculture and Vietnam. Jenny is a drug-taking, antiwar-demonstrating, sexually promiscuous flower-child whose "liberation" begets addiction and physical abuse. Thomas Byers suggests that Jenny embodies "the revisionist version of the counterculture, which collapses together (as 'liberal' and 'evil') any and all behaviors that deviate from the repressive norms of the 1950s."[55] Jenny becomes a single mother in the 1980s and eventually dies of an AIDS-like virus, fulfilling conservative fears about moral breakdown and its effects. Lieutenant Dan is a career soldier, an officer in Vietnam who cannot readjust on return and becomes bitter, resentful and alcoholic. With the film's tendency to evade political critique, Dan's bitterness is the result of being crippled, not his experience of the war or the political fallout that questioned America's entire involvement. Both Jenny and Dan are rescued from emotional and spiritual tail-spins by the integrity and generosity of Forrest. This is brought together with meta-phorical brio toward the end of the film, when Forrest and Jenny get married—less a culmination of romance than of lives rescued by a family ideal. Attended by Lieutenant Dan and his Asian fiancée, the wedding is a ceremony of healing and reconciliation: victims of the counterculture and Vietnam are brought together by Gump in a concluding allegorical scene of national restoration.

In *Schindler's List*, it is Oskar's complexity of character that motivates the film. He is a hero despite himself, transforming from an opportunist with a taste for the good life to a morally resolute figure whose goodness preserves the value of life itself. In *Forrest Gump*, it is Gump's simplicity and innocence that motivate the film. He is also a hero despite himself, although more because he is unable to recognize his agency upon people and events than through any necessary personal transformation or moral awakening. While *Schindler's List* sets a charismatic figure of male authority in relation to victims of historical oppression, *Forrest Gump* sets an innocent child–man in relation to victims compromised by a histori-cal period. Although markedly different, both films structure relation-ships that depend fundamentally on a redeeming male figure, saving, healing, and establishing the basis for a future generation. Both films are a product, and must be seen in the context, of the early 1990s. In a time when the white heterosexual middle-class man had become a bogey of oppression, *Schindler's List* and *Forrest Gump* gave him the capacity of saving victims, not creating them; both films traffick in a certain kind of nostalgia for white, male, agency and authority.

Drawing *Schindler's List* and *Forrest Gump* together may seem to go against the critical grain, especially when compared on the grounds of documentary nostalgia. However, by concentrating on cinematic style, situating the movies in relation to contemporary film genericity, and considering their projection of white male identity, the techniques and terms of remembrance in each are not entirely at odds. Implied in my consideration of *Schindler's List* and *Forrest Gump* is a relationship be-tween the mode of the two films and their articulation of white mascu-line authority. The black-and-white image is significant in each case, although taken up in different ways. In *Schindler*, black and white is instrumental to the film's claim of cultural and cinematic authenticity. While bound in the rehabilitation of Spielberg's move from hack director to artistic historian, black and white establishes different visual registers—documentary, archival, elegiac, nostalgic—that contribute to the film's multilayered memory effect. Black and white creates an authenticating historical aesthetic that also, and at the same time, codes a particular memory of Hollywood classicism.

In *Gump*, black and white is one of a number of textual codes that help create a terrain of American postwar pastness. Monochrome is part of an iconic repertoire and is used without any particular reverence for its representational and/or historical authenticity; it contributes to the more general breakdown of distinctions between fact and fiction, representation and experience, which Vivien Sobchack relates to the film's historically self-conscious mode (incorporating the position of the individual *within* history).[56] In bringing the two films together, black and white provides the most available comparative distinction of their respective strategies of sincerity and eclecticism. In each film, monochrome is used to create a documentary effect, but one that is inflected with nostalgia. Engendered by the visuality of black and white as a temporal and archival mode, each film creates a register of media memory that contributes, at some level, to a more generalized patterning of cultural remembrance focusing on the vivified power of the white, male subject.

Considering the attempt in 1990s film to rearticulate the cultural narratives that define America, newly accounting for the nation's polycultural reality, Robert Burgoyne writes of a "desire to remake . . . the 'dominant fiction,' the ideological reality, or the 'image of social consensus' within which members of a society are asked to identify themselves."[57] He argues that those on the cultural margins have increasingly been brought to the center of the national imaginary, compelling a new configuration of America's self-image and of the nation's collective past. This is not the whole story, however. As Burgoyne's consideration of *Forrest Gump* is forced to acknowledge, along with the proliferation of identities and histories treated in contemporary American film, there has been an attempt to stabilize a sense of common memory based around, and serving the interests of, centered (that is to say white, male, heterosexual) identity and power. *Gump* is an aggressive example of the attempt to restore investments in narratives of nation that are unburdened by, or have silenced, the claims of cultural difference. *Schindler's List* may operate in relation to a different set of cultural discourses, but, like *Gump*, it attempts to fix an incorporative master memory based on regenerative masculine authority. In tone and style, it may appear that *Schindler's List* and *Forrest Gump* could not be further apart. However, their respective cultural memories are figured in ways that can be set in a similar context, respond to similar demands, and are structured in a similar way. Both proffered documentary master memories at a juncture where the cultural past was becoming a site of increasing fracture and debate, and both served to congratulate a benevolent and redeeming white "father" in a cultural moment of destabilized patriarchal legitimacy.

NOTES

1. See Marcia Landy, ed., *The Historical Film: History and Memory in Media* (London: The Athlone Press, 2001).

2. Marita Sturken, *Tangled Memories: The Vietnam War, the AIDS Epidemic and the Politics of Remembering* (Berkeley, CA: University of California Press, 1997): 2.

3. Robert Sklar, *Movie-Made America: A Cultural History of American Movies* (New York: Vintage Books, 1994): 358.

4. Liam Kennedy, "Alien Nation: White Male Paranoia and Imperial Culture in the United States," *Journal of American Studies*, 30, no. 1 (1996): 87.

5. Miriam Bratu Hansen, "*Schindler's List* is not *Shoah*: The Second Commandment, Popular Modernism and Public Memory," *Critical Inquiry*, 22 (Winter 1996): 292.

6. Yosefa Loshitsky, "Introduction," in Yosefa Loshitsky, ed., *Spielberg's Holocaust: Critical Perspectives on Schindler's List* (Bloomington, IN: Indiana University Press, 1997): 2.

7. Martin Walker, "Making Saccharine Taste Sour," *Sight and Sound*, 4, no. 10 (1994): 16.

8. Cited in Richard Schickel, "Heart of Darkness," *Time*, 13 December 1993: 49.

9. Cited in Walker, "Making Saccharine Taste Sour": 17.

10. Robert Burgoyne, *Film Nation: Hollywood Looks at U.S. History* (Minneapolis, MN: University of Minnesota Press, 1997): 121.

11. James E. Young, "Holocaust Documentary Fiction," *Writing and Rewriting the Holocaust: Narrative and the Consequences of Interpretation* (Bloomington, IN: Indiana University Press, 1988): 51–63. Spielberg inherited a documentary-based narrative from Thomas Keneally's *Schindler's Ark*, the book on which Steven Zaillian's screenplay was based.

12. Robert A. Rosenstone, *Visions of the Past: The Challenge of Film to Our Idea of History* (Cambridge, MA: Harvard University Press, 1995): 45–79. Rosenstone suggests that "drama" and "document" both personalize and dramatize history, telling it as a story with progressive and moral messages, and both insist on history as the story of individuals, using the special capabilities of the filmic medium to heighten and intensify feeling. In short, he argues that documenting the historical past depends on many of the same codes and cinematic conventions that shape its more overt dramatization.

13. Paul Arthur, "Jargons of Authenticity (Three American Moments)," in Michael Renov, ed., *Theorizing Documentary* (New York: Routledge, 1993): 108.

14. Renov, *Theorizing Documentary*.

15. Jim Collins, "Genericity in the Nineties: Eclectic Irony and the New Sincerity," in Jim Collins, Hilary Radner, and Ava Preacher Collins, eds., *Film Theory Goes to the Movies* (New York: Routledge, 1993): 242–260.

16. Collins, "Genericity in the Nineties": 254.

17. David Ansen, "Spielberg's Obsession," *Newsweek*, 21 Dec 1993: 43.

18. Collins, "Genericity in the Nineties": 262.

19. Saul Friedlander, *Reflections of Nazism: An Essay on Kitsch and Death* (Bloomington, IN: Indiana University Press, 1993).

20. See, in particular, Fred Pfeil, *White Guys: Studies in Postmodern Difference and Domination* (London: Verso, 1995); Richard Dyer, *White* (London: Routledge, 1997); and Kennedy, "Alien Nation": 87–100.

21. Sklar, *Movie-Made America*: 371.

22. Thomas B. Byers, "History Re-membered: *Forrest Gump*, Postfeminist Masculinity, and the Burial of the Counterculture," *Modern Fiction Studies*, 42, no. 2 (1996): 426.

23. Cited in Friedlander, *Reflections of Nazism*: epigraph.

24. Cited in Edward Guthman, "Spielberg's List," *San Francisco Chronicle*, 12 December 1993, in Thomas Fensch, ed., *Oskar Schindler and His List: The Man, the Book, the Film, the Holocaust and Its Survivors* (Vermont: Paul S. Eriksson, 1995): 51.

25. Cited in Karen Erbach, "*Schindler's List* Finds Heroism Amidst Holocaust," *American Cinematographer* (January 1994): 49.

26. Cited in Curt Schleier, "Steven Spielberg's New Direction," *Jewish Monthly*, 108, no. 4 (1994): 12.

27. The same framing device is used in *Malcolm X*, suggesting connections between the lived present and the remembered past. The film begins with documentary footage of the Rodney King beating and ends with a selection of images that include children proclaiming "I am Malcolm X," Nelson Mandela teaching children in a classroom, and black stars like Bill Cosby and Janet Jackson wearing "X" caps. Black and white is used in both *Malcolm X* and *JFK* to reinforce the aura of documentary authenticity, although each film is in color.

28. A pointed illustration of intertextuality, using the effect of a red dress, can be found in the advertising of a car manufacturer, which deployed a "Schindler aesthetic" to sell one of its models. A television ad for the Peugot 306 (Britain, 1997) is entirely black and white except for a cherubic girl with a colorized red dress. She appears several times within a montage of images that show, together with a man driving a car, life scenes of passion, emotion, and distress. The girl stands in a road where a truck bears down upon her. The ad concludes with the man, whom we have by now seen driving the car, running to catch and save the girl. The ad plays out to a hit by M People with the refrain, "Search for the Hero Inside Yourself." Black and white recreates the visual character of *Schindler's List* in a narrative of character-building heroism.

29. Cited in Guthman, "Spielberg's List": 54.

30. Leon Wieseltier, "Close Encounters of the Nazi Kind," *New Republic*, 24 January 1994: 42.

31. Terrence Rafferty, "A Man of Transactions," *The New Yorker*, 21 December 1993, in Fensch, *Oskar Schindler and His List*: 88.

32. John H. Richardson, "Steven's Choice," *Premiere* (January 1994): 66.

33. Hansen, "*Schindler's List* is not *Shoah*": 310.

34. Yosefa Loshitzky, "Holocaust Others: Spielberg's *Schindler's List* versus Lanzmann's *Shoah*," in Loshitzky, *Spielberg's Holocaust*: 109.

35. Wieseltier, "Close Encounters": 42.

36. Friedlander, *Reflections of Nazism*: 21.

37. Collins, "Genericity in the Nineties": 257.

38. Cited in Paula Parisi, "Forrest Gump Gallops through Time," *American Cinematographer* (October 1994): 40.

39. Music is a key demarcation of period "zones" and is used according to various cultural associations that have developed between artists and events. While Jimi Hendrix is used for the rock 'n' roll soundtrack of Vietnam, Bob Dylan and Paul Simon play out the counterculture. Notably, the 1980s are evoked by hits of the time but from artists with a baby-boom pedigree like Fleetwood Mac and Willie Nelson. *Forrest Gump* is very much about the boomer generation and the impact and legacy of the pivotal 1960s.

40. Dyer, *White*.

41. The film rights to *Schindler's List* were purchased in 1983. In accounting for the timing of the film, Spielberg has explained the lapse of time before making the film by several related factors: the problems of adapting a suitable screenplay, his own need to mature as a director, and the pressing conditions that gave the film significance, like the atrocities in Bosnia and the declining number of Holocaust survivors. Emphasizing the "crisis of white male identity" does not negate practical criteria of production or preclude different kinds of reading. Instead, it situates *Schindler's List* in relation to an important contextual discourse that moves beyond the discussion of Holocaust memory and that bears upon specific debates within the American cultural sphere.

42. Robert Hughes, *Culture of Complaint: The Fraying of America* (New York: Oxford University Press, 1993).

43. Kennedy, "Alien Nation": 90.

44. Pfeil, *White Guys*: 238.

45. James E. Young, *The Texture of Memory: Holocaust Memorials and Meaning* (New Haven, CT: Yale University Press, 1993). Young concentrates on memorials. He argues that while in Israel memorials frequently relate to the birth of the state, those in Germany invariably focus upon guilt and Jewish absence. American memorials often remember the Holocaust through ideals of liberty, pluralism, and the experience of immigration.

46. See Jeffrey Shandler, "Schindler's Discourse: America Discusses the Holocaust and Its Mediation, from NBC's Miniseries to Spielberg's Film," in Loshitsky, ed., *Spielberg's Holocaust*: 153–168; and Marcia Landy, *Cinematic Uses of the Past* (Minneapolis, MN: University of Minnesota Press, 1996).

47. Considering the tension between Jews and African–Americans over the significance and degree of racial oppression in their respective histories, it is not incidental that Spielberg's next historical film, *Amistad*, should be about slavery.

48. Sara R. Horowitz, "But is it Good for the Jews?: Spielberg's Schindler and the Aesthetics of Atrocity," in Loshitsky, *Spielberg's Holocaust*: 136.

49. See Susan Jeffords, "Can Masculinity be Terminated?" in Steven Cohen and Ina Rae Hark, eds., *Screening the Male: Exploring Masculinities in Hollywood Cinema* (London: Routledge, 1993): 245–260; and "The Big Switch: Hollywood Masculinity in the Nineties," in Jim Collins, Hilary Radner, Ava Preacher Collins, eds., *Film Theory Goes to the Movies*: 196–208.

50. Byers, "History Re-membered": 439. Byers suggests that the "emptying out" effects of nostalgia art are not ends in themselves, as implied in Jameson's postmodern theory, but can equip a terrain of pastness that can then be rewritten for particular, hegemonic, purposes.

51. Burgoyne, *Film Nation*: 117.

52. For persuasive arguments of this position, see Byers, "History Re-membered"; Pfeil, *White Guys;* and Burgoyne, *Film Nation.*

53. Burgoyne, *Film Nation:* 121.

54. The film recognizes racism but then denies it by turning it into something incomprehensible or silly, like the slogan-filled rants of a Black Panther or the portrayal of the Ku Klux Klan as men in bed-sheets, ridiculous more than repressive.

55. Byers, "History Re-membered": 432.

56. Vivien Sobchack, "History Happens," in Vivien Sobchack, ed., *The Persistence of History: Cinema, Television and the Modern Event* (New York: Routledge, 1996): 1–14.

57. Burgoyne, *Film Nation:* 1.

6

Reclaiming Heritage:
Colorization and the Culture War

It has so far been my argument that a discourse of "black-and-white-ness" developed in different cultural media during the 1990s. I have essentially been concerned with the way that monochrome was deployed in the dominant media: how it was used to create particular temporal and authenticity effects and how these became linked to particular figurations of national history and memory. In this final chapter I consider the way that black and white was *defended* in cultural debates that sought, in the late 1980s and early 1990s, to affirm an idea of cultural inheritance through recourse to the principle, and preservation, of monochrome memory. Highlighting the discursive continuities between a specifically liberal defense of cultural patrimony, evident in the debate over film colorization, and the culture war critique associated with neoconservatism, I relate the black-and-white image to a particular, and politicized, discussion about the configuration and transmission of American cultural identity. The chapter makes explicit some of the connotative ascriptions that underlie the discourse of "black-and-white-ness" in 1990s image culture, demonstrating a particular equation drawn at the beginning of the decade between the visuality of monochrome and the negotiation of nation. Of central concern are questions about taste, critical authority, and the relation of black and white to specific debates fought over the preservation of aesthetic and cultural integrity.

In the late 1980s, a skirmish broke out over the issue of film colorization, a culture war of a particular sort. The brouhaha began in March

1986, when Ted Turner bought MGM Entertainment and swiftly announced a plan to convert to color twenty-four films in his new back
catalogue, among them *The Maltese Falcon* and *Father of the Bride*. As an
economic venture, colorization would give new profit potential to films
that had lost their market viability through age and the visual hindrance
of being in black and white. Proponents of color conversion—like Turner
and the Hal Roach Company, which helped develop the conversion
process—argued that technological enhancement would represent nothing short of "the rebirth of the film classics of yesteryear."[1] Opponents
were less sanguine about the virtues of colorization, bodies like the
American Film Institute and the Directors Guild of America, along with
figures such as Woody Allen and John Huston, denouncing the process
as a threat to the originality of the art work and the moral rights of the
creator. The colorization debate set art against commerce, creative rights
against ownership, monochrome against the dastard color of money.
Fought in the media and then in court, it raised questions about intellectual property but also, and significantly, about authenticity and cultural
heritage.

   At the same time as the colorization fracas was taking place, another
more pernicious culture war was beginning to unfold. In 1987, Allan
Bloom published *The Closing of the American Mind*, a conservative jer-
emiad on higher education that would set the tone for a proliferating
number of right-wing broadsides against the legacy of 1960s radicalism
in American universities and the development of an invidious new
relativism. From William Bennett and Lynne Cheney to Roger Kimball
and Dinesh D'Souza, a crisis was being defined, "tenured radicals"
conspiring to politicize knowledge, undermine the Great Books of literature, and to threaten core values, liberal education, and Western Civilization generally. As with colorization, the preservation of cultural
heritage—or what Bennett would call reclaiming a legacy—became central to the barbed conflicts over educational standards and the challenge
of multiculturalism.[2]

   The colorization debate and the conflict over higher education have
very different political stakes. If the former is a question of personal
property in relation to moral rights and popular memory, the latter is a
far more significant issue concerning the status of the university, the
circulation of knowledge, and the representation of peoples and identities within what counts as legitimate knowledge and culture. One became a minor issue that had snuffed itself out by 1989, while the other
became a defining controversy that would burn through the 1990s, creating with it the smoke and bluster of "political correctness." Colorization and multiculturalism are different in scope and scale, but they
reveal similarities in the way they were and are defined in public discourse. Narratives of decline have been mobilized in each case, focusing

upon the authenticity of the art work and the status of national heritage. If colorization and multiculturalism can be examined together, a significant basis for comparison is perhaps their disrespect for the preserves of cultural tradition. More specifically, they (are seen to) disrupt a certain concept of tradition grounding particular ideas about educational practice and the popular circulation of cultural texts. At the end of the 1980s, the process of colorizing film and the politics of "colorizing" the curriculum induced a sense of discontinuity that gave nostalgia a concerted rhetorical currency within American cultural politics.

In their appeal to a lost authenticity, the nostalgics of the culture war were most readily observed on the right, typified by Allan Bloom and his best-selling requiem for cultural authority and the Great Books. While nostalgia may underscore the polemical tenor of much conservative criticism, however, this does not limit the extent to which its rhetorical strategies have been engaged across the political spectrum. The left developed its own narratives of decline in battles fought over multiculturalism. This focused principally upon what was seen as the baleful emergence of academic theory and the parochial nature of identity politics, what Todd Gitlin described as a "grim and hermetic bravado celebrating victimization and stylized marginality."[3] Beset by cant and cosmetic political triumphs, left/liberal critics like Gitlin, Russell Jacoby, and Robert Hughes chastized the shallow politics of a beleaguered left that had come to fight politics from the library, protest by means of abstract theory, could not build majorities, and saw political action in the confines of curricular revision. According to Andrew Ross, the focus on marginality in the academy in the late 1980s and early 1990s had "run up against the same reactionary consensus of left and right, each unswervingly loyal to their own narratives of decline: charges of post-1960s fragmentation and academification from unreconstructed voices on the left, and warnings of doom and moral degeneracy from Cassandras on the Right."[4] If Bloom was an angel of doom within this scheme, Gitlin makes a case for unreconstructed leftism.

In general terms, a politics of nostalgia can emerge from multiple, not simply conservative, conceptions of loss. On occasion, this has produced some intriguing parallels that cross the political divide. My interest in the colorization debate stems from the character of nostalgia it engendered among ranks of the liberal-left, and the discursive continuities this revealed with key tenets of neoconservative critique. Colorization gave rise to a liberal nostalgia that understood loss in terms of threatened cultural heritage. The status of the "classic" text, the principles of aesthetic distinction, and the importance of cultural inheritance all became points of issue for a liberal lobby seeking to fend off the deleterious encroachments of commerce in the cultural sphere. In many respects, the anticolorization camp trafficked in what Joan Wallach Scott has called the "fetishizing of tradition" in contemporary discourse.[5] Scott associates this with conservative endeavors to shore up the "integrity" of American identity (and its structures of privilege) against multicultural discordance. The discourse of tradition has also been mobilized and refined by the left, however. The colorization debate complicates the discursive "territories" of left and right, joining rather curiously the likes of Woody Allen and Allan Bloom, Martin Scorsese and George Will, in a common defense of heritage and cultural transmission.

The colorization debate set liberal artisan guilds, film organizations, critics, directors, and Democratic senators against the powerful economic interests of Turner Broadcasting Systems, CBS/Fox, Hal Roach Studios, Colorization Inc., and Color Systems Technology. In framing their opposition to the conversion process, liberals rushed to the defense of the classic work; they justified the policing of taste against commercial opportunism and the vulgarities of consumer preference; they sought to counter the debilitating effects of postmodern technology and its digital manipulation of the visual image. These were similar, however, to the terms being deployed by the conservative assault on multiculturalism as it developed in the same cultural moment. Right-wing critics abhorred the attack on classic works of literature; arguments were made about the onset of ignorance and superficiality with the "politicization" of the humanities; conservatives sought to challenge postmodern theory and its corrosive impact on sense, clarity, and standards of value. Colorization and multiculturalism created respective barbarisms against which defenders of culture, heritage, and good taste could unite. The significant difference between the two was the axis determining from where exactly rhetoric of nostalgia, linked to particular notions of authenticity, was being voiced. Colorization was fought with rhetorical grapeshot compared with the heavy weapons wheeled out for the battles over multiculturalism. Both debates nevertheless reveal a similar resistance, in a comparable language, to challenges made upon the "fixity" of tradition, the stability of artistic canons, and the formation of American cultural identity.

COLORIZATION

It has been said that "postmodernism's politics will be a struggle for control—not over the means of production, but over the means of replication."[6] This speaks, in part, of the licensed reprivatization of culture, where capitalist energies enforce laws of copyright and ownership within areas that are, or should be, public. Colorization is one such example. Both the Hal Roach Studios and Turner Broadcasting saw the opportunity of forging new copyrights for old works through techniques of color conversion. Adding color would, it was hoped, be recognized as "new creativity" by the Copyright Office (which it was in 1987), color-ized films therefore becoming an "original work of authorship." Ted Turner sought to maximize the profit potential of works he already owned by securing copyrights for them as new commodities. This had the effect of creating private property out of an ostensibly public re-source. While opponents tried moving the issue onto moral grounds—namely, was colorization a breach of the moral rights of the original creators?—there was short legal mileage to be gained from this argu-ment. In 1988, President Reagan signed legislation for America to be-come party to the Bern Convention, an agreement for the protection of literary and artistic works, but with a provision that effectively meant that moral rights would not be recognized in America. Colorization was a legal victory for owners above artists, a triumph for those holding property rights and a digital paint brush.[7]

Colorization was first and foremost about money. As Ted Turner explains: "Movies were made to be profitable. They were not made as art, they were made to make money . . . anything that could make more money has always been considered to be OK."[8] The vehicle and medium for the colorized film was television; profit would be made through syndication and video release. In 1986, Turner announced that he would market a series of color-converted films—including *Yankee Doodle Dandy, White Heat, High Sierra, Father of the Bride, Dark Victory,* and *The Maltese Falcon*—on a barter basis. These were sold to television stations as part of the Color Classic Network. By 1987, the vice-president of marketing for Turner Broadcasting, David Copp, reported that 85 sta-tions had decided to participate in the network, earning the company substantial revenues. For example, two colorized Errol Flynn movies (*Captain Blood* and *Sea Hawk*) grossed $800,000 in less than a year. In black and white, these had earned only $200,000 apiece. It was difficult to anticipate the failure of colorization from the initial furor that it caused.

Charles R. Acland suggests—rightly, in my opinion—that it is not color that attracts audiences but the very fact of colorization, "the specta-cle of the re-finished product, a creation of technological wizardry." He argues that "people are intrigued by the seemingly profane reworking of definitive moments in their collective cultural history."[9] There is per-haps a curiosity in digital alteration, of seeing a film artfully doctored in the name of creating what Acland calls the "new classic." The fact that colorization failed to establish itself, that demand was eventually low and companies lost millions in the gamble, may illustrate the momen-tary fascination. Colorization became a fad, a short-lived exercise that expired with the public's waning interest. By 1994, the *New York Times* wrote that "the mad dash to colorize classic black-and-white movies appears to be over."[10] After issuing 120 colorized films, Turner closed down his operations. For all its wizardry, color conversion could not deliver a convincing visual spectacle or compete with the revival of black-and-white movies on cable channels such as American Movie Classics. In the end, colorization became little more than a digitally inspired novelty.

What interests me is not so much the fact that colorization failed in popular, if not in legal, terms, but the manner in which it rallied opposition. While the debate was principally waged over rights (ownership versus the moral entitlements of the creator), the rhetoric of the conflict focused upon a few central themes, prominent among them those of authenticity, canonicity, and cultural heritage. Notions of originality and authenticity have been problematized in a climate where cultural production has become ever more hybrid, intertextual, and digitally reproduced.[11] Authenticity remains a powerful cultural category, however, as is evident in the colorization debate. Opponents decried the process of color conversion as a "desecration" of the art work (Martin Scorsese), a "mutilation" (Woody Allen), an impropriety not unlike "robbing a grave" (Robert Redford). The Directors Guild of America called color conversion "cultural butchery." Colorization was portrayed as an encroachment on the rights of the creator, but moral arguments were often linked to an idea of the authentic—that is to say, black-and-white—work of art.

Authenticity is conceptually linked to the idea and possibility of fraud. Exactly how fraudulent the colorized film is or can be said to be was basic to the legal and aesthetic debates that governed the issue of color conversion within public discourse. There were two main areas of discussion. The aesthetic debate questioned the grounds on which colorization was (im)moral (*should it be done?*) and the legal debate questioned the grounds on which colorization was (il)legal (*can it be done?*). There is considerable overlap between the two, for, as I have said, legal arguments were fought in terms of moral rights. The concept of authenticity was framed somewhat differently in each case, however. While the legal debate contested the degree of control a film-maker could expect to have over his or her original (authentic) work, the aesthetic debate focused more upon the formal properties of black and white in defining a work's very originality (authenticity).

Flo Leibowitz argues that black and white can affect the entire mood of a film; monochrome performs expressive work in its own right. A monochrome movie is not simply a film without color—it has a tonal quality that is often used quite deliberately in genres like film noir.[12] Describing the high-contrast tones of black-and-white film stock, used to great effect in film noir "mystery lighting," James Naremore suggests that "certain directors and cinematographers—even when they work in color—repeatedly aspire to *the condition of black and white*" (italics added).[13] Monochrome, in this view, is an aesthetic modality with particular conventions and connotations. Whether for its graphic quality, its dependence on light and shade, its association with gritty realism or with aesthetic refinement, black and white has specific properties that have been taken up in various genre forms and film traditions. Woody Allen writes that "The different effect between color and black and white is often so wide it alters the meaning of scenes."[14] One line of defense in the anticolorization campaign was that monochrome, even in the heyday of the black-and-white movie, was not used out of pure technical necessity but was, and remains, intrinsic to the creation of film mood and atmosphere.

By giving the black-and-white image an aesthetic value in its own right, the anticolorization lobby could better advance its case for preserving the art work in the (monochrome) form intended by the original artist. At stake was the issue, and potential abuse, of creative intentionality. Woody Allen said that colorization is "an ugly practice, totally venal, antiartistic and against the integrity of every filmmaker."[15] Fred Zinnemann—who as expatriate president of the Directors Guild of Britain initiated anticolorization protest by calling for a limited number of classics to be "saved"—called the process "a cultural crime of the first order."[16] Liberal proclamations put a value on the authenticity of the art work. In framing this as an absolute principle, however, the anticolorization lobby failed to acknowledge that authenticity has never been a fixed value in cultural life. Michael Schudson wrote in *Society*: "To make color versions of black-and-white films does not seem essentially different from other ways people update, to be vulgar, or reinterpret, to be precise, old works of art."[17] Of course, colorization does not restage an art work, as in the performing arts—it visually reconfigures it. To the likes of Allen and Zinnemann, this would no doubt be a crucial difference. It remains the case, however, that colorization does not alter or destroy the *original* form of any art work. By transferring a film image from the master copy to videotape, the colorization procedure represents a modification rather than a mutilation of the original film text; the process does not destroy the single instantiation of the art work—it is, instead, based on the digital production of colorized *copies*.[18] The perception of colorization as "venal" and "a crime" was a form of hyperbole that developed from a somewhat fetishized notion of artistic authenticity.

There are numerous examples in cultural life where authenticity could (but has not) become an issue. This may pose questions about the particularity of film colorization's threat. Musicians such as Frank Zappa, for instance, have used digital technologies to correct "flaws" in recordings made decades earlier; a host of CD reissues have "improved" sound recordings from the beginning and middle of the century by ridding them of various acoustic imperfections; digital technology has been used to remaster old films, notably demonstrated by the 1997 rerelease of George Lucas's enhanced and extended version of *Star Wars*. In no single case have the digital modifications in these examples been specifically questioned or opposed. This would suggest that the defense of authenticity in cultural and creative life is not consistently fought but is linked to the context and circumstances of modification. Hypothetically, this could apply to colorization itself. There may have been a different response in liberal critique, for example, if Frank Capra and not Ted Turner had been responsible for colorizing *It's a Wonderful Life*. Color conversion may have become a more legitimate enterprise if carried out in the name of artistic experimentation rather than profit. The point to make here is that authenticity is not a fixed state and standard. In the clamor to condemn colorization, however, authenticity became just that, pinned to the status and value of the black-and-white image. An editorial in *American Cinematographer* typified the tone of liberal reproach by suggesting that "An artist's original intent is what is most valuable to his or her culture and most characteristic of genius."[19] In media comment and film critique, authenticity—by implication, the authenticity of monochrome—became a hardened principle used in the name—and taken up in the defense—of artistry and cultural integrity.

If the question and protection of textual authenticity depends on the context and conditions of modification, there are several reasons for the particular, and vociferous, liberal outcry over film colorization. First, color conversion was a flagrantly commercial venture with no artistic pretensions; it was bankrolled by a media magnate for whom property rights were paramount. Turner saw in colorization a way to recoup his substantial overpayment for the MGM back catalogue and, brandishing entitlements as legal owner, carried forth the less-than-conciliatory view that "if the director of *The Maltese Falcon* didn't want it colorized, he should have wrote [sic] that into the contract when he went to work."[20] Anticolorization was, in a primary sense, a fight against big business. Second, color conversion fed the enduring perception in liberal discourse of the degradation of art through the medium of television; colorization was seen as the latest manifestation of television's capacity to exploit the vulgarities of public taste for commercial profit. In the words of the National Society of Film Critics, the conversion and syndication of colorized movies was a "betrayal . . . of film as an art form."[21] Third, and the point I develop: adding color to black-and-white films upset notions of film classicism that were, in turn, linked to ideas of cultural heritage. While panning and scanning has long altered the original format of movies for the viewing demands of television, there was something about the modification of aesthetics that made the issue of colorization more grave. By digitally reinterpreting a monochrome movie, colorization was seen by its detractors to compromise not only a film's authenticity, but also its place within cinematic history. If panning and scanning had never raised the hackles of the film community before, it was arguably because the classic (chromatic) status of the film, and the demarcation of cinematic tradition, had not been challenged in quite the same way.

The last point is significant, for it situates the anticolorization lobby within a more general critical reaction in the late 1980s and early 1990s to transformations brought about by electronic media culture. Ava Collins suggests that a revolution based on computer, cable, and video technologies has had "a profound effect (on) the way that information is disseminated, exchanged and circulated within the culture, with profound ramifications for those institutions involved in the cultural production and exchange of information and knowledge."[22] Collins is concerned with the relationship between popular culture and pedagogy, but her argument is useful in demonstrating a parallel fear on the right and the left regarding the challenge of popular cultural forms to evaluative criteria and to prescriptions of cultural tradition. She suggests that one consequence of the increasing centrality of popular culture in everyday life, brought about by new information technologies, has been for critics to reassert "true Culture" and "to demonize popular culture as pure commodity product, inauthentic, mindlessly repetitive, imposed from above by a cabalistic culture industry that threatens civilization as we know it."[23] Collins has in mind here staunch cultural warriors in the education debate, like William Bennett, Allan Bloom, and Roger Kimball, all of whom sought to banish popular culture from the classroom and reinstate the primacy of "classic" Western literature. However, the same principle of restoring a corpus of authentic works, defining a specific legacy and/or cultural tradition, can also be witnessed in the anticolorization campaign. In each case, and in their own terms, classicism and canonicity became articles of faith, set against the ruinous encroachments of new and stupefying cultural forms enabled by the technological facilities and textual flexibilities of capitalist postmodernity.

It was the perception of an imminent threat to national heritage that came, in the end, to define the anticolorization campaign. Rather than fight Turner and the colorization process by attacking the hegemonic dominance of property rights within American life, the anticolorization campaign appealed in somewhat righteous tones to the "authenticity" of creative genius and to the vitality of cultural tradition. The fight against big business focused not on the terms and limits of ownership, but on the defense of defining art works. In his seminal essay "The Work of Art in the Age of Mechanical Reproduction," Walter Benjamin describes the effect of technical reproduction on the authenticity, or aura, of the art object.[24] The production of copies, he argues, detaches the art object from the domain of tradition. Discussing colorization and the formation of popular histories through cultural works, Charles Acland adapts Benjamin's argument. In a culture where authorship and originality have been undermined as never before in the age of digital reproduction, he writes: "There is a lot at stake in the establishment of stable reference points and in the reinstallation of the aura, what might be referred to as the *reproduction of the authentic*" (italics added).[25] Acland suggests that the colorization debate—much like the conflict over the curriculum in higher education—revealed the need to construct a fixed history, to assemble a "consensual cultural heritage," from works commonly agreed upon as "classic." By the terms of the debate, the black-and-white image became equated semiotically with artistic authenticity, but also, and crucially, with the aesthetic temporality of film classicism.

The black-and-white "classic" became a fulcrum of the colorization controversy, giving rise to the issue of cinematic canons. Episodes of *Gilligan's Island* could be colorized, but God forbid anyone should touch *Citizen Kane*. It was the digital threat to an assemblage of perceivable "classics" that inspired legal initiatives. In 1987, Democrat Representative Richard Gephardt put forward the Film Integrity Act. This was designed to give a measure of copyright protection to a film's creator, but also to safeguard the classic motion picture. Senate hearings focused upon the Gephardt bill, and testimony was given by Steven Spielberg (Directors Guild of America), George Lucas (Writers Guild of America), Ginger Rogers (Screen Actors Guild), and a panel consisting of Woody Allen, Sydney Pollack, Elliot Silverstein, and Milos Forman. While the Congressional hearings failed to uphold the principle of moral rights—reluctant to follow France, Germany, and Italy and establish concrete legal protections for artists as well as owners[26]—the Senate decreed that a limited number of films that were "culturally, historically and aesthetically significant" should be included in a National Film Registry. These films would not be exempt from digital alteration but would carry a label acknowledging the fact *of* alteration. It was a limited victory for the anticolorization lobby, but interesting in what it revealed about the role of government in preserving "classic" works of art and the stakes fought over the cultural transmission of canonical artifacts and the particular histories they designate.

A pivotal argument used by opponents of color conversion was the effect it would have on heritage, memory, and national identity. John Huston denounced colorization, saying that "it would almost seem as though a conspiracy exists to degrade our national character." Fred Zinnemann echoed this sentiment, saying that color conversion was "against the national interest." Bonita Granville Wrather, chairperson of the American Film Institute, said that coloring "will destroy our national film history and the rich heritage which it represents."[27] Although master copies of original films are always left intact after color conversion and may even be better preserved, this fact was thought to be insignificant all the time a powerful entertainment industry controls distribution, circulation, and access. With time, it was argued, a colorized film would replace the original version in the public memory; works of art would be replaced by inferior commercial spectacles. This would have severe consequences for any real understanding of film history and cinematic tradition.

It was in this context that in 1988 Congress published findings that led to the creation of the National Film Preservation Board. It drew three main conclusions. First, that "motion pictures are an indigenous American art form that has been emulated throughout the world"; second, that "certain motion pictures represent an enduring part of our nation's historical and cultural heritage"; and, third, that "it is appropriate and necessary for the Federal Government to recognize motion pictures as a significant art form deserving of protection."[28] The National Film Preservation Board was a committee of thirteen people who in 1990, under the auspices of the Library of Congress, began to consider a list of 1,500 films nominated by the public for selection as cinematic landmarks. Twenty-five titles would be chosen each year, the Library of Congress requiring the copyright owner to submit a high-quality print or negative to its archive and obliging colorized versions to carry a sticker that read: "This is a colorized version of a film originally marketed and distributed to the public in black and white. It has been altered without the participation of the principal director, screenwriter and other creators of the original film." Notwithstanding its legal infirmity, this was a rather toothless gesture, undermined by the fact that Turner simply put the label on everything he colorized, irrespective of whether or not the film had been given the revered status of cinematic landmark. As a political gesture, however, the decision appeared conciliatory: the government established an apparatus that could decide upon the fixed constituency of national heritage but that did not substantially affect property rights. Protecting copyright ownership, but acknowledging the importance of film heritage, the federal ruling on colorization put the legal primacy on property while, at the same time, it validated the *principle* of artistic inheritance.

One link between colorization and multiculturalism is that concerning the role of government in upholding standards and values within a notional cultural policy. This would become a hotly contested issue in the war over political correctness, focusing upon the level of public funding (administered by the National Endowment for the Arts and Humanities) given famously to artists such as Robert Mapplethorpe and Andres Serrano. While the standards in this case were about the protection of public morality—should the government sponsor work that is "pornographic" and "anti-Christian"?—and were, in fact, linked to Republican efforts to cut the NEA budget, the standards upheld by the colorization ruling were, in a different sense, about the protection of *public memory*. Government took steps to articulate a concept of heritage through its commitment—however empty it may have been in practical terms—to "classic" film. In a climate where the preservation of national tradition was gathering a discursive and polemical weight—especially in cultural debates over educational standards—the federal ruling symbolically affirmed, and formally endorsed, a collective inheritance of canonical texts: heritage was defined in a nationalist framework based upon the selection, and sanctification, of seminal art works.

The threat imposed to the transmission of heritage became a key issue in American cultural politics in the late 1980s and early 1990s. Colorization disturbed conventions of memory by visually reinterpreting artifacts of film history. Unlike the (multicultural) revisioning of history and canonicity within museal and academic discourse, colorization had pecuniary rather than political motivations. Similar issues about historical representation were at stake, however, and similar complaints were made against the perception of sacrilegious tampering. Compare these statements by John Huston, addressing the U.S. Congress in 1987 on the issue of color conversion, and George Will, writing in *Newsweek* in 1991 about political correctness.[29]

We are all custodians of our culture. Our culture defines not who we are but who and what we were. Those of us who have labored a lifetime to create a body of work look to you for the preservation of that work in the form we chose to make it. I believe we have that right. [John Huston]

The transmission of the culture that unites, even defines America—transmission through knowledge of literature and history—is faltering. The result is collective amnesia and deculturation. That prefigures social disintegration, which is the political goal of the victim revolution that is sweeping campuses. [George Will]

These comments are different in that in one the emphasis is on the question of artistic choice and in the other on the question of cultural literacy. However, both examples ground their arguments in the custody and carriage of American identity; they both invoke a threatened tradition integral to the conception, and maintenance, of national heritage and culture. If the colorization debate illustrates some of the rhetorical tropes utilized in New Right attacks on multiculturalism, the main agent of "deculturation" for the anticolorization lobby was never a tenured radical or member of the loony left but Ted Turner (hardly a radical, even if he was married to Jane Fonda). In the late 1980s, a defense began to mount, in two different areas of cultural life and from different political positions, a discourse of tradition seeking to enclose and protect cultural heritage from insidious, or at best self-serving, corporate and pedagogical interlopers.

Heritage is a capacious term, and battles fought in its name reveal different political constellations and commitments. In America, conservatives have spoken of the importance of "reclaiming heritage" in education, but they have been instrumental in slashing federal funds to the National Trust and introducing property rights legislation that has crippled preservation efforts to save old buildings and communities.[30] Meanwhile, the anticolorization lobby was adamant about the protection of black-and-white film heritage but tended to neglect, or sideline, issues about the material threat to fragile nitrate-based film stock. Stuart Klawans notes that one of the ironies of colorization was that Ted Turner spent more money and did more to preserve film heritage than any federal effort by storing and making safe the catalogue of an entire studio (MGM). He suggests that, in the end, the anticolorization campaign did more harm than good by redirecting valuable resources away from efforts to physically preserve degradable film stock genuinely threatened by age.[31] The point to make from these examples is that heritage has often become less a question of material preservation than one of maintaining continuities of knowledge, of defending specific histories inscribed in cultural texts. Barbara Kirschenblatt-Gimblett suggests that "Heritage is not lost and found, stolen and reclaimed . . . [but] produces something new in the present that has recourse to the past."[32] In the burgeoning culture wars of the late 1980s and early 1990s, heritage became an issue principally fought over *representation*. In political terms, this can be understood in terms of the negotiation of critical authority, cultural hegemony, and the determination of taste and tradition. It is the discursive continuities between anticolorization and opposition to multiculturalism, evident in this fight, that I now consider briefly.

MULTICULTURALISM

"Colorization represents the mutilation of history, the vandalism of our common past, not merely as it relates to film, but as it affects society's perception of itself."[33] So read a committee letter by the Directors Guild of America, submitted at the Senate hearings on moral rights. The tone here could be mistaken for that leveled against Afrocentrism and the "cult of ethnicity" in the work of a critic such as Arthur Schlesinger, Jr. In 1991, Schlesinger published *The Disuniting of America*, a best-seller that delivered a prognosis on the "new ethnic gospel" being instilled through education and the teaching of history. This was a book that, as Michael Bérubé suggests, served to delegitimize multiculturalism and authorize a backlash. It is not my purpose to examine Schlesinger, but he

does illustrate similar discursive ground occupied by the anticolorization lobby in its concern with historical mutilations and vandalism.
Lamenting the use of education to build self-esteem in minority groups,
he argues that history should not be tampered with in the service of
cultural therapy. How else but through the invocation of history, he
suggests, "can a people establish the legitimacy of its personality, the
continuity of its tradition, the correctness of its course."[34] The colorization debate never entertained the polemics of ethnic difference, but it
did raise issues of pedagogy and historical transmission that were being
expressed in the conflict over multiculturalism.

If we are to be precise, colorization was more about taste than about
pedagogy defined in any institutional sense. In his attack on colorization, Jerrold Levinson argues that "it is a bad thing to foster the degradation of taste in the general populace since this leads, at least for viewers
who are not literally constitutionally unable to deal with black-and-
white film, to lives intrinsically worse than they might otherwise be."[35]
This elitist view seeks to police the standards of value for those impres-
sionable souls unable to distinguish between monochrome quality and
colorized trash, heritage, and heresy. It is left to those with enough
cultural acumen to recognize and regulate the difference. A similar
premise underwrites *The Closing of the American Mind*. Allan Bloom's
Arnoldian sense of cultural tradition seeks to preserve distinctions between high and low culture in the perpetuation of a discernible (Western) cultural heritage. He suggests that "For Americans the works of the
great writers could be the bright sunlit uplands where they could find
the outside, the authentic liberation for which this essay is a plea."[36]
Authenticity is a byword for *true* cultural value; it is basic to a critique
that decries superficiality, ignorance, fakers, and those who no doubt
traffic in postmodern theory.

If colorization and multiculturalism both created barbarisms against
which defenders of culture, heritage, and good taste could unite, this
particular form of cultural brutishness is an expression of effects that
might usefully be called postmodern. In the case of colorization, the
conversion process is enabled by digital technologies that allow the film
image to be altered in ways that previous techniques of tinting and
toning could never achieve. Colorization was seen to create a simulacrum of the classic film, undermining representational authenticity and
tampering with tradition. In the multicultural debate, postmodern
theory became a perceivable menace to originality and heritage, classic
works of literature coming under the relativist cosh. While a complex
movement with diverse political investments, multiculturalism was relentlessly stigmatized in public discourse and by the media press. Reflecting upon the culture wars, Frederick Buell wrote at the end of the
1990s: "'Multiculturalism' was repeatedly spoken of as a singular, easily

labeled position, one that amounted to 1) separatism and 2) cultural relativism."[37] The "barbarism" attached to multiculturalism was a particular conflation of these two elements. The questions that the multicultural movement posed to the stability of artistic canons—namely, the concept of common culture—were linked, and often confused, with an assault on the very status of nationhood (the concept of common society). I realize that I am using the word "multiculturalism" without accounting for its ubiquitous use and meaning in social and political discourse.[38] However, its conceptual and political diversity was never something its detractors were careful to preserve. If the "barbarism" of multiculturalism can be compared with that of colorization, it is on the grounds that each was seen fundamentally to disturb the relationship between cultural canonicity and national identity.

Tropes of universal worth and timeless value can be witnessed in both debates. George Lucas said at the Senate hearings that technological advances "will alter, mutilate and destroy for future generations the subtle human truths and higher human feelings that talented individuals within our society have created."[39] This implies an idea of cultural uplift (higher feelings) in works that transmit enduring values (subtle truths). It is reminiscent of the bright sunlit uplands that Bloom finds in the great writers, those talented individuals of the literary world. Film colorization problematized the status of the classic by showing that, as a concept, it could be challenged, redefined, and essentially fought over. This produced an outpouring of commentary in film journals lambasting the proponents and practitioners of colorization, "people who are unreachable by cultural, artistic or social appeals" and who possess "shriveled sensibilities."[40] The status of the classic work also became the crux of the canon debate within higher education; the classic literary text was supposedly devalued through a process of "politicization" inspired by new left-wing orthodoxies. This produced a different, but contiguous, media outpouring leveled against academic "terrorists" and their "crimes against humanity."[41] In different ways, opponents of multiculturalism and colorization saw the ritual sacrifice of aesthetic and cultural standards in ill-considered attempts to accommodate injured visual and / or political sensibilities.

This "accommodation" was seen to have a powerful commercial dimension. Colorization was clear evidence to its critics of the vulgarities of the marketplace, corporate impresarios out to make a ready buck through the base exploitation of (a created) consumer fancy. Colorization was seen as an expression of impersonal market forces, global magnates seeking to extend their command over lucrative new markets. Ted Turner was no cultural patron but, as *American Film* literally pictured him, a dangerous "raider of the last archive."[42] The market-based challenge to aesthetic value and cultural heritage also distinguished conservative complaints about multiculturalism within education. Academics, it was thought, were becoming self-aggrandizing careerists; disciplines like cultural studies were emerging as lucrative cottage industries; the university was succumbing to a new consumerism less concerned with maintaining the "autonomy of knowledge" than with showcasing a graduating roster of satisfied customers. Within a broad context, these kinds of criticism can be seen as a response to the substantial weakening of local identity at a time when transnational flow (of persons, technologies, finance, information, and ideology) had come increasingly to undermine the basis of national tradition, including the social function of the university as it had been linked to ideas of national culture.[43]

In the context of discussion about the formation and effects of capitalist postmodernity, Ien Ang writes: "The desire to keep national identity and national culture wholesome and pristine is not only becoming increasingly unrealistic, but is also, at a more theoretical level, damagingly oblivious to the contradictions that are condensed in the very concept of national identity."[44] At some level, it is the desire to essentialize national culture through (the defense of) some conceptually authentic heritage that joins the liberal anticolorization campaign and the neoconservative critique of multiculturalism. It is not my intention in this section to trace the intricate contours of the academic culture wars. The debates over higher education had multiple stakes, various fronts, and many complex turns. A full account would have to contend with a range of issues: curricular revision, speech codes, affirmative action, the backlash against "theory," and the fiscal crisis facing the humanities.[45] It would also have to account for the manifold alliances and antagonisms that developed in and between the cultural left and cultural right. This was especially marked in conflicts about the status and principle of "common culture."[46] I do not want to involve myself deeply in these issues; my aim is not to examine the culture war as such, but to read the colorization debate through certain of its dominant themes. In each case, canonicity—broadly understood as the formalization of knowledge and cultural literacy in key, or "classic," texts—became a site of critical contestation: an issue that revealed a mutual resistance to challenges brought to bear on the basis and determination of identity, inheritance, community, and culture.

There are common themes in the colorization and multicultural debates, despite their difference in political scale. Both engaged rhetoric of opposition based upon the stability of tradition, the need to maintain aesthetic value, the preservation of authenticity against fakery, the impositions of the marketplace, and the continuities of cultural and historical transmission. I do not want to bludgeon the similarities between quite different types of culture war, but each debate was distinguished by a narrative of decline. Nostalgia became an idiom of cultural complaint for the left as much as the right, an undertone extending itself in debates that, while separate, emerged in the same cultural moment. Colorization may have been local and slight compared with multiculturalism, which has become embracing and pivotal, but the discourse opposing them both was energized and thickened by a concept of loss advanced by conservatives *and* liberals. While fighting different enemies—left-wing "thought police" in one case and big business in the other—each used similar basic terms. Cultural manifestations in education and popular culture—call them postmodern, if you like—were seen to undermine the systems of meaning that give order and unity to American tradition and, with it, national identity.

NOSTALGIA

The allure of nostalgia became an emotive issue that cut across conventional political demarcations in the late 1980s and early 1990s. If similar rhetorical modes were marshaled in the colorization and multicultural debates, these were figured around battles for cultural authority waged by right and left, what became struggles over the guardianship of taste and the protection of tradition. With certitudes of artistic value and cultural identity coming under increasing pressure, liberal and conservative factions sought to affirm a stable, authentic heritage inscribed within "legitimate" forms of cultural representation. Raising issues of cultural distinction, each debate can demonstrate the way in which intellectuals and tastemakers of the left and right have mutually conceived the public as cultural dupes, in danger of being cretinized without the proper recognition and regulation of "timeless" cultural value. Nostalgia was embroiled in attempts to "reclaim" cultural heritage, a process of rescuing the stupefied public from both cultural fragmentation and their own ignorance. Michael Schudson writes: "Defending the purity of the 'classic' is as often an assertion of the privileged stance of a professional group defending its turf as it is a selfless allegiance to art."[47] So it can be said of the nostalgic defenders of authenticity, classicism, and heritage in specific culture-war debates of the late 1980s and early 1990s.

The anticolorization campaign was arguably structured by two forms of nostalgia, buried within the legal contestation of moral rights: nostalgia for authenticity and the value attached to authentic nostalgia. It is here that one can relate the colorization debate more directly to the status and meaning ascribed to the black-and-white image. In one sense, the debate demonstrates the strategic validation of black and white as a mode of temporality and authenticity. At another level, the colorization controversy affords a precise illustration of the way that monochrome became discursively entwined with negotiations of American identity. If colorization can demonstrate the aesthetic politics of "black-and-white-ness," it is in the way that monochrome became the crux of, and point of defense within, a struggle to affirm visual meaning and national memory at a time when both seemed under threat.

Nostalgia for authenticity can be witnessed in a cultural moment where authorship and originality have been profoundly challenged by the capacity of new technologies to refigure cultural texts. Colorized movies were seen and discussed by the anticolorization lobby in a way that made them akin to the postmodern retro film described by Jean Baudrillard—what he defines as being "to those one knew what the android is to man: marvelous artifacts, without weakness, pleasing simulacra that lack only the imaginary, and the hallucination inherent to cinema."[48] Color conversion was seen to create a depthless artifice with little or no artistic worth. While Color Systems Technology declared that scrupulous efforts were made by research teams to achieve "authentic" color values (unlike Colorization Inc., which tried to make films look as modern as possible), any alteration to the color and tone of the black-and-white original was seen by the anticolorization lobby as an act of "destructive reinterpretation."[49] Authenticity was a black-and-white issue, and resistance came in righteous tones that called the coloring process a moral abomination.

Andreas Huyssen has written: "It is no coincidence that the 'work of art' has come back in this age of unlimited reproduction, dissemination, and simulation. The desire for history, for the original work of art, the original museal object is parallel, I think, to the desire for the real at a time when reality eludes us more than ever."[50] The status of the black-and-white image in the colorization debate was linked, in one sense, to the recovery of aura in a world of media spectacle and technological simulation. This was not without its political ramifications, however. In defending the integrity of the work of art, the anticolorization campaign absorbed binary metaphors of (modernist) depth and (postmodernist) surface in rhetoric that sought to affirm traditional modes of critical evaluation, as well as historical understanding. Privileging the creative originality and historical temporality of monochrome "depth," set against the textual hybridity and amnesiac spatiality of colorized "surface," the anticolorization lobby appealed to a principle of timeless value, directorial genius, and, by implication, to the forms of critical authority that can designate their manifestation in "classic" texts.[51]

The callous disregard for the work of art in the colorization process was seen to have grave implications for authorship and creativity, but also—and perhaps more profoundly—for heritage and popular memory. The value attached to "authentic nostalgia" put monochrome in direct relation to the question, and protection, of historicity and cultural identity. If the past must be represented in order to be remembered, colorization was seen by its detractors to have serious implications for cultural memory. By erasing the authentic artifact (the original representation), it was thought that the contours of film history would be mapped differently, or at least modified within the recall of the nation's cinematic sensibilities. Andreas Huyssen has asked what a postmodern memory would look like in a world where the technological media affect the way we perceive and live our temporality.[52] For those suspicious of meddlesome digital effects, it no doubt looked very much like a colorized film: false, crude, and inherently amnesiac.

The colorized film is a digital product of algorithms stored in computer memory; it is simultaneously of the past *and* the present. The concept of authentic nostalgia was a critical response to the presentness of the "new classic," and to the fear that memory is being short-changed in the reign of postmodern simulacra. Woody Allen wrote: "Part of the artistic experience of seeing old Ginger Rogers and Fred Astaire movies is the period quality: the black-and-white photography gives it its entire feel."[53] The digital alteration of a movie's color was seen as destroying the intrinsic visual pastness that might register a film within cultural memory; colorization was a contrivance that made it impossible for the work of art to be watched with the appropriate degree of visual nostalgia that might locate it within historical time. Theoretically, this view corresponds at some level with Fredric Jameson's anxiety about the profound waning or blockage of historicity in postmodern culture. Like the "nostalgia film" that Jameson famously treats, colorized movies would provide further evidence of what he suggests to be an incumbent memory crisis.[54] In appealing to authentic nostalgia, the anticolorization lobby tried to revitalize a sense of the past unthreatened by the mutability of postmodern simulacra. "Authentic nostalgia" was valued against the specter of postmodern forgetting. As a concept, it underwrote liberal-left complaints about the *ahistorical* experience of the colorized film, a crude cinematic spectacle caught symptomatically between the very words "new" and "classic."

Ted Turner believed that the "new classic" would maintain memory in alternative, more contemporary, forms, affirming that "consumers have voted, they like it."[55] Popular endorsement did not stem the fears of the anticolorization lobby, however. The "sugar-water" of colorization, as John Huston put it, only proved that the public were lacking in the critical capacities that might safeguard creative authenticity and preserve the integrity of national tradition. As a mode of authenticity and temporality, monochrome became the rhetorical locus of a campaign that sought, in the late 1980s and early 1990s, to establish the archival essence of American (film) heritage. The nonrepresentational status of "black and whiteness" was at the focal center of attempts to arrest meaning within, and stabilize identity against, the critical and cultural indeterminacy of postmodernism and its deconstructive impact on aesthetic values and national memory.

THE CULTURE WAR

The anticolorization campaign set out to resist postmodern configurations of cultural transmission whereby artifacts of history can be digitally altered and made to circulate in ways that undermine conceptions of authorship, originality, and fixed tradition. The debate over multiculturalism, while more varied and consequential and generating higher degrees of political venom, raised similar issues. This was notable in what conservatives saw as the crumbling foundations of Western cultural heritage in higher education and the humanities. It has not been my intention either to condone or to condemn colorization. Instead, I have sought to illustrate some of the discursive continuities between two debates that emerged in the same cultural moment and engaged left and right quite differently but with similar presuppositions. In each case, narratives of decline were mobilized, barbarians identified, and tradition sanctified.

While the anticolorization lobby was predominantly liberal in orientation, this should not imply that conservatives were, by implication, *for* the whole process. Considering the regimes of taste that organize and structure symbolic domination in the cultural field, Andrew Ross has discussed a mutual distrust between intellectuals and tastemakers of the left and right regarding "new technologies and the monstrous mass cultures to which they give birth." He says:

For the right this demonology takes the form of a brutally mechanical possession of the last cultural outposts of high civilization. For the left, the specter of hypercapitalism is omnipresent, looming up behind the cretinizing, stupor-inducing cultural forms produced by a dying system in the last throes of economic and ideological reorganization. Both strains of thought share a generally pessimistic view of cultural decline hurried on by the forces of technological rationality or determinism.[56]

Colorization was a new digital technology sponsored by corporate finance; the "new classic" was industrially produced to make profit, a cultural form that for many compromised the borders of legitimate taste and fostered the idiocy of its popular audience. As a cultural and aesthetic issue, colorization received condemnation from left and right alike. It was in terms of ownership and property rights that colorization became more specifically mapped (although not specifically argued) as a liberal/Democrat crusade. Even the black-and-white film star Ronald Reagan could not, in his new role as president, be moved to intervene and save the monochrome classic if it meant doing so at the expense of business principles and copyright law.

My interest in this chapter has been the means by which liberal criticism of colorization arguably helped to strengthen the legitimacy of right-wing discourse in its fetishizing of "traditional" knowledge and culture. Authenticity, canonicity, and tradition became vital to right-wing rhetoric in its attack on superficiality, ignorance, and politicization within American universities. These same terms were also used by the anticolorization lobby, however. Before multiculturalism ever became a national issue, but at the same moment that conservatives were gathering steam, the defense of cultural heritage was being fought by the right *and* by the left. At the end of the 1980s, nostalgia developed a polemical currency in two separate debates. In each case, this was linked to issues of value, taste, and cultural heritage. Opposition to both colorization and multiculturalism was, in part, the result of technological and intellectual transformations that disturbed values and identities inscribed in a selection of "untouchable" texts. By rehearsing a particular common sense about the preservation of heritage and the status of the classic, the anticolorization campaign fortified principles of cultural authority threatened by new postmodern connections between art, evaluation, education, and the archive. I would argue that in their rhetorical nostalgia for the work of art and consensual cultural heritage, the liberal-left helped to articulate themes that would reverberate powerfully in right-wing bromides against the "therapeutic" and "separatist" tendencies of multiculturalism. Effectively, the anticolorization lobby enriched a discourse that advanced the vitality of traditional knowledge, the value of aesthetic taste, and the virtue of cultural inheritance: a discourse that would be developed, defined, and deployed strategically by the right in the hegemonic "war of positions" waged to control the terms of the multicultural debate.

A politics of nostalgia is commonly associated with conservative critique. This can understate, however, the degree to which it has shaped liberal anxieties about a jeopardized cultural heritage. The threat to historical transmission, whether by tenured radical or corporate parvenu, has been met with resistance in major *and* minor culture wars, producing oppositional configurations with a shared investment in principles of authenticity, historical continuity, and consensual heritage. Rhetoric has developed *across political lines*, roping off and defending versions of cultural heritage. This may feed different debates with different discursive histories—namely, the critique of mass culture and the contested function of the university—but in the late 1980s concerns sharpened, for liberals and for conservatives, upon a similar basic fear: the dawning possibility that in being exposed to odious forms of PC (popular culture, political correctness, postmodern critique), American students and consumers were becoming—to use politically correct argot—"culturally challenged."

CODA

Critics from Todd Gitlin to Nikhal Pal Singh have discussed the origins and context of the culture wars shaping public discourse in the late 1980s and early 1990s.[57] Although providing different political interpretations, they both point to the political and economic, as well as specifically cultural, histories informing the struggles over multiculturalism. The culture wars were a symptom of a "crisis" of national identity brought about by a confluence of transformations associated with capitalist postmodernity—from transnational political and economic restructuring to an emergent politics of difference, from the revolution in information technology and its impact on the circulation of information and knowledge to the redefinition of international commitments in the wake of the cold war. While the culture war debates had run their course by the middle of the 1990s, including the jeremiads on the compromised nature of American tradition, the need to articulate a coherent sense of nation and national memory remained. If the desire to stabilize the configuration and perceived transmission of American cultural identity was a defining aspect of hegemonic memory politics in the 1990s, "black-and-whiteness" became a significant visual discourse in this context. Monochrome is a style. It is also a matter of taste. It performed cultural work in the 1990s, however, by helping to aestheticize a sense of archival history and memory for a culture whose ideologies of national coherence had come under particular, and intensified, strain.

NOTES

1. Quoted from a promotional videotape made by the Hal Roach Studios, cited in "Homevideo," *Cineaste,* 2 (1986): 56.

2. William Bennett, *To Reclaim a Legacy: A Report on the Humanities in Higher Education* (Washington DC: National Endowment for the Humanities, 1984).

3. Todd Gitlin, "The Rise of Identity Politics," in Michael Bérubé and Cary Nelson, eds., *Higher Education Under Fire: Politics, Economics, and the Crisis of the Humanities* (New York: Routledge, 1994): 311.

4. Andrew Ross, *No Respect: Intellectuals and Popular Culture* (New York: Routledge, 1989): 211. There are, of course, interests at stake with any sense of loss. Gitlin has been accused of nostalgia by critics who point to his own threatened authority as a white male politico, someone who resists the challenge made by a new generation of academics and who, himself, can afford to disclaim identity politics because there is little personally at stake. Gitlin denies the charge of nostalgia, suggesting that there is no golden age to which he aspires or which he seeks to recover. This does not explain away the narrative of decline in his work, however, largely figured around the

waning political capacities of an effective left, matched with a certain wistfulness for a spirit of change associated with, or remembered in, the early New Left.

5. Joan Wallach Scott, "The Campaign Against Political Correctness: What's Really at Stake," in Jeffrey Williams, ed., *PC Wars: Politics and Theory in the Academy* (New York: Routledge, 1995): 23–43.

6. Michael Bérubé, *Public Access: Literary Theory and American Cultural Politics* (London: Verso, 1994): 127.

7. For a comprehensive treatment of the legal turns of the colorization debate, see Stuart Klawans, "Colorization: Rose-Tinted Spectacles," in Mark Crispin Miller, ed., *Seeing through Movies* (New York: Pantheon, 1990): 150–185; see also Craig A. Wagner, "Motion Picture Colorization, Authenticity and the Elusive Moral Right," *New York University Law Review*, 64, no. 3 (1989): 628–725.

8. Greg Dawson, "Ted Turner" (interview), *American Film*, 14, no. 4 (1989): 39.

9. Charles R. Acland, "Tampering with the Inventory: Colorization and Popular Histories," *Wide Angle*, 12, no. 2 (1990): 15.

10. Bill Carter, "Colorized Films Losing Appeal," *New York Times*, 19 December 1994: 10.

11. On the issue of digital technology in film see Stephen Prince, "True Lies: Perceptual Realism, Digital Images and Film Theory," *Film Quarterly*, 49, no. 3 (1996): 27–37.

12. Flo Leibowitz, "Movie Colorization and the Expression of Mood," *British Journal of Aesthetics*, 49, no. 4 (1991): 363–365.

13. James Naremore, *More Than Night: Film Noir in Its Contexts* (Berkeley, CA: University of California Press, 1998): 196.

14. Woody Allen, "True Colors," *New York Review of Books*, 13 August 1987: 13.

15. Cited in Klawans, "Colorization": 160.

16. Cited in David Wilson, "Colour Box," *Sight and Sound*, 55, no. 3 (1986): 147.

17. Michael Schudson, "Colorization and Authenticity," *Society*, 24, no. 4 (1987): 18.

18. For a useful summary of the moral and philosophical dimensions of this issue, see Julie Van Camp, "The Colorization Controversy," *The Journal of Value Inquiry*, 29, no. 4 (1995): 447–468.

19. Mathew Lee and Nora Lee, "Are Filmmakers Artists? Do They Have Rights?" *American Cinematographer*, 72, no. 11 (1991): 112.

20. Cited in Dawson, "Ted Turner": 52.

21. Cited in Wagner, "Motion Picture Colorization": 644, fn. 91.

22. Ava Collins, "Intellectuals, Power and Quality Television," *Cultural Studies*, 7, no. 1 (1993): 29.

23. Collins, "Intellectuals, Power": 34.

24. Walter Benjamin, *Illuminations*, trans. Harry Zohn (London: Fontana Press, 1992): 211–244.

25. Acland, "Tampering with the Inventory": 16.

26. In 1988, a French trial court permanently banned the television broadcast of a colorized version of John Huston's *The Asphalt Jungle* on the basis that it would cause "unmendable and intolerable damage" to the integrity of the work and would therefore compromise Huston's moral rights.

27. Huston is cited in Klawans, "Colorization": 165; Zinnemann is cited in Wilson, "Colour Box": 147; Wrather is cited in Susan Linfield, "The Color of Money," *American Film*, 12, no. 4 (1987): 35.

28. Cited in Wagner, "Motion Picture Colorization": 631, fn. 22.

29. John Huston is cited in Lee and Lee, "Are Filmmakers Artists?" 112; George Will, "Literary Politics," _Newsweek,_ 22 April 1991: 72.

30. Since 1981 rehabilitation tax credits had given incentives to investors to channel money into historic preservation. This changed when the right of ownership was championed by conservatives who gave support to a principle of compensation for those whose land and/or property encountered regulation in the name of preservation. Financial entitlements were established for those unable to realize the worth of their assets. For a good account, see Mike Wallace, _Mickey Mouse History and Other Essays on American Memory_ (Philadelphia, PA: Temple University Press, 1996): 224–246.

31. Klawans, "Colorization: Rose-Tinted Spectacles": 182–184.

32. Barbara Kirschenblatt-Gimblett, _Destination Culture: Tourism, Museums and Heritage_ (Berkeley, CA: University of California Press, 1998): 149.

33. Cited in Wagner, "Motion Picture Colorization": 645, fn. 95.

34. Arthur Schlesinger Jr, _The Disuniting of America: Reflections on a Multicultural Society_ (New York: W. W. Norton, 1991): 48. For a perceptive critique of _Disuniting,_ see Bérubé, _Public Access,_ 225–241.

35. Jerrold Levinson, "Colourization Ill-Defended," _British Journal of Aesthetics,_ 30, no. 1 (1990): 65.

36. Allan Bloom, _The Closing of the American Mind_ (New York: Simon and Schuster, 1987): 48.

37. Frederick Buell, "National Postnationalism: Globalist Discourse in Contemporary American Culture," _American Quarterly,_ 50, no. 3 (1998): 555.

38. See Avery F. Gordon and Christopher Newfield, eds., _Mapping Multiculturalism_ (Minneapolis, MN: University of Minnesota Press, 1996).

39. Cited in Wagner, "Motion Picture Colorization": 645, fn. 95.

40. Michael Dempsey, "Colorization," _Film Quarterly,_ 40, no. 2 (1986–87): 3.

41. These comments were made, respectively, by Eugene Genovese in _The New Republic_ and by an editorial in the _Chicago Tribune._ They are cited in two perceptive articles on the constitution of political correctness as a media issue: Jim Neilson, "The Great PC Scare: Tyrannies of the Left, Rhetoric of the Right," in Jeffrey Williams, ed., _PC Wars: Politics and Theory in the Academy_ (New York: Routledge, 1995): 60–89; and Michael Bérubé, "Public Image Limited: Political Correctness and the Media's Big Lie," _Village Voice,_ 18 June 1991: 31–37.

42. The cover of the January 1989 edition of _American Film_ shows Turner dressed as Indiana Jones, wearing a stetson and sporting a rifle.

43. See Bill Readings, _The University in Ruins_ (Cambridge, MA: Harvard University Press, 1996).

44. Ien Ang, _Living Room Wars: Rethinking Media Audiences for a Postmodern World_ (London: Routledge, 1996): 144.

45. Two valuable collections dealing with many of these issues are Jeffrey Williams, ed., _PC Wars: Politics and Theory in the Academy_ (New York: Routledge, 1995); and Michael Bérubé and Cary Nelson, eds., _Higher Education Under Fire: Politics, Economics and the Crisis of the Humanities_ (New York: Routledge, 1994).

46. Conservatives like Roger Kimball and Diane Ravitch argued that common culture should be valued against the threat posed by an incipient, and unruly, tribalism in American life. Writing from a different political position, Todd Gitlin also warned against "American-style tribalism." Lambasting the multicultural attack on commonality, he made attempts to rescue the political and civic legacies of the Enlightenment from antifoundational theory and the praxis of marginality. In 1992,

Gitlin wrote: "Authentic liberals have good reason to worry that the elevation of 'difference' to a first principle is undermining everyone's capacity to see, or change, the world as a whole." Typical of much liberal-left critique hostile to multiculturalism, Gitlin plays upon a concept of "authentic" political leftism, set against the vogueish and critically facile radicalism of identity politics. In contradistinction to those who see cultural commonality as a social imperative and politically strategic necessity, left-wing critics such as Janice Radway and Joan Scott have challenged the dominant set of assumptions, values, and beliefs that underlie prescriptions of a national and cultural "commons." Radway argues that "the future of a diverse population will depend on the capacity to articulate a conception of shared public culture that will both depend upon difference and protect and celebrate it as well." Scott frames this within a reconfigured concept of community (and commonality) that moves away from models of consensus and that recognizes that "conflict and contest are inherent in communities of difference." See Roger Kimball, *Tenured Radicals: How Politics Has Corrupted Our Higher Education* (New York: Routledge, 1991); Diane Ravitch, "The War on Standards," *Partisan Review,* 60 (1993): 685–692; Todd Gitlin, "On the Virtues of a Loose Canon," in Patricia Aufderheide, ed., *Beyond PC: Towards a Politics of Understanding* (St. Paul, MN: Graywolf Press, 1992): 185–190; Janice Radway, "What's in a Name? Presidential Address to the American Studies Association, 20 November, 1998," *American Quarterly,* 51, no. 1 (1999): 1–32; and Scott, "The Campaign Against Political Correctness": 22–43.

47. Schudson, "Colorization and Authenticity": 19.

48. Jean Baudrillard, *Simulacra and Simulations,* trans., Sheila Faria Glaser (Ann Arbor, MI: University of Michigan Press, 1994): 45.

49. Lee and Lee, "Are Filmmakers Artists?": 112.

50. Andreas Huyssen, *Twilight Memories: Marking Time in a Culture of Amnesia* (New York: Routledge, 1995): 101.

51. For a discussion of the depth/surface metaphor and its problematization in postmodern culture, see Philip E. Simmons, *Deep Surfaces: Mass Culture and History in Postmodern American Fiction* (Athens, GA: University of Georgia Press, 1997): 1–21.

52. Huyssen, *Twilight Memories*: 101.

53. Allen, "True Colors": 38.

54. Fredric Jameson, *Postmodernism, or, The Cultural Logic of Late Capitalism* (London: Verso, 1991): 21. In contrast to Jameson, Linda Hutcheon argues that postmodernism "does not deny the existence of the past: it does question whether we can *know* that past other than through its textualized remains." Underpinning her argument is the view that the recycling, hybridizing (perhaps even the colorizing) of past styles need not prefigure a postmodern "crisis of historicity" but may instead suggest a discursive rearticulation of the past. Linda Hutcheon, "Beginning to Theorize Postmodernism," *Textual Practice*, 1, no. 1 (1987): 10–33.

55. Cited in Dawson, "Ted Turner": 39.

56. Ross, *No Respect*: 209.

57. Todd Gitlin, *The Twilight of Common Dreams: Why America is Wracked by Culture Wars* (New York: Henry Holt, 1995); Nikhal Pal Singh, "Culture/Wars: Recoding Empire in an Age of Democracy," *American Quarterly,* 50, no. 3 (1998): 471–522.

Conclusion:
Visual / Global / Nostalgia

Create a timeless memory . . . next time why not try a Black & White
film in your camera.

Advertisement for Ilford film processing, 1995

Moving into the twenty-first century, the black-and-white image remains a popular visual style, although there are signs that its stock is
beginning to diminish. While home improvement wholesalers appear
less disposed toward black and white in their current picture catalogues,
fashion advertising has rediscovered color promotion, demonstrated not
least by the transition of Giorgio Armani in the late 1990s—the stalwart
of black-and-white fashion advertising—to color campaigns.[1] When, in
1998, *Pleasantville* dramatized the incursions of a color present into a
black-and-white past, creating a narrative based on the cultural apothe-
osis, "not everything is as simple as black and white," the temporal and
authenticity effects of monochrome seemed distinctly lackluster. Whereas the colorization debate had fetishized the black-and-white image in
the face of digital manipulation and the shock of technological excess,
Pleasantville helped demonstrate the cultural domestication of coloring
technique and the return of monochrome to visual associations with an
arcane past. Black and white retains a special currency in punctuating
the norms of visual reception. Arguably, however, it no longer enjoys
the heightened popularity and visual cachet that it experienced for
much of the 1990s: a cultural moment that, alongside and perhaps in
response to new digital capacities for transforming and circulating

(color) imagery, produced a particular impetus toward idioms of authenticity and time.

This book is not, in any strict sense, *about* the black-and-white image. Instead, it has been concerned with a specific discourse of "black-and-whiteness" that emerged in the 1990s, a visual mode that became linked to questions about the construction, representation and preservation of American national memory. Of course, the use and popularity of the black-and-white image is not specific to the United States; monochrome was used in the 1990s within cultural forms that have a global, rather than a purely domestic, reach. It would be wrong to associate the resurgence of black-and-white imagery with American visual culture alone. Monochrome has been taken up and made popular in a range of national contexts and visual markets; the figuration of stylized temporality has become something of a transnational trend. This has a lot to do with the international growth of, and the patterning of taste by, commercial image industries. However, the disposition toward modes of aestheticized memory can also be given a wider cultural significance.

Writing about the reconceptualization of the past in contemporary life, Andreas Huyssen suggests that the new obsession with history and memory may indicate a temporal shift in the (Western) utopian imagination. He suggests that since the 1970s it has moved from a futuristic pole based on narratives of emancipation and liberation, toward the pole of remembrance. This has been experienced "not in the sense of a radical turn, but in the sense of a shift of emphasis."[2] Huyssen's theory is based on assumptions about the breakdown of attitudes, beliefs, values, and meanings organized around notions of progressive history.[3] It is also argued in relation to the threat posed to memory and the temporal order by new technologies of electronic communication. While Huyssen's thesis runs the risk of reducing all evocations of the past to a postmodern condition distinguished by the need and desire to confront the exhaustion of once commanding metanarratives, and the fevered impulse to somehow "mark time," it does raise the important question of *legitimation*, of the means by which national/cultural ideologies have come to be sustained and authorized in contemporary life.

If the past has taken on a broad discursive significance in the way that cultural identities are forged, the resurgence of the black-and-white image in American media culture can be related to particular negotiations of nation in the 1990s. From the end of the cold war and the inflated discussions about the "end of history" to the emergence of the culture war and its numerous debates about morality, memory, history, and identity, the 1990s witnessed a particular struggle to define the terms of American cultural nationalism. Under particular pressure from the forces of geopolitical change, the challenge of multiculturalism, and the global restructuring of capital were tenets of a liberal consensus that has based its authority in the postwar period on ideas of common culture, capital growth, and the integrity of the nation state, bound within frameworks of social and political exceptionalism. In historical and discursive terms, the United States was forced in the 1990s to realize and confront its place as a node within an enveloping, and uncertain, transnational order. Writing of "the frictions and disjunctions brought about by the slow but inexorable erosion of national formations," Paul Giles suggests that transnationalism can be seen as a "highly contested situation where traditional identities find themselves traversed by the forces of difference."[4] Seen in this context, the American culture wars of the early decade were a specific reaction against the perceived evisceration of national coherence by the pressures of difference and the "attack" on traditional determinants of cultural value and authenticity.

If the early 1990s were marked by a rhetoric of disuniting and crisis and a proliferation of discourses about lost national foundations, Frederick Buell suggests that, by the end of the decade, U.S. culture had become marked by attempts to "recreate official culture out of the very heterogeneity and heteroglossia that were supposedly undoing it."[5] Nationalism, in other words, was reconstituted in ways that came to embrace and accommodate transformations that had once seemed unsettling to the moorings of American identity. While the discursive context of national identity formation changed during the 1990s, influenced by America's growing engagement in the emerging order of neoliberal globalization, the concept of cultural nationalism hardly disappeared. Indeed, while the idea of national culture has become more problematic in a globalized sphere, it still retains a long and potent half-life.[6] Arguably, the potency of this half-life helped to contribute to the context and conditions for a media discourse of "black-and-whiteness" in the 1990s; it established a provision for the aestheticization of American memory in a range of cultural media and popular forms.

In accounting for the resurgence of memory in contemporary culture, Susannah Radstone suggests that memory has become a site within which particular cultural equivocations are expressed. Rather than read memory diagnostically, as a utopian or a dystopian "syndrome" of late modernism, she understands it as a locus through which specific doubts and uncertainties are worked through.[7] In political terms, this process of working through can be seen to involve particular struggles of hegemonic legitimation. Specifically, and with regard to the United States, memory has come to bear upon the ambivalence attending to the conceptual location of national identity within the ideological, economic, and media flows/configurations of the global cultural economy. In a period distinguished by what Arjun Appadurai calls the "peculiar chronicities"[8] of late capitalism—meaning in this case a juncture where images of the past are no longer, or necessarily, attached to resolute or territorialized experiences of national memory—the contingency of the remembered past has been met with a counterimpulse to stabilize memory's particular look and feel. On these terms, monochrome was taken up in the 1990s in attempts to consolidate ideas (and images) of permanence, stability, cultural foundations. In one sense, the black-and-white image served to arrest meaning within, and suggest something outside, an image world of color simulacra. Read politically, however, and judged in specific media contexts, monochrome also helped to infuse particular constructions of national and cultural identity with archival legitimacy.

Discussing media representations of America by U.S.-based multinational media corporations, Lawrence Grossberg suggests that a struggle is being waged "over the construction of the United States and its place in the world. This is a struggle not merely over identity, but over its spaces and territories, a struggle to remap the United States, its population and capital."[9] Inferred here are new configurations of identity and hegemony that are emerging in the spatial matrix of global capitalism, *transcending* national interests and imperatives.[10] It would, of course, be wrong to suggest that globalization somehow diminishes American national influence and power. If global processes materialize in national territories, the United States is a key site of economic, military, legal, cultural, and ideological capital. However, it would also be wrong to *conflate* globalization with the exertions of America, or to suggest that U.S. national culture and society has not been altered by its place and engagement in the global sphere. In cultural terms, the 1990s can be seen as the beginning of an unfinished period where the determinants of American nationhood came to be reconfigured in light of changes brought about by an emerging transnational juncture.

As the United States moves into the twenty-first century, questions of cultural nationalism have become, and will continue to be, challenged in and by the global sphere. While America is undoubtedly a key geopolitical player in what Saskia Sassen calls the "new geography of power,"[11] the internal coherence and global influence of the United States is far from assured or unchallenged. In a material sense, transnational capitalism has become far less dependent on the nation as a legal, political, and cultural entity. While capitalist modes of production have long operated below and across national sites, the nation-state has assumed a far less significant position as capitalist activity has become more mobile and global. This has produced a situation of increasing geocultural complexity and interaction, involving rapid alterations in the circulation of knowledge and in the narratives of history that support national identities and ideologies. If the United States has been compelled to renegotiate the basis of its domestic coherence and international influence, memory has become a strategic site for the articulation of national and postnational identity; it has been mobilized by dominant power forma-tions attempting to recoup and reaestheticize a sense of continuity in the face of cultural and ideological change.

If it is true that when economic capital seeks flight, cultural capital seeks stable moorings, I would suggest that monochrome became part of cultural attempts to address transitions in the status and authority of national identity. The black-and-white image performed cultural work in the 1990s by shoring up, and helping to incorporate difference within, an aestheticized rendering of a national and postnational past. As a visual nostalgia mode, the black-and-white image was used affectively in the dominant media to stabilize history and memory against the vicissitudes of a heterogeneous, multivocal, and increasingly decentered order. While not specific to the visual culture of the United States, "black-and-whiteness" was nevertheless bound discursively in the at-tempt to legitimate a past that, in both representational and nonrepre-sentational terms, made efforts to stabilize archival "America" in the imaginary landscapes of a transforming world. It remains to be seen how and to what extent the idea of timeless memory, and the broader aestheticization of national memory, can perform a legitimating func-tion in a period where traditional regimes of temporality and formations of nationalism continue to be radically compromised.

NOTES

1. See Colin McDowell, "A Man for All Seasons," *Sunday Times Magazine*, 25 July 1999: 13–16.

2. Andreas Huyssen, *Twilight Memories: Marking Time in a Culture of Amnesia* (New York: Routledge, 1995): 88.

3. This has been engendered by factors such as environmental disaster, the growth of unaccountable capitalism, seismic technological change, and the processes of decolonization and globalization. More specific to America, one could point to the erosion of a postwar liberal consensus that based its particular articulation of nation-hood upon ideas of exceptionalism, progress, political freedom, and social and eco-nomic opportunity—an erosion that was largely caused by divisions in the 1960s and 1970s based around the Vietnam war, economic crisis, and the rise of civil rights and the new social movements.

4. Paul Giles, "Foreword," in Will Kaufman and Heidi Slettedaht Macpherson, eds. *Transatlantic Studies* (Lanham, NY: University Press of America, 2000): x.

5. Frederick Buell, "Nationalist Postnationalism: Globalist Discourse in Contem-porary American Culture," *American Quarterly*, 50, no. 3 (1998): 552.

6. This argument is made by David Morley and Kevin Robins in *Spaces of Identity: Global Media, Electronic Landscapes and Cultural Boundaries* (London: Routledge, 1995): 108.

7. Susannah Radstone, "Working with Memory," in Susannah Radstone, ed. *Memory and Methodology* (Oxford: Berg, 2000): 1–22.

8. Arjun Appadurai, "Disjuncture and Difference in the Global Cultural Econo-my," *Public Culture*, 2, no. 2 (1990): 1–24.

9. Lawrence Grossberg, *Dancing in Spite of Myself: Essays on Popular Culture* (Durham, NC: Duke University Press, 1997): 254.

10. Jonathan Friedman relates this situation to the relative decline of Western and U.S. hegemony, based around the fragmentation of old territorial units and the simultaneous formation of global elites enthralled by neoliberal ideologies and "cosmopolitan internationalism. See Jonathan Friedman, "Americans Again, or the New Age of Imperial Reason?" *Theory, Culture & Society*, 17, no. 1 (2000): 139–146.

11. Saskia Sassen, *Losing Control: Sovereignty in an Age of Globalization* (New York: Columbia University Press, 1996): xi.

Bibliography

Acland, Charles R. "Tampering with the Inventory: Colorization and Popular Histories." *Wide Angle,* 12, no. 2 (1990): 12–20.

Allen, Woody. "True Colors." *New York Review of Books,* 13 August 1987: 13.

Ang, Ien. *Living Room Wars: Rethinking Media Audiences for a Postmodern World.* London: Routledge, 1996.

Ansen, David. "Spielberg's Obsession." *Newsweek,* 21 December 1993: 43–46.

Anthony, Andrew. "There's One Good Thing about the Nineties." *Observer Review,* 14 July 1998: 5.

Appadurai, Arjun. "Disjuncture and Difference in the Global Cultural Economy." *Public Culture,* 2, no. 2 (1990): 1–24.

Arthur, Paul. "Jargons of Authenticity (Three American Moments)." In *Theorizing Documentary,* edited by Michael Renov. New York: Routledge, 1993: 108–134.

Barthes, Roland. *Image Music Text.* Trans. Stephen Heath. London: Fontana, 1977.

Barthes, Roland. *Camera Lucida.* Trans. Richard Howard. London: Vintage, 1993.

Bassin, Donna. "Maternal Subjectivity in the Culture of Nostalgia: Mourning and Melancholia." In *Representations of Motherhood,* edited by Donna Bassin. New Haven, CT: Yale University Press, 1994: 162–173.

Baudrillard, Jean. *Simulacra and Simulations.* Trans. Sheila Faria Glaser. Ann Arbor, MI: University of Michigan Press, 1994.

Bauman, Zygmunt. *Intimations of Postmodernity.* London: Routledge, 1992.

Becker, Jane S. *Selling Tradition: Appalachia and the Construction of an American Folk 1930–1940.* Chapel Hill, NC: North Carolina University Press, 1998.

Benjamin, Walter. *Illuminations*. Trans. Harry Zohn. London: Fontana, 1992.

Bennett, Laurence I. "It's Not Quite Over." *Time*, 2 November 1992: 32.

Bennett, Susan. *Performing Nostalgia: Shifting Shakespeare and the Contemporary Past*. London: Routledge, 1996.

Bennett, William. *To Reclaim a Legacy: A Report on the Humanities in Higher Education*. Washington, DC: National Endowment of the Humanities, 1984.

Bérubé, Michael. "Public Image Limited: Political Correctness and the Media's Big Lie." *Village Voice*, 18 June 1991: 31–37.

Bérubé, Michael. *Public Access: Literary Theory and American Cultural Politics*. London: Verso, 1994.

Bérubé, Michael, and Cary Nelson, eds. *Higher Education under Fire: Politics, Economics, and the Crisis of the Humanities*. New York: Routledge, 1994.

Berger, John. *Ways of Seeing*. London: BBC and Penguin, 1972.

Bloom, Allan. *The Closing of the American Mind: How Higher Education Has Failed Democracy and Impoverished the Souls of Today's Students*. New York: Simon and Schuster, 1987.

Blumenthal, Sidney, and Thomas Byrne, eds. *The Reagan Legacy*. New York: Pantheon Books, 1988.

Booth, Cathy. "Steve's Job: Restart Apple." *Time*, 18 August 1997: 34–40.

Boyer, M. Christine. *The City of Collective Memory: Its Historical Imagery and Architectural Entertainments*. Cambridge, MA: MIT Press, 1994.

Brett, David. *The Construction of Heritage*. Cork: Cork University Press, 1996.

Bruner, Edward. "Abraham Lincoln as Authentic Reproduction: A Critique of Postmodernism." *American Anthropologist*, 96, no. 2 (1994): 394–415.

Buell, Frederick. *National Culture and the New Global System*. Baltimore, MD: Johns Hopkins University Press, 1994.

Buell, Frederick. "Nationalist Postnationalism: Globalist Discourse in Contemporary American Culture." *American Quarterly*, 50, no. 3 (1998): 548–591.

Burgin, Victor, ed. *Thinking Photography*. London: Macmillan, 1982.

Burgoyne, Robert. *Film Nation: Hollywood Looks at U.S. History*. Minneapolis, MN: University of Minnesota Press, 1997.

Byers, Thomas B. "History Re-membered: *Forrest Gump*, Postfeminist Masculinity, and the Burial of the Counterculture." *Modern Fiction Studies*, 42, no. 2 (1996): 419–444.

Carmody, Deirdre. "One More Time: Magazine Is Reborn." *New York Times*, 13 April 1992: 1.

Carter, Bill. "Colorized Films Losing Appeal." *New York Times*, 19 December 1994: 10.

Cavell, Stanley. *The World Viewed: Reflections on the Ontology of Film*. New York: Viking Press, 1971.

Chalmers, Sarah. "Confessions of a New Age Man." *Daily Mail*, 3 April 1997: 39.

Chase, Malcolm, and Christopher Shaw. *The Imagined Past: History and Nostalgia*. Manchester, U.K.: Manchester University Press, 1989.

Cheney, Lynne. *American Memory: A Report on the Humanities in the Nation's Public Schools.* Washington, D.C.: National Endowment for the Humanities, 1987.

Clarke, Gerald. "The Meaning of Nostalgia." *Time,* 3 May 1971: 77.

Collins, Ava. "Intellectuals, Power and Quality Television." *Cultural Studies,* 7, no. 1 (1993): 28–45.

Collins, Jim. *Uncommon Cultures: Popular Culture and Post-Modernism.* New York: Routledge, 1989.

Collins, Jim, Hilary Radner, and Ava Preacher Collins, eds. *Film Theory Goes to the Movies.* New York: Routledge, 1993.

Collins, Jim. *Architectures of Excess: Cultural Life in the Information Age.* New York: Routledge, 1995.

Combs, James. *The Reagan Range: The Nostalgic Myth in American Politics.* Bowling Green, KY: Bowling Green State University Press, 1993.

Comor, Edward A. "The Re-Tooling of American Hegemony: U.S. Foreign Communications Policy from Free Flow to Free Trade." In *Media in a Global Context: A Reader,* edited by Annabelle Sreberny-Mohammadi, Dwayne Winseck, Jim McKenna, and Oliver Boyd-Barrett. London: Arnold, 1997: 194–206.

Cook, Richard. "Nostalgia." *Gramophone,* August 1997: 102–104.

Coontz, Stephanie. *The Way We Never Were: American Families and the Nostalgia Trap.* New York: Basic Books, 1992.

Cringley, Robert X. *Accidental Empires: How the Boys of Silicon Valley Made Their Millions, Battle Foreign Competition and Still Can't Get a Date.* London: Penguin, 1992.

Cruz, Jon. "From Farce to Tragedy: Reflections on the Reification of Race at Century's End." In *Mapping Multiculturalism,* edited by Avery F. Gordon and Christopher Newfield. Minneapolis, MN: University of Minnesota Press, 1996: 19–39.

Cubitt, Sean. *Timeshift: On Video Culture.* London: Routledge, 1991.

Cullen, Jim. *The Art of Democracy: A Concise History of Popular Culture in the United States.* New York: Monthly Review Press, 1996.

Davidov, Judith Fryer. *Women's Camera Work: Self/Body/Other in American Visual Culture.* Durham, NC: Duke University Press, 1998.

Davies, Jude, and Carol R. Smith. *Gender, Ethnicity and Sexuality in Contemporary American Film.* Keele, U.K.: Keele University Press, 1997.

Davis, Fred. *Yearning for Yesterday: A Sociology of Nostalgia.* New York: Free Press, 1979.

Dawson, Greg. "Ted Turner" interview. *American Film,* 14, no. 4 (1989): 36–39, 52.

Dempsey, Michael. "Colorization." *Film Quarterly,* 40, no. 2 (1986–87): 2–3.

Dionne, E. J., Jr. *Why Americans Hate Politics.* New York: Touchstone, 1991.

Doane, Janice, and Devon Hodges. *Nostalgia and Sexual Difference: The Resistance to Contemporary Feminism.* New York: Methuen, 1987.

Dyer, Richard. *Only Entertainment.* London: Routledge, 1992.

Dyer, Richard. *White.* London: Routledge, 1997.

Eco, Umberto. "Innovation and Repetition: Between Modern and Post-Modern Aesthetics." *Diogenes,* 114, no. 4 (1985): 161–184.

Edelman, Rob. "Homevideo." *Cineaste,* 12, no. 2 (1986): 56–57.

Elliot, Stuart. "New Apple Ad Lifts off from Disney's Land." *New York Times,* 29 September 1997: 13.

Erbach, Karen. "*Schindler's List* Finds Heroism Amidst Holocaust." *American Cinematographer,* January 1994: 48–57.

Fabre, Genevieve, and Robert O'Meally, eds. *History and Memory in African-American Culture.* New York: Oxford University Press, 1994.

Falk, Pasi. "The Benetton–Toscani Affair: Testing the Limits of Conventional Advertising," in *Buy This Book: Studies in Advertising and Consumption,* edited by Mica Nava. London: Routledge, 1997: 64–83.

Fensch, Thomas, ed. *Oskar Schindler and His List: The Man, the Book, the Film, the Holocaust and Its Survivors.* Middlebury, VT: Eriksson, 1995.

Fiske, John. *Power Plays, Power Works.* London: Verso, 1993.

Flinn, Caryl. *Strains of Utopia: Gender, Nostalgia and Hollywood Film Music.* Princeton, NJ: Princeton University Press, 1992.

Frank, Thomas. *The Conquest of Cool: Business Culture, Counterculture, and the Rise of Hip Consumption.* Chicago, IL: University of Chicago Press, 1997.

Frazer, June, and Timothy C. Frazer. "'Father Knows Best' and 'The Cosby Show': Nostalgia and Sitcom Tradition." *Journal of Popular Culture,* 27, no. 3 (1993): 163–174.

Freud, Sigmund. *On Metapsychology, Vol. II.* Trans. and ed. James Strachey. London: Penguin, 1991.

Friedlander, Saul. *Reflections of Nazism: An Essay on Kitsch and Death.* Bloomington, IN: Indiana University Press, 1993.

Frow, John. "Tourism and the Semiotics of Nostalgia." *October,* 57 (1991): 123–151.

Geary, James. "A Trip Down Memory's Lanes." *Time,* 5 May 1997: 43–49.

Giles, Paul. "Virtual Americas: The Internationalization of American Studies and the Ideology of Exchange." *American Quarterly,* 50, no. 3 (1998): 523–547.

Giles, Paul. "Foreword," in Will Kaufman and Heidi Slettedaht Macpherson, eds., *Transatlantic Studies.* Lanham, MD: University Press of America, 2000: ix–xi.

Giroux, Henry. "Post-Colonial University Pressures and Democratic Possibilities: Multiculturalism as Anti-Racist Pedagogy." *Cultural Critique,* 21 (1992): 5–40.

Gitlin, Todd. "On the Virtues of a Loose Canon." In *Beyond PC: Towards a Politics of Understanding,* edited by Patricia Aufderheide. St. Paul, MN: Graywolf Press, 1992: 185–190.

Gitlin, Todd. *The Sixties: Years of Hope, Days of Rage.* New York: Bantam Books, 1993.

Gitlin, Todd. "The Rise of Identity Politics: An Examination and Critique." In *Higher Education Under Fire: Politics, Economics, and the Crisis of the Humanities,* edited by Michael Bérubé and Cary Nelson. New York: Routledge, 1994: 308–325.

Gitlin, Todd. *The Twilight of Common Dreams: Why America Is Wracked by Culture Wars.* New York: Henry Holt, 1995.

Glaberson, William. "Newspapers Adoption of Color Nearly Complete." *New York Times*, 31 May 1993: 41.

Gomery, Douglas. *Shared Pleasures: A History of Movie Presentation in the United States*. Madison, WI: University of Wisconsin Press, 1992.

Gordon, Avery F., and Christopher Newfield, eds. *Mapping Multiculturalism*. Minneapolis, MN: University of Minnesota Press, 1996.

Graham, Allison. "History, Nostalgia and the Criminality of Popular Culture." *Georgia Review*, 38, no. 2 (1984): 348–364.

Grainge, P. "Global Media and the Ambiguities of Resonant Americanization," *American Studies International*, 39, no. 3 (2001): 4–24.

Grainge, P. "Remembering the American Century: Media Memory and the *Time* 100 List," *The International Journal of Cultural Studies*, 5, no. 2 (2002): 367–385.

Gray, Paul. "Whose America?" *Time*, 8 July 1991: 23–27.

Grossberg, Lawrence. *We Gotta Get Out of This Place: Popular Conservatism and Popular Culture*. New York: Routledge, 1992.

Grossberg, Lawrence. *Bringing It All Back Home: Essays on Cultural Studies*. Durham, NC: Duke University Press, 1997.

Grossberg, Lawrence. *Dancing in Spite of Myself: Essays on Popular Culture*. Durham, NC: Duke University Press, 1997.

Guimond, James. *American Photography and the American Dream*. Chapel Hill, NC: North Carolina University Press, 1991.

Halbwachs, Maurice. *On Collective Memory*. Trans. and ed. Lewis Coser. Chicago, IL: University of Chicago Press, 1992.

Hale, Grace Elizabeth, and Beth Loffreda. "Clocks for Seeing: Technologies of Memory, Popular Aesthetics and the Home Movie." *Radical History Review*, 66 (Fall 1996): 163–171.

Hall, Stuart. "Cultural Studies and Its Theoretical Legacies." In *Stuart Hall: Critical Dialogues in Cultural Studies*, edited by David Morley and Kuan-Hsing Chen. London: Routledge, 1995: 262–275.

Hamilton, "France and Frenchness in Post-War Humanist Photography." In *Representations: Cultural Representations and Signifying Practices*, edited by Stuart Hall. London: Sage, 1997: 75–150.

Hansen, Miriam Bratu. "*Schindler's List* Is Not *Shoah*: The Second Commandment, Popular Modernism and Public Memory." *Critical Inquiry*, 22 (Winter 1996): 292–312.

Harper, Ralph. *Nostalgia: An Existential Exploration of Longing and Fulfillment in the Modern Age*. Cleveland, OH: Press of the Western Reserve University, 1966.

Harvey, David. *The Condition of Postmodernity*. Oxford: Blackwell, 1989.

Havlena, William J., and Susan L. Holak. "The Good Old Days: Observations on Nostalgia and Its Role in Consumer Behaviour." *Advances in Consumer Research*, 18 1991: 323–329.

Hayward, Susan. *French National Cinema*. London: Routledge, 1993.

Herron, Jerry. "Homer Simpson's Eyes and the Culture of Late Nostalgia." *Representations*, 43 (Summer 1993): 1–26.

Hewison, Robert. *The Heritage Industry: Britain in a Climate of Decline*. London: Methuen, 1987.

Hobsbawm, Eric, and Terence Ranger, eds. *The Invention of Tradition.* Cambridge, U.K.: Cambridge University Press, 1983.

Hofer, Johannas. "Medical Dissertation on Nostalgia." Trans. Carolyn K. Anspach. *Bulletin of the History of Medicine,* 2 (1934): 376–391.

Hollard, Bernard. "New Nostalgia on Record." *Herald Tribune,* 4 June 1997: 12.

Horowitz, Sara R. "But Is It Good for the Jews? Spielberg's Schindler and the Aesthetics of Atrocity." In *Spielberg's Holocaust: Critical Perspectives on Schindler's List,* edited by Yosefa Loshitsky. Bloomington, IN: Indiana University Press, 1997: 119–140.

Hughes, Robert. "The Fraying of America." *Time,* 3 February 1992: 84–89.

Hughes, Robert. *Culture of Complaint: The Fraying of America.* New York: Oxford University Press, 1993.

Hunter, James Davison. *Culture Wars: The Struggle to Define America.* New York: Basic Books, 1991.

Hutcheon, Linda. "Beginning to Theorize Postmodernism." *Textual Practice,* 1, no. 1 (1987): 10–33.

Hutcheon, Linda. *A Poetics of Postmodernism: History, Theory, Fiction.* London: Routledge, 1988.

Hutcheon, Linda. *The Politics of Postmodernism.* London: Routledge, 1989.

Huyssen, Andreas. *After the Great Divide: Modernism, Mass Culture, Postmodernism.* London: Macmillan, 1986.

Huyssen, Andreas. *Twilight Memories: Marking Time in a Culture of Amnesia.* New York: Routledge, 1995.

"iMac Is Too Hot to Handle." *San Francisco Chronicle,* 8 September 1998: 6.

Isaacson, Walter. "Luce's Values—Then and Now." *Time,* 9 March 1998: 103.

Jacoby, Russell. *The Last Intellectuals: American Culture in the Age of Academe.* New York: Noonday Press, 1987.

Jameson, Fredric. "Walter Benjamin, or Nostalgia." *Salmagundi,* 10–11 (1969): 52–68.

Jameson, Fredric. "Periodizing the Sixties." In *The Sixties Without Apologies,* edited by Sonya Sayres et al. Minneapolis, MN: University of Minnesota Press, 1984: 178–209.

Jameson, Fredric. "Postmodernism and Consumer Society." In *Postmodernism and Its Discontents,* edited by E. Ann Kaplan. London: Verso, 1990: 13–29.

Jameson, Fredric. *Signatures of the Visible.* New York: Routledge, 1990.

Jameson, Fredric. *Postmodernism, or, The Cultural Logic of Late Capitalism.* London: Verso, 1991.

Jeffords, Susan. "Can Masculinity Be Terminated?" In *Screening the Male: Exploring Masculinities in Hollywood Cinema,* edited by Steven Cohen and Ina Rae Hark. London: Routledge, 1993: 245–260.

Jeffords, Susan. "The Big Switch: Hollywood Masculinity in the Nineties." In *Film Theory Goes to the Movies,* edited by Jim Collins, Hilary Radner and Ava Preacher Collins. New York: Routledge, 1993: 196–208.

Jenkins, Keith, ed. *The Postmodern History Reader.* London: Routledge, 1997.

Kammen, Michael. *Mystic Chords of Memory: The Transformation of Tradition in American Culture.* New York: Vintage, 1993.

Kammen, Michael. *In the Past Lane: Historical Perspectives on American Culture.* New York: Oxford University Press, 1997.

Kaplan, Amy, and Donald E. Pease, eds. *Cultures of United States Imperialism.* Durham, NC: Duke University Press, 1993.

Kaye, Harvey J. *The Powers of the Past: Reflections on the Crisis and the Promise of History.* New York: Harvester Wheatsheaf, 1991.

Kennedy, Liam. "Alien Nation: White Male Paranoia and Imperial Culture in the United States." *Journal of American Studies,* 30, no. 1 (1996): 87–100.

Kimball, Roger. *Tenured Radicals: How Politics Has Corrupted Higher Education.* New York: Routledge, 1991.

Kindem, Gorham A. "Hollywood's Conversion to Color: The Technological, Economic and Aesthetic Factors." *Journal of the University Film Association,* 31, no. 2 (1979): 29–36.

King, Richard. "Memory and Phantasy." *Modern Language Notes,* 98 (1983): 1197–1213.

Kirschenblatt-Gimblett, Barbara. *Destination Culture: Tourism, Museums, and Heritage.* Berkeley, CA: University of California Press, 1998.

Klawans, Stuart. "Colorization: Rose-tinted Spectacles." In *Seeing through Movies,* edited by Mark Crispin Miller. New York: Pantheon: 150–185.

Klein, Naomi. *No Logo.* London: Flamingo Press, 2000.

Kundera, Milan. *Slowness.* London: Faber & Faber, 1996.

Landy, Marcia. *Cinematic Uses of the Past.* Minneapolis, MN: University of Minnesota Press, 1996.

Landy, Marcia, ed. *The Historical Film: History and Memory in Media.* London: The Athlone Press, 2001.

Lasch, Christopher. "The Politics of Nostalgia." *Harper's,* November 1984: 65–70.

Lears, Jackson. *Fables of Abundance: A Cultural History of Advertising in America.* New York: Basic Books, 1994.

Lears, Jackson. "Looking Backward: In Defense of Nostalgia." *Lingua Franca,* December/January 1998: 59–66.

Lee, A. Robert. "Shooting America: American Images: Photography 1945–1980." *Journal of American Studies* 20, no. 2 (1986): 294–298.

Lee, Mathew and Nora Lee. "Are Filmmakers Artists? Do They Have Rights?" *American Cinematographer,* 72, no. 11 (1991): 112.

Leibowitz, Flo. "Movie Colorization and the Expression of Mood." *British Journal of Aesthetics,* 49, no. 4 (1991): 363–365.

Levine, Lawrence. *The Unpredictable Past: Explorations in American Cultural History.* New York: Oxford University Press, 1993.

Levinson, Jerrold. "Colourization Ill-Defended." *British Journal of Aesthetics,* 30, no. 1 (1990): 62–67.

Linfield, Susan. "The Color of Money." *American Film,* 12, no. 4 (1987): 29–36.

Lipsitz, George. *Time Passages: Collective Memory and American Popular Culture.* Minneapolis, MN: University of Minnesota Press, 1990.

Loshitsky, Yosefa, ed. *Spielberg's Holocaust: Critical Perspectives on Schindler's List.* Bloomington, IN: Indiana University Press, 1997.

Lowenthal, David. *The Past Is a Foreign Country.* Cambridge, U.K.: Cambridge University Press, 1985.

Lowenthal, David. "Nostalgia Tells It Like It Wasn't." In *The Imagined Past: History and Nostalgia,* edited by Malcolm Chase and Christopher Shaw. Manchester, U.K.: Manchester University Press, 1989: 18–32.

McDowell, Colin. "A Man for All Seasons." *Sunday Times Magazine,* 25 July 1999: 13–16.

McKay, George, ed. *Yankee Go Home (& Take Me With You): Americanization and Popular Culture.* Sheffield, U.K.: Sheffield Academic Press, 1997.

Mitchell, Susan. *American Attitudes: Who Thinks What about the Issues That Shape Our Lives.* Ithaca, NY: New Strategists Publications, 1998.

Morley, David, and Kevin Robins. *Spaces of Identity: Global Media, Electronic Landscapes and Cultural Boundaries.* London: Routledge, 1995.

Morley, David, and Kuan-Hsin Chen, eds. *Stuart Hall: Critical Dialogues in Cultural Studies.* London: Routledge, 1996.

Morrow, Lance. "Man of the Year: The Torch Is Passed." *Time,* 4 January 1992: 27.

Morrow, Lance. "The Time of Our Lives." *Time,* 9 March 1998: 25–31.

Munslow, Alan. *Deconstructing History.* London: Routledge, 1997.

Naremore, James. *More Than Night: Film Noir in Its Contexts.* Berkeley, CA: University of California Press, 1998.

Neale, Steve. *Cinema and Technology: Image, Sound, Colour.* London: Macmillan, 1985.

Neilson, Jim. "The Great PC Scare: Tyrannies of the Left, Rhetoric of the Right." In *PC Wars: Politics and Theory in the Academy,* edited by Jeffrey Williams. New York: Routledge, 1995: 23–27.

Nora, Pierre. "Between Memory and History: Les Lieux de Mémoire." Trans. Marc Roudebush. *Representations,* 26 (Spring 1989): 7–25.

Orvell, Miles. *The Real Thing: Imitation and Authenticity in American Culture 1880–1940.* Chapel Hill, NC: North Carolina University Press, 1989.

"Papering the Nation." *Time,* 9 March 1998: 99.

Parisi, Paula. "Forrest Gump Gallops through Time." *American Cinematographer,* October 1994: 38–52.

Pease, Donald E. "New Americanists: Revisionist Interventions into the Canon." *Boundary 2,* 17, no. 1 (1990): 1–37.

Pfeil, Fred. *White Guys: Studies in Postmodern Difference and Domination.* London: Verso, 1995.

Pickering, Jean, and Suzanne Kehde, eds. *Narratives of Nostalgia, Gender and Nationalism.* Basingstoke, U.K.: Macmillan, 1997.

Preston, Peter. "The Last Picture Show." *Guardian Weekend,* 28 November 1998: 28.

Prince, Stephen. "True Lies: Perceptual Realism, Digital Images and Film Theory." *Film Quarterly,* 49, no. 3 (1996): 27–37.

Radstone, Susannah, ed. *Memory and Methodology.* Oxford, U.K.: Berg, 2000.

Radway, Janice. "What's in a Name? Presidential Address to the American Studies Association, 20 November 1998." *American Quarterly,* 51, no. 1 (1999): 1–32.

Ravitch, Diane. "The War on Standards." *Partisan Review,* 60 (1993): 685–692.

Readings, Bill. *The University in Ruins*. Cambridge, MA: Harvard University Press, 1996.

Reimer, Robert C., and Carol J. Reimer. *Nazi-Retro Film: How German Cinema Remembers the Past*. New York: Twayne, 1992.

Richardson, John H. "Steven's Choice." *Premiere,* January 1994: 66.

Ritchen, Fred. "Photojournalism in the Age of Computers." In *The Critical Image: Essays on Contemporary Photography*, edited by Carol Squiers. London: Lawrence and Wishart, 1990: 28–37.

Rogin, Michael. "Spielberg's List." *New Left Review,* July–August 1998: 153–160.

Rose, Gillian. *The Melancholy Science: An Introduction to the Work of Theodor W. Adorno.* London: Macmillan, 1978.

Rosenblatt, Roger. "Prologue: In Black and White." In P. F. Bentley, *Clinton*: *Portrait of Victory*. New York: Warner Books, 1993.

Rosenstone, Robert A. *Visions of the Past: The Challenge of Film to Our Idea of History*. Cambridge, MA: Harvard University Press, 1995.

Rosenzweig, Roy, and David Thelan. *The Presence of the Past: Popular Uses of History in American Life*. New York: Colombia University Press, 1998.

Ross, Andrew. *No Respect: Intellectuals and Popular Culture*. New York: Routledge, 1989.

Ross, Andrew. *Real Love: In Pursuit of Cultural Justice*. New York: Routledge, 1998.

Rushdie, Salman. "Mohandas Gandhi." *Time,* 13 April 1998: 70–74.

Russell, Cheryl. *The Master Trend: How the Baby-boom Generation Is Remaking America*. Reading, U.K.: Perseus Books, 1993.

Samuel, Raphael. *Theatres of Memory: Past and Present in Contemporary Culture*. London: Verso, 1994.

Sarchett, Barry S. "Russell Jacoby, Antiprofessionalism, and the Cultural Politics of Nostalgia." In *PC Wars: Politics and Theory in the Academy*, edited by Jeffrey Williams. New York: Routledge, 1995: 253–278.

Sassen, Saskia. *Losing Control: Sovereignty in an Age of Globalization.* New York: Columbia University Press, 1996.

Schatz, Thomas. "The New Hollywood." In *Film Theory Goes to the Movies*, edited by Jim Collins, Hilary Radner, and Ava Preacher Collins. New York: Routledge, 1993: 8–36.

Schickel, Richard. "Heart of Darkness." *Time,* 13 December 1993: 49–51.

Schleier, Curt. "Steven Spielberg's New Direction." *Jewish Monthly*, 108, no. 4 (1994): 12.

Schlesinger, Arthur, Jr. *The Disuniting of America: Reflections on a Multicultural Society*. New York: W. W. Norton, 1991.

Schlesinger, Arthur, Jr. "The Cult of Ethnicity, Good and Bad." *Time,* 8 July 1991: 28.

Schudson, Michael. "Colorization and Authenticity." *Society*, 24, no. 4 (1987): 18–19.

Schwartz, Barry. "The Social Context of Commemoration: A Study in Collective Memory." *Social Forces,* 61, no. 2 (1982): 374–402.

Scott, Joan Wallach. "The Campaign Against Political Correctness: What's Really at Stake." In *PC Wars: Politics and Theory in the Academy*, edited by Jeffrey Williams. New York: Routledge, 1995: 22–43.

Shandler, Jeffrey. "Schindler's Discourse: America Discusses the Holocaust from NBC's Miniseries to Spielberg's Film." In *Spielberg's Holocaust: Critical Perspectives on Schindler's List*, edited by Yosefa Loshitsky. Bloomington, IN: Indiana University Press, 1997: 153–168.

Silverman, Kaja. "Fragments of a Feminist Discourse." In *Studies in Entertainment: Critical Approaches to Mass Culture*, edited by Tania Modleski. Bloomington, IN: Indiana University Press, 1986: 139–152.

Simmons, Philip E. *Deep Surfaces: Mass Culture and History in Postmodern American Fiction*. Athens, GA: University of Georgia Press, 1997.

Singh, Nikhal Pal. "Culture/Wars: Recoding Empire in an Age of Democracy." *American Quarterly*, 50, no. 3 (1998): 471–522.

Sklar, Robert. *Movie-Made America: A Cultural History of American Movies*. New York: Vintage Books, 1994.

Skolnick, Arlene. *Embattled Paradise: The American Family in an Age of Uncertainty*. New York: HarperCollins, 1991.

Sobchack, Vivien, ed. *The Persistence of History: Cinema, Television and the Modern Event*. New York: Routledge, 1996.

Sontag, Susan. *On Photography*. London: Penguin, 1979.

Spigel, Lynn. "From the Dark Ages to the Golden Age: Women's Memories and Television Reruns." *Screen*, 36, no. 1 (1995): 16–33.

Sreberny-Mohammadi, Annabelle. "The Global and Local in International Communications." In *Mass Media and Society*, edited by James Curran and Michael Gurevitch. London: Arnold, 1996: 177–203.

Starobinski, Jean. "The Idea of Nostalgia." Trans. William S. Kemp. *Diogenes*, 54 (1966): 81–103.

Stauth, Georg, and Bryan S. Turner. "Nostalgia, Postmodernism and the Critique of Mass Culture." *Theory, Society & Culture*, 5 (1988): 509–526.

Stephanson, Anders. "Regarding Postmodernism: A Conversation with Fredric Jameson." In *Postmodernism/Jameson/Critique*, edited by Douglas Kellner. Washington, DC: Maisonneive Press, 1989: 43–74.

Stephens, Michelle A. "Black Transnationalism and the Politics of National Identity." *American Quarterly*, 50, no. 3 (1998): 592–608.

Stern, Barbara B. "Nostalgia in Advertising Text: Romancing the Past." *Advances in Consumer Research*, 19 (1992): 388–389.

Stern, Barbara B. "Historical and Personal Nostalgia in Advertising Text: The Fin de Siècle Effect." *Journal of Advertising Studies* 21, no. 2 (1992): 11–22.

Stewart, Susan. *On Longing: Narratives of the Miniature, the Gigantic, the Souvenir, the Collection*. Baltimore, MD: Johns Hopkins University Press, 1984.

Stobart, Paul, ed. *Brand Power*. London: Macmillan, 1994.

Sturken, Marita. *Tangled Memories: The Vietnam War, the AIDS Epidemic and the Politics of Remembering*. Berkeley, CA: University of California Press, 1997.

Tagg, John. *The Burden of Representation: Essays on Photographies and Histories*. London: Macmillan, 1988.

Tannock, Stuart. "Nostalgia Critique." *Cultural Studies,* 9, no. 3 (1995): 453–464.

Terdiman, Richard. *Present Past: Modernity and the Memory Crisis.* Ithaca, NY: Cornell University Press, 1993.

Tomlinson, John. *Globalization and Culture.* Cambridge, U.K.: Polity Press, 1999.

Toor, Matt. "Different Strokes." *MacUser,* 14, no. 8 (1998): 61–69.

Turner, Bryan S. "A Note on Nostalgia." *Theory, Culture & Society,* 4, no. 1 (1987): 147–156.

Van Camp, Julie. "The Colorization Controversy." *The Journal of Value Inquiry,* 29, no. 4 (1995): 447–468.

Wagner, Craig A. "Motion Picture Colorization, Authenticity and the Elusive Moral Right." *New York University Law Review,* 64, no. 3 (1989): 628–725.

Wakefield, Neville. *Postmodernism: The Twilight of the Real.* London: Pluto, 1990.

Walker, Martin. "Making Saccharine Taste Sour." *Sight and Sound,* 4, no. 10 (1994): 16–17.

Wallace, Mike. *Mickey Mouse History and Other Essays in American Collective Memory.* Philadelphia, PA: Temple University Press, 1996.

Wasko, Janet. *Hollywood in the Information Age.* Cambridge, U.K.: Polity Press, 1994.

Wernick, Andrew. *Promotional Culture: Advertising, Ideology and Symbolic Expression.* London: Sage, 1991.

Wernick, Andrew. "Resort to Nostalgia: Mountains, Memories and Myths of Time." In *Buy This Book: Studies in Advertising and Consumption,* edited by Mica Nava, Andrew Blake, Iain MacRury, Barry Richards. London: Routledge, 1997: 207–223.

Wieseltier, Leon. "Close Encounters of the Nazi Kind." *New Republic,* 24 January 1994: 42.

Will, George. "Literary Politics." *Newsweek,* 22 April 1991: 72.

Williams, Jeffrey, ed. *PC Wars: Politics and Theory in the Academy.* New York: Routledge, 1995.

Williams, Phil. "Feeding off the Past: The Evolution of the Television Rerun." *Journal of Popular Film and Television,* 21, no. 4 (1994): 162–175.

Williamson, Judith. *Decoding Advertisements: Ideology and Meaning in Advertising.* London: Martin Boyers, 1978.

Wills, Gary. *Reagan's America.* New York: Penguin, 1988.

Wilson, David. "Colour Box." *Sight and Sound,* 55, no. 3 (1986): 147.

Wilson, Rob, and Wimal Dissanayake, eds. *Global/Local: Cultural Production and the Transnational Imaginary.* Durham, NC: Duke University Press, 1996.

Young, James E. *Writing and Rewriting the Holocaust: Narrative and the Consequences of Interpretation.* Bloomington, IN: Indiana University Press, 1988.

Young, James E. *The Texture of Memory: Holocaust Memorials and Meaning.* New Haven, CT: Yale University Press, 1993.

Index

King, Martin Luther, 105, 106, 111, 116, 148
King, Rodney, 82, 84, 152
Kirschenblatt-Gimblett, Barbara, 57, 167
Klawans, Stuart, 167
Klein, Naomi, 102
Kundera, Milan, 32

Lake Wobegon Days (1985), 47
Lange, Dorothea, 70
Lanzmann, Claude, 138
LA riots, 82–83
Lasch, Christopher, 20, 37, 44
Last Picture Show, The (1971), 71
Late capitalism, 6, 30, 57
Lears, Jackson, 24
Le Baiser de l'Hôtel de Ville, 68
Lee, A. Robert, 94
Leibowitz, Flo, 160
Levin, Gerald, 90
Levine, Lawrence, 4
Lieux de mémoire, 34, 93
Lipsitz, George, 14
Longing, 6, 12, 21, 27, 37, 58; absence of, 37, 46, 51; nostalgic, 11
Loshitsky, Yosefa, 127, 138
Loss: of memory and time, 4–7; nostalgic, 18, 22; as theoretical assumption, 21, 23–27, 32, 36
Lowenthal, David, 20
Lucas, George, 169
Luce, Henry, 77, 84

Madonna, 69
Magnum, 71, 78
Maltese Falcon, The (1941), 162
Manhattan (1979), 1–2
Mapplethorpe, Robert, 68, 165
Melancholy, 20, 23
Memorabilia, 54
Memory: American national, 13; collective, 20, 56; common sense of, 9, 150; construction of, 11, 36; contingency of, 35; as critical debate, 3; cultural, 33, 125, 127, 135, 173; as field of negotiation, 126–128; marketing of, 53; master, 126–128, 132, 134, 139, 141–142, 150–151; timeless, 35, 52, 111, 171, 172, 181, 185
Memory crisis, 4–11, 21, 173

Microsoft, 91, 104, 106, 107
Monochrome: *see* black-and-white image
Morley, David, 10
Morrow, Lance, 83, 86
Mourning, 23, 86, 128
Muller, Henry, 75
Multiculturalism: and American identity, 118, 119–120, 126; and colorization debate, 157, 158, 165, 167–171; and education, 7–8, 79–81; as lightning rod, 7, 8, 82

Nachtway, James, 78
Naremore, James, 160
National Endowment for the Humanities (NEH), 4, 165
National Film Preservation Board, 165
National identity: American cultural nationalism, 59–60, 115, 121, 183; crisis of, 7, 12; narratives of, 8, 10, 84, 115, 119; negotiations of, 10, 13, 72, 129, 170, 176
Neale, Steve, 36
Neoconservativism, 4, 7–8, 26; and culture war discourse, 155–157; and Reagan, 43–47
Neoliberalism, 10, 115, 121
Newfield, Christopher, 8, 119
Newsweek, 74, 75, 79, 99, 108
New Yorker, 99, 137
New York Times, 74, 111, 116, 159
Niche marketing, 48–50, 51
Nick at Nite, 48, 50
Nickelodeon, 50
Nonrepresentational codes, 14, 35–38, 69, 92, 111, 173
Nora, Pierre, 22, 32, 34–35, 56, 93
Nostalgia: in advertising, 103–104; affective economies of, 6, 36–37; and authenticity, 171–174; commercial boom, 44; commodification of, 11, 20, 27–29, 37, 41–43, 47–53; as creative exhaustion, 42; as cultural style, 11–15, 22, 36–38, 41–43, 58, 98; and decline, 4, 43, 171; as discourse, 43; and loss, 23, 51, 55, 58, 171; in media production, 47–53; as mode, 4, 6, 11, 27–35, 43, 51, 131, 142, 185; as mood, 11, 23–27; ontological condition, 22; origins of term, 19, 23; politics of, 43–47, 157–158,

About the Author

PAUL GRAINGE is lecturer in the Institute of Film Studies, part of the School of American and Canadian Studies at the University of Nottingham, U.K. His work on memory and contemporary American media has appeared in *Cultural Studies, The Journal of American Studies, American Studies, The International Journal of Cultural Studies,* and *The Journal of American and Comparative Cultures.* He is the editor of *Memory and Popular Film* (2003).